Alvin Plantinga

Few thinkers have had as much impact on contemporary philosophy as has Alvin Plantinga. The work of this quintessential analytic philosopher has in many respects set the tone for the debate in the fields of modal metaphysics and epistemology, and he is arguably the most important philosopher of religion of our time. In this volume, a distinguished team of today's leading philosophers address the central aspects of Plantinga's philosophy – his views on natural theology, his responses to the problem of evil, his contributions to the field of modal metaphysics, the controversial evolutionary argument against naturalism, his model of epistemic warrant and his view of epistemic defeat, his argument for warranted Christian belief, his response to the challenge of religious pluralism, and his recent work on mind-body dualism. Also included is an appendix containing Plantinga's often referred to, but previously unpublished, lecture notes entitled "Two Dozen (or so) Theistic Arguments," with a substantial preface to the appendix written by Plantinga specifically for this volume.

Deane-Peter Baker is a Senior Lecturer in the School of Philosophy and Ethics at the University of KwaZulu-Natal (South Africa). He is the author of *Tayloring Reformed Epistemology: Charles Taylor, Alvin Plantinga and the De Jure Challenge to Christian Belief*.

Contemporary Philosophy in Focus

Contemporary Philosophy in Focus offers a series of introductory volumes to many of the dominant philosophical thinkers of the current age. Each volume consists of newly commissioned essays that cover major contributions of a preeminent philosopher in a systematic and accessible manner. Comparable in scope and rationale to the highly successful series **Cambridge Companions to Philosophy**, the volumes do not presuppose that readers are already intimately familiar with the details of each philosopher's work. They thus combine exposition and critical analysis in a manner that will appeal to students of philosophy and to professionals as well as to students across the humanities and social sciences.

FORTHCOMING VOLUMES:

Jerry Fodor edited by Tim Crane
Saul Kripke edited by Alan Berger
David Lewis edited by Theodore Sider and Dean Zimmermann
Bernard Williams edited by Alan Thomas

PUBLISHED VOLUMES:

Stanley Cavell edited by Richard Eldridge
Paul Churchland edited by Brian Keeley
Donald Davidson edited by Kirk Ludwig
Daniel Dennett edited by Andrew Brook and Don Ross
Ronald Dworkin edited by Arthur Ripstein
Thomas Kuhn edited by Thomas Nickles
Alasdair MacIntyre edited by Mark Murphy
Richard Rorty edited by Charles Guignon and David Hiley
John Searle edited by Barry Smith
Charles Taylor edited by Ruth Abbey

Alvin Plantinga

Edited by

DEANE-PETER BAKER
University of KwaZulu-Natal

CAMBRIDGE
UNIVERSITY PRESS

CAMBRIDGE UNIVERSITY PRESS
Cambridge, New York, Melbourne, Madrid, Cape Town, Singapore, São Paulo

Cambridge University Press
32 Avenue of the Americas, New York, NY 10013-2473, USA

www.cambridge.org
Information on this title: www.cambridge.org/9780521855310

© Cambridge University Press 2007

First published 2007

Printed in the United States of America

A catalog record for this publication is available from the British Library.

Library of Congress Cataloging in Publication Data
Alvin Plantinga / [edited by] Deane-Peter Baker.
  p.   cm. – (Contemporary philosophy in focus)
Includes bibliographical references and index.
ISBN-13: 978-0-521-85531-0 (hardback)
ISBN-13: 978-0-521-67143-9 (pbk.)
1. Plantinga, Alvin. I. Baker, Deane-Peter. II. Title. III. Series.
B931.P454A76   2007
191–dc22   2006035658

ISBN   978-0-521-85531-0 hardback
ISBN   978-0-521-67143-9 paperback

Contents

Contributors

DEANE-PETER BAKER is a Senior Lecturer in the School of Philosophy and Ethics at the University of KwaZulu-Natal (South Africa). He is the author of *Tayloring Reformed Epistemology: Charles Taylor, Alvin Plantinga and the De Jure Challenge to Christian Belief.*

JAMES BEILBY is Associate Professor of Philosophical and Systematic Theology at Bethel University. His publications include *Epistemology as Theology: An Evaluation of Alvin Plantinga's Religious Epistemology* (Ashgate, 2005); (ed.) *For Faith and Clarity: Philosophical Contributions to Christian Theology* (Baker Academic, 2006); and (ed.) *Naturalism Defeated? Essays on Plantinga's Evolutionary Argument Against Naturalism* (Cornell University Press, 2002).

KELLY JAMES CLARK is Professor of Philosophy at Calvin College. His publications include *The Story of Ethics: Human Nature and Human Fulfillment*, with Anne Poortenga (Prentice-Hall, 2003); *Reader in Philosophy of Religion* (Broadview, 2000); *Five Views on Apologetics*, with William Lane Craig, Gary Habermas, John Frame, and Paul Feinberg (Zondervan, 2000); and *Return to Reason* (Eerdmans, 1990). He has also edited *Our Knowledge of God: Essays on Natural and Philosophical Theology* (Kluwer, 1992).

JOHN DIVERS is Reader in Philosophy at the University of Sheffield. In recent years Divers has been concentrating on modality, and he is currently preparing a sequel, *Dispensing with Possible Worlds*, to his book *Possible Worlds* (Routledge, 2002). He is presently a Fellow of the AHRB ARCHE project on the metaphysics and epistemology of modality at the University of St. Andrews and was awarded a British Academy Readership for 2003–2005.

RICHARD M. GALE is Professor of Philosophy and Fellow of the Center for Philosophy of Science at the University of Pittsburgh. Recent publications include *The Divided Self of William James* (Cambridge, 1999), and he is the editor of *The Philosophy of Time* (Anchor Doubleday, 1967), *The Blackwell Companion to Metaphysics* (2002), and (with Alexander Pruss) *The Existence of God* (Dartmouth, 2003).

JONATHAN KVANVIG is Professor of Philosophy and Department Chair at the University of Missouri. His publications include *The Possibility of an All-Knowing God* (Macmillan, 1986); *The Intellectual Virtues and the Life of the Mind* (Rowman & Littlefield, 1992); *The Problem of Hell* (Oxford, 1993); (ed.) *Warrant in Contemporary Epistemology: Essays in Honor of Plantinga's Theory of Knowledge* (Rowman & Littlefield, 1996); and *The Value of Knowledge and the Pursuit of Understanding* (Cambridge, 2003).

GRAHAM OPPY is Associate Dean of Research at Monash University. Recent publications include *Ontological Arguments and Belief in God* (1995); *Arguing About Gods* (2006); and *Philosophical Perspectives on Infinity* (2006), all from Cambridge University Press.

ERNEST SOSA is Romeo Elton Professor of Natural Theology and Professor of Philosophy at Brown University and Distinguished Visiting Professor at Rutgers University. His recent publications include *Knowledge in Perspective: Selected Essays in Epistemology* (Cambridge University Press, 1991); *Epistemic Justification: Internalism vs. Externalism, Foundations vs. Virtues* (a debate between Sosa and Laurence Bonjour) (Blackwell, 2003); and *Contemporary Debates in Epistemology* (ed., with Mattias Steup) (Blackwell, 2005).

PETER VAN INWAGEN is John Cardinal O'Hara Professor of Philosophy at the University of Notre Dame. His recent works include *Material Beings* (Cornell, 1995); *God, Knowledge & Mystery: Essays in Philosophical Theology* (Cornell, 1995); *The Possibility of Resurrection and Other Essays in Christian Apologetics* (Westview, 1997); *Ontology, Identity, and Modality: Essays in Metaphysics* (Cambridge, 2001); and *Metaphysics* (Westview, 2002).

Acknowledgements

In preparing this volume I have been overwhelmed by the positive reaction to it by philosophers of the highest calibre, many of whom contributed the chapters that follow. Among those who do not appear herein, William Alston must be singled out. Because of an unfortunate bout of ill health, Professor Alston was not able to write a chapter for this volume, but his support and encouragement for the project has been greatly valued. I am also grateful to Ruth Abbey, who encouraged me to pursue this project and whose excellent book *Charles Taylor*, which appeared earlier in this series, was the ideal template. Thanks must also go to my colleague, friend, and mentor Simon Beck, whose support and wise guidance has always been crucial. Finally, I owe a great debt of gratitude to Alvin Plantinga himself, who generously gave of his time when I needed it, and whose example as philosopher and Christian has been a real inspiration to me and many others.

Introduction: Alvin Plantinga, God's Philosopher

DEANE-PETER BAKER

INTRODUCTION

The dominance of logical empiricism's verification principle in the middle part of the twentieth century forced philosophy of religion almost entirely out of the philosophy curriculum, and, with a few notable exceptions, few philosophers willingly identified themselves as Christians. However, logical empiricism collapsed under the weight of its own principles, and in the spring of 1980 *Time* magazine reported that in a "quiet revolution in thought and arguments that hardly anyone could have foreseen only two decades ago, God is making a comeback. Most intriguingly, this is happening not among theologians or ordinary believers... but in the crisp, intellectual circles of academic philosophers, where the consensus had long banished the Almighty from fruitful discourse."[1]

Alvin Plantinga, one of those who had played a role in the demise of the verification principle, was identified by *Time* as a central figure in this 'quiet revolution'. In fact, the article went so far as to label him the "world's leading Protestant philosopher of God."[2] Being singled out in this way by arguably the world's foremost news magazine is made all the more remarkable by the fact that, at the time, Plantinga was a professor of philosophy at a small Calvinist college, whose most important work was yet to come.

The intervening years since *Time*'s report have seen Plantinga emerge as one of contemporary Western philosophy's leading thinkers of any stripe. While the general thrust of his work has remained focused on questions that fall within the bounds of the philosophy of religion (or, as Plantinga would prefer to describe it, Christian philosophy), his career has also been characterised by important contributions to other areas of philosophy – such as the metaphysics of modality and, most importantly, epistemic theory – that have earned him the (sometimes grudging) respect of his most notable peers. The aspect of Plantinga's thought that has had the greatest impact to date is the central role he has played in the emergence and growth of the 'Reformed epistemology' movement, with its emphasis on the proper basicality of

1

religious belief. This epistemological thesis is central to Plantinga's magnum opus, *Warranted Christian Belief* (Oxford University Press, 2000), which has established him as without doubt the preeminent figure in contemporary philosophy of religion. Indeed, one reviewer favourably compares the importance of this book to Aquinas's *Summa Theologica* and Karl Barth's *Church Dogmatics*.[3]

Plantinga's impact has not, however, been limited to his writings – he has, as a past president of the American Philosophical Association (Central Division), played a role in the development of philosophy in the Anglo-American world. His greatest impact, however, has been on the development of specifically *Christian* philosophy – through his foundational role in the forming of the Society of Christian Philosophers in 1978 (which has grown into one of the largest such organisations within the APA), and through papers such as his "Advice to Christian Philosophers."[4]

Alvin Plantinga is unquestionably one of the leading philosophers of our time, whose work undoubtedly warrants a dedicated volume of the *Contemporary Philosophy in Focus* series. In keeping with the other volumes in the series, the goal of this book is to introduce thoughtful readers to the most important features of Plantinga's philosophy.

PROFILE

Alvin Plantinga was born on the fifteenth of November 1932, a week after Franklin D. Roosevelt won the U.S. presidential election in a landslide victory over Herbert Hoover.[5] Plantinga's parents, Cornelius A. Plantinga and Lettie Plantinga (née Bossenbroek), were then living in Ann Arbor, Michigan, where Cornelius was at the time a graduate student in philosophy at the University of Michigan. Though Lettie was born in the United States, her family originally hailed from the province of Gelderland in the Netherlands. Cornelius was born in the Netherlands, though in the province of Friesland, inhabitants of which are fond of viewing themselves as a separate nation altogether.

As a young boy, Alvin moved around fairly regularly as the family followed Cornelius first to Duke University in North Carolina, where he earned a Ph.D. in philosophy and a Master's degree in psychology; then to South Dakota where he taught philosophy at Huron College; and then to North Dakota where he taught Latin, Greek, philosophy and psychology at Jamestown College. It was in North Dakota that Alvin encountered philosophy for the first time – his father supplemented his high school curriculum with some Latin and Plato's *Dialogues* – and where, at age fourteen, he resolved to become a philosopher. Contrary to stereotypes, this did not make young Alvin a bookish nerd – indeed, he was an enthusiastic participant in high school football, basketball and tennis.

Although Plantinga cannot remember ever not having been convinced of the claims of the Christian religion, it was when he was around eight or nine years old that he first began to seriously wrestle with the tenets of the Calvinism he encountered in the churches he attended alongside his parents (he particularly remembers struggling to come to grips with the Calvinist view of total depravity). He writes: "I spent a good deal of time as a child thinking about these doctrines, and a couple of years later, when I was ten or eleven or so, I got involved in many very enthusiastic but undirected discussions of human freedom, determinism (theological or otherwise), divine foreknowledge, predestination and allied topics."[6] Cornelius Plantinga was an active lay preacher, and there is no question that what Alvin learned of the Christian faith from his parents laid an essential foundation for his future life and work. That said, it must not be thought that Alvin Plantinga's upbringing was without its difficulties – in 1993 he wrote that his father, Cornelius, had suffered from manic-depressive psychosis "for fifty years and more,"[7] which cannot have made life easy in the Plantinga household. Alvin credits his mother, Lettie, with playing a crucial role in holding the family together, bearing the responsibility for caring for and helping Cornelius with "magnificent generosity," "unstinting devotion" and "a sort of cheerful courage that is wonderful to behold."[8]

At his father's urging, Alvin reluctantly skipped over his senior year of high school and enrolled in Jamestown College. The enrolment was short-lived, however, for during Alvin's first semester, Cornelius was invited to join the psychology department at his alma mater, Calvin College. Alvin (again reluctantly) made the move to Grand Rapids, Michigan, but in a rebellious move applied for a scholarship to Harvard during his first semester at Calvin. To his surprise the scholarship was awarded, and in the fall of 1950 he relocated to Cambridge, Massachusetts.

The undergraduate Plantinga found Harvard to be a most impressive and enjoyable place. He also found it to be the locus of his first real spiritual challenge. For the first time he came across serious non-Christian thought 'in the flesh', and like many undergraduates found his faith shaken. In a telling passage, which suggests the beginnings of Plantinga's approach to Christian philosophy, he writes:

My attitude gradually became one of a mixture of doubt and bravado. On the one hand I began to think it questionable that what I had been taught and had always believed could be right, given that there were all these others who thought so differently (and [who] were so much more intellectually accomplished than I). On the other hand, I thought to myself, what really is so great about these people? Why should I believe *them*? . . . [W]hat, precisely, is the *substance* of their objections to Christianity? Or to theism? Do these objections really *have* much by way of substance? And if, as I strongly suspected, *not*, why should their taking the views they did be relevant to what *I* thought? The doubts (in that form anyway) didn't last long, but something like the bravado, I suppose, has remained.[9]

One of the events that dispelled the doubts Plantinga experienced at Harvard was a moment in which he experienced what he was convinced was the presence of God, something which he describes as a rare but important event in his spiritual walk. The other crucial event in this regard took place during a trip home, when he had the opportunity to attend some classes at Calvin College. Here he encountered something that held an even stronger attraction for him than the stimulating environment at Harvard – William Harry Jellema's philosophy classes. Harry Jellema was, in Plantinga's own words, "by all odds . . . the most gifted teacher of philosophy I have ever encountered."[10] More than this, Jellema was "obviously in dead earnest about Christianity; he was also a magnificently thoughtful and reflective Christian."[11] Deeply affected by Jellema's teaching and his response to the modern philosophical critique of Christianity, Plantinga resolved after only two semesters at Harvard to return to Calvin, a decision he never regretted.

Under the direction of Jellema and Henry Stob, Plantinga and his classmates (who included Dewey Hoitenga and Nicholas Wolterstorff) spent much of their time on the history of philosophy, particularly Plato, Aristotle, Augustine, Aquinas, Descartes, Leibniz and Kant. In order to read some of these philosophers' works in the original languages, Plantinga also spent a significant amount of time studying French, German and Greek (having already learned Latin from his father while in high school). Apart from philosophy, Plantinga also majored in psychology (taking six courses from his father) and English literature.

In January 1954 Plantinga left Calvin for the University of Michigan, where he commenced his graduate studies. There he studied under William Alston, Richard Cartwright and William K. Frankena. Plantinga enjoyed his studies at Michigan, and the connection made there with Alston was to be one of the more important friendships that grew out of his philosophical career (Plantinga dedicated *Warranted Christian Belief* to Alston, with the words "Mentor, Model, Friend"). Moving on to graduate studies was not the only threshold crossed during this period of Plantinga's life. It was while at Calvin, in 1953, that Plantinga had met Kathleen De Boer, then a Calvin senior. Plantinga describes himself as having been "captivated by her generous spirit and mischievous, elfin sense of humor."[12] In 1955 they were married and in the intervening years have become proud parents to four children – Carl, Jane, William Harry and Ann. It was through Kathleen's relatives that Plantinga was introduced to the pleasures of rock climbing and mountaineering, which became an enduring passion.

Shortly after her marriage to Alvin, Kathleen Plantinga endured the first of what is to date almost twenty relocations – this time to Yale. Despite enjoying Michigan, and there developing a strong interest in the philosophical challenges mounted against theism, Plantinga had felt that philosophy there was "too piecemeal and too remote from the big questions."[13] Yale seemed to offer a solution, and so the newlywed Plantingas made the move to New Haven. Though he was impressed by teachers like Paul Weiss and Brand Blanshard, Yale turned out to be something of a disappointment for Plantinga. He found the high level of generality in the courses on offer to be perplexing and frustrating: "The problem at Yale was that no one seemed prepared to show a neophyte philosopher how to go about the subject – what to *do*, how to think about a problem to some effect."[14]

It was in the fall of 1957 that Plantinga had his first taste of teaching – focusing on the history of metaphysics and epistemology – which he describes as a harrowing experience, one familiar to many new academics:

> I spent most of the summer preparing for my classes in the fall; when September rolled around I had perhaps forty or fifty pages of notes. I met my first class with great trepidation, which wasn't eased by the preppy, sophisticated, almost world-weary attitude of these incoming freshmen. Fortified by my fifty pages of material, I launched or perhaps lunged into the course. At the end of the second day I discovered, to my horror, that I'd gone through half of my material; and by the end of the first week I'd squandered my entire summer's horde. The semester stretched before me, bleak, frightening, nearly interminable. That's when I discovered the value of the Socratic method of teaching.[15]

Plantinga's lack of teaching experience was not something that in any way dampened the enthusiastic advances of George Nakhnikian of Detroit's Wayne State University, who in that same year began tirelessly to pursue Plantinga for his department. Despite initial reservations Plantinga eventually gave in to Nakhnikian, and in the fall of 1958 the Philosophy Department at Wayne became Plantinga's first faculty home. Looking back, Plantinga considers the move to be "one of the best decisions I ever made."[16]

Plantinga's colleagues at Wayne State were Nakhnikian, Hector Castañeda, Edmund Gettier, John Collinson, Raymond Hoekstra and Robert C. Sleigh. Collinson left soon after Plantinga arrived, and the department was boosted a couple of years later by the arrival of Richard Cartwright and Keith Lehrer. In contrast to Yale, Plantinga found the Wayne approach to philosophy a lot more to his liking: "There wasn't nearly as much talk *about* philosophy – what various philosophers or philosophical traditions said – and a lot more attempts actually to figure things out."[17] Among the central topics of discussion at Wayne during Plantinga's years there were Wittgenstein's private language argument and the place of modal concepts in philosophy. This latter topic particularly fascinated Plantinga, an interest that is evident in much of his published work. It was here, too, that his interest in epistemology began to grow. Cartwright and Sleigh had both been students of Roderick Chisholm at Brown University, a consequence of which was a series of seminars between the Wayne and Brown departments. This turn of events brought Chisholm's work to Plantinga's attention, and looking back he opines that "there is no other contemporary philosopher from whom I have learned more over the years."[18]

After five happy years at Wayne State University, Plantinga was invited to replace the retiring Harry Jellema at Calvin College. He found it a difficult decision to make, though not for the reasons many of his friends saw as obvious. For those with no previous connection with Calvin, there seemed little reason to leave the lively and impressive Philosophy Department at Wayne State, which Plantinga had found to be enormously stimulating and enjoyable, for a little-known Christian college in western Michigan. For Plantinga, however, the call to Calvin was all but irresistible. It was only his trepidation at stepping into Jellema's shoes that made the decision a difficult one. Calvin was a natural home for Plantinga – it was a place build on a deep commitment to the Reformed Christianity that had been the central plank of his life since early childhood; the philosophical topics in which his was most interested (many of which centred around the relationship between Christianity and philosophy) could be most naturally pursued at Calvin; and Calvin and Plantinga shared a common belief in the idea that the academic enterprise cannot be viewed as religiously neutral, and that there is therefore a need for university education build upon Christian fundamentals. Thus, overcoming his trepidations, Plantinga moved to Calvin College in 1963, and remained there for the following nineteen years.

The longevity of Plantinga's stay at Calvin is a reflection of the natural home that the department was for him. In his "Self-Profile," Plantinga singles out two aspects of life in the Philosophy Department at Calvin that he particularly appreciated. Firstly, the department was characterised by the same outlook on philosophy as that held by Plantinga – that the purpose of "doing philosophy" (for Christians, at least) is to contribute to specifically *Christian* scholarship, and that this endeavour is a communal one. The other characteristic of life at Calvin of which he writes with great approval is related to this communal effort, namely, that Calvin's size made it possible to interact with, and form friendships with, colleagues in other disciplines. Among the philosophers and other colleagues whom Plantinga credits with having been of great help to his scholarly growth in his time at Calvin, he singles out Peter de Vos, Del Ratzsch, Kenneth Konyndyk, Thomas Jager (mathematics) and particularly Nicholas Wolterstorff and Paul J. Zwier (mathematics). Also significant was the period (1979–1980) when Plantinga (along with Wolterstorff, George Mavrodes, William Alston, David Holwerda, George Marsden, Ronald Feenstra and Michael Hakkenberg) was a fellow in the Calvin Centre for Christian Scholarship. During that time these scholars dedicated themselves to a yearlong project entitled "Toward a Reformed View of Faith and Reason," the result of which was the publication in 1983 of a book, *Faith and Rationality* (edited by Wolterstorff and Plantinga) that has the best claim of any work to being the first comprehensive account of the Reformed epistemology project.

The latter years of Plantinga's tenure at Calvin also saw some of his greatest involvement in service to the philosophical community. In 1980–1981 he served as vice-president of the Central Division of the American Philosophical Association, and subsequently, in 1981–1982, he became president thereof. Following this service, he took on the mantle of president of the Society of Christian Philosophers, a position he held from 1983 until 1986.

In 1982 Plantinga made the move to his current academic home, at the University of Notre Dame. Before this transition he described the prospect of leaving Calvin as "disturbing and in fact genuinely painful."[19] Despite this, the reasons for the move were for him straightforward. The prospect of teaching primarily graduate students was a central motivating factor. The other was linked to Plantinga's ongoing goal of exploring what it means to be a Christian in philosophy. Despite being a university firmly shaped by Roman Catholicism, Notre Dame boasted (and boasts) a very large concentration of philosophy graduates who share the same essential belief framework as Plantinga. His desire to pass on to these 'new' Christian philosophers some of what he has learned along the way was a significant reason for the move to Notre Dame.

Plantinga has now been at Notre Dame for more than two decades, and there is no question that it has been a productive environment. Notre Dame boasts possibly the largest philosophy faculty in the United States, some of whom have reputations to rival even Plantinga's. Added to the obvious benefits gained from presenting work at staff seminars in such an intellectually rich environment, Plantinga has certainly benefited from teaching an impressively bright group of graduate students. Many of those students – Michael Bergmann, Kelly James Clark, Robin Collins, Thomas Crisp, Thomas Flint, Trenton Merricks and Michael Rea among them – are increasingly recognised as the vanguard of the next generation of Protestant Christian philosophers. It might be argued, only partially in jest, that the lack of a single Dutch surname among this group shows that Plantinga's move to Notre Dame has done much to widen the membership of the Protestant Christian philosophers' club! During his time at Notre Dame Plantinga has published some of his most important work, including his magnum opus, *Warranted Christian Belief*, and has twice been invited to present the prestigious Gifford Lectures, a rare honour indeed.

Another important aspect of Plantinga's tenure at Notre Dame has been his involvement with the Centre for Philosophy of Religion, established in 1976. The centre's focus is today twofold: firstly, the original goal of promoting scholarly work in traditional philosophy of religion, and secondly, to encourage research relevant to Christian philosophy, where this is conceived of as philosophy that takes Christianity for granted and works out philosophical issues on that basis. This latter goal, in particular, reflects the central theme of Plantinga's philosophical work, and there can be no question of his contribution to the centre's goals in this regard. He took over the directorship of the centre in 1984, and only relinquished that duty in the summer of 2002. At the time of writing Plantinga remains a member of the centre's board, and he was honoured in 2003 by having one of the centre's key fellowships (formerly the "Distinguished Scholar Fellowship") named for him. It is described as being intended "to provide time for reflection and writing to those whose work is in the forefront of current research in the philosophy of religion and Christian philosophy."[20]

THE WAY AHEAD

One of my chief interests over the years has been in philosophical theology and apologetics: the attempt to defend Christianity (or more broadly, theism) against the various sorts of attacks brought against it.[21]

A reader first encountering this statement might be forgiven for presuming that a central thrust of Plantinga's work has been what is traditionally called natural theology, the attempt to prove God's existence or facts about God's nature by rational argument based on ordinary experience. In fact, however, as Graham Oppy points out in Chapter 1 of this book, Plantinga's early work (particularly in his *God and Other Minds*) was characterised by a clear conviction that the project of natural theology is a failure. This has not meant that natural theology has been of no use to Plantinga in his attempt to defend belief in God against its detractors – the heart of his argument in *God and Other Minds* is that the arguments of natural theology are *no worse than* the arguments for the existence of other minds, and that therefore we have as much reason to believe in God as in other minds. Still, this negative view of natural theology, which characterised Plantinga's early work, has contributed to the view that Plantinga and those who share his approach to philosophy are constitutionally opposed to the natural theology project. At least one book, *Rational Faith: Catholic Responses to Reformed Epistemology*,[22] is in large part dedicated to defending natural theology against Plantinga and his ilk. Graham Oppy, however, argues that a survey of Plantinga's work shows an increasing acceptance of the value of natural theology. Oppy, himself an opponent of natural theology, argues that the later Plantinga's more positive view is in fact a step backwards, and that his earlier position is the better supported.

There is one observation that seems to me worth making here about Oppy's chapter. The reader will observe that Oppy is reluctantly willing to concede that many of Plantinga's arguments are, or could be, successful in showing that Christianity or theism is not irrational, though he argues that this on its own does not show atheism to be irrational. Whether or not Oppy's arguments here are successful, his concession is striking when considered in the light of the recent history of Western philosophy. When Plantinga first entered the world of academic philosophy, logical positivism still exerted a strong influence, and it was widely considered that the verifiability criterion of meaning showed that the claims of Christianity and theism are little more than nonsense.[23] That we have come to a point where a leading atheologian like Oppy feels compelled to defend the rationality of atheism against Plantinga's arguments shows the immense growth in credibility that theism has achieved in philosophical circles in recent decades, a development for which Plantinga himself is in large part responsible.

Where Chapter 1 of this book provides, through Oppy's survey of Plantinga's views on natural theology, a very useful overview of Plantinga's work, Chapter 2 focuses on one particular challenge against which Plantinga has long been at pains to defend the Christian faith – the problem of evil. Indeed, he has gone as far as to claim that "of all the antitheistic arguments only the argument from evil deserves to be taken really seriously."[24] Richard Gale begins his contribution to this volume by pointing out that Plantinga's responses to the problem of evil address two different forms of the problem: the logical form (in which it is argued that there is a logical contradiction in the notion that both God and evil exist, and given that evil clearly does exist it is therefore impossible that God does exist) and the evidential form (which points to the evidence of all the evil there is in the world as grounds for the claim that it is very unlikely that God exists). Plantinga has been careful to ensure that his readers know he intends neither of these defences to be *theodicies*, in which it is claimed that some particular state of affairs makes it such that God has a morally sufficient reason for allowing evil. Instead, he has contended that Christians must accept that they do not know in detail why God permits evil.[25] Thus, the form of Plantinga's defences against this particular challenge to the faith he holds so dear is to argue that it is *likely* there are reasons that would justify God in allowing evil, even if we do not know what those reasons are. Against the logical form of the problem of evil Plantinga offers his well-known free will defence, while he responds to the evidential challenge of evil with an argument from theistic skepticism, which in its roughest and most general form is the claim that the 'problem' of evil only looks like a problem because of our limited knowledge and perspective. If we knew all God knows, then we'd see that there's no problem. In his chapter Gale addresses both of these arguments and offers a thorough critique of Plantinga's position.

Plantinga's response to the problem of evil exists against the background of his exceptional work on the metaphysics of modality. As mentioned earlier, this is an interest that extends back at least as far as his Wayne State days, in the late 1950s and early 1960s. In recent years it is perhaps only David Lewis (who is the focus of another volume in this series) who can be singled out alongside Plantinga as having developed influential and fully fledged theories of modal metaphysics and ontology. In Chapter 3 John Divers begins by setting Plantinga's work in the context of the recent history of thought in this area. He then outlines twelve distinctive features of Plantinga's position, before briefly pointing the reader towards perhaps the three most important lines of critique that have been directed against Plantinga in this regard.

In the fourth chapter Ernest Sosa considers what has become known as Plantinga's evolutionary argument against naturalism. In this argument, which Plantinga first outlined in 1991,[26] the traditional relationship between theology and atheology is turned on its head, for now the claim is that it is atheology (or more specifically, evolution-based naturalism) that is irrational. The argument, in its crudest form, takes as its starting point the idea that in evolutionary theory the only value is survival value, and that this is therefore the only measure that can be applied to our cognitive faculties, including those that we would generally think of as truth-directed. But, argues Plantinga, if our cognitive faculties have evolved purely because they have had survival value in the past, and given that in any particular situation there are generally considerably more beliefs with survival value than there are true beliefs, then the likelihood of our cognitive faculties enabling us to have true beliefs is rather low, and we therefore have a defeater for the belief that our cognitive faculties are reliable. Given that those beliefs (if one is an evolutionary naturalist) include the belief that evolutionary naturalism is true, we must, argues Plantinga, conclude that evolutionary naturalism is a self-undermining doctrine. It is an argument that has received considerable attention in philosophical circles, including an entire book dedicated to it.[27] Another indication of the impact of this argument is the fact that in Chapter 4 of our volume, as distinguished a scholar as Ernest Sosa returns to address this argument for a second time.[28]

The notion of epistemic defeat is an essential feature of Plantinga's evolutionary argument against naturalism, as well as his work on warrant. It is thus fitting that between Sosa's chapter and James Beilby's account of Plantinga on warranted Christian belief lies Jonathan Kvanvig's analysis of epistemic defeat. Using the image of a house to represent epistemic theory, Kvanvig distinguishes between two approaches to the concept of defeat, the 'front-door' and the 'backdoor' approach. He characterises Plantinga's approach as an example of a backdoor approach – that is, "one which assumes a context of actual belief and an existent, complete noetic system, and which describes epistemic defeat in terms of what sort of doxastic and noetic responses would be appropriate to the addition of particular pieces of information." Against this Kvanvig defends a front-door approach, which "begins with propositional relationships, only by implication describing what happens in the context of a noetic system."

In shaping a volume dedicated to as prolific and important a philosopher as Plantinga, it is no easy task to decide what to include and what, of necessity, must be left out. What has not been difficult, however, has been the decision to dedicate a greater proportion of the overall word count to the chapter devoted to expounding Plantinga's *Warranted Christian Belief*. In many ways this book represents the confluence of all of the most central strands of Plantinga's philosophical career, and James Beilby offers a thorough account of this work and its origins in Chapter 6. Beilby's central critiques – that Plantinga undermines the impact of his model of warranted Christian belief by a) failing to argue for its truth, b) focusing on the paradigmatic case of belief rather than belief as it is typically held by actual Christians, and c) failing to fully articulate the theological details of how warranted Christian beliefs are formed – are all articulated against a background recognition that Plantinga's theory is the most comprehensive attempt in existence to produce a work of distinctly Christian philosophy, and that no such work can possibly cover every desirable piece of philosophical ground.

Perhaps the most vigorously contested questions that have arisen among those who have felt the impact of *Warranted Christian Belief* are the ones surrounding the implications of religious diversity for Plantinga's model of belief. It is widely held among critics of the sort of religious exclusivism held by Plantinga that religious diversity acts as a defeater for the warrant one might otherwise have for exclusive religious beliefs. Not surprisingly, Plantinga has contested this claim, arguing that Christian belief can be warranted even in circumstances in which one is acutely aware of the existence of other religions. In Chapter 7 of this book, Kelly James Clark scrutinises both sides of this debate before concluding that Plantinga's critics are mistaken in believing that the existence of religious diversity *must* decrease the warrant for Christian belief, but that nonetheless, this *may* result in some cases.

Plantinga, of course, remains a vigorous and prolific contributor to contemporary philosophy. In recognition of this, the final chapter is dedicated to a philosophical question on which Plantinga has only recently focused his attention, the issue of mind-body dualism. While this is new ground for Plantinga, it will be obvious by now that this is a topic that falls comfortably within the range of the broad thrust of his Christian philosophy. In defence of mind-body dualism, Plantinga has recently offered an argument that asks us to imagine a fictional but possible scenario in which, while seated in his chair reading the comics section of the newspaper, all the parts of his body are, in rapid sequence, removed and replaced, without at any point disrupting the phenomenology of his comic-reading enjoyment. Peter van Inwagen draws this tribute to Plantinga's work to a close by setting up the many implications and inherent assumptions of this argument, and outlining his own point of departure from Plantinga's position.

Mention must also be made of the appendix to this volume, entitled "Two Dozen (or so) Theistic Arguments." As Plantinga explains in his brief introduction, the appendix consists of a set of lecture notes that were never intended for publication. However, as Oppy's chapter makes clear, through Internet distribution these notes have become an essential part of the Plantinga corpus, and are often referred to in the secondary literature. With Professor Plantinga's permission they are published here – in unaltered format – for the first time, in recognition of their importance in understanding his views on natural theology. It is hoped that doing so will provide scholars of his work a reliably citable source in this regard.

The range of Plantinga's published work is such that a volume like this one is inevitably incomplete. The incompleteness is pleasingly exacerbated by the fact that Plantinga is as prolific as ever – readers can in the near future expect to see in print the fruits of his 2005 Gifford Lectures at the University of St Andrews, entitled "Science and Religion: Conflict or Concord?" Despite these limitations, it is the ardent hope of all of the contributors to this volume that it will be a useful contribution to the scholarship surrounding the exceptional work of Alvin Plantinga.

Notes

1. Quoted by Philip Blosser, "God Among the Philosophers," in *New Oxford Review* 66, no. 9 (October 1999), p. 39.
2. Ibid.
3. Andrew Chignell, "Epistemology for Saints: Alvin Plantinga's Magnum Opus," *Books and Culture*, March/April 2002, online edition.
4. *Faith and Philosophy* 1(1984), pp. 253–271.
5. The material in this section draws on Plantinga's "Self-Profile," which appears in *Alvin Plantinga*, James E. Tomberlin and Peter van Inwagen (eds.), 1985, Dordrecht: D. Reidel Publishing, pp. 3–97; his "A Christian Life Partly Lived," which appears in *Philosophers Who Believe: The Spiritual Journeys of 11 Leading Thinkers*, Kelly James Clark (ed.), 1993, Downers Grove, IL: InterVarsity, pp. 45–82; and an interview with Professor Plantinga kindly granted the editor, which took place on 15 November 2005. What is offered here is the barest sketch – interested readers are encouraged to read the most enjoyable self-descriptions given by Plantinga that appear in print in the books just mentioned.
6. Plantinga, "A Christian Life Partly Lived," p. 49.
7. Ibid., p. 68.
8. Ibid.
9. Ibid., p. 51.
10. Plantinga, "Self-Profile," p. 9.
11. Plantinga, "A Christian Life Partly Lived," p. 53.
12. Plantinga, "Self-Profile," p. 14.
13. Ibid., p. 18.

14. Ibid., p. 20.
15. Ibid., pp. 21–22.
16. Ibid., p. 22.
17. Ibid., p. 23.
18. Ibid., p. 29.
19. Ibid., p. 33.
20. http://www.nd.edu/~cprelig/activities.html, accessed 26 April 2006.
21. Plantinga, "A Christian Life Partly Lived," pp. 68–69.
22. Linda Zagzebski (ed.), 1993, Notre Dame, IN: University of Notre Dame Press.
23. Plantinga points out that Rudolph Carnap mused that the 'meaningless' sentences of theology and metaphysics might be best understood as a form of music (Plantinga, *Warranted Christian Belief*, p. 8).
24. Plantinga, "A Christian Life Partly Lived," p. 72.
25. See, for example "A Christian Life Partly Lived," p. 70. However, it must be noted that, as Plantinga pointed out in a recent e-mail communication with the editor, his "Supralapsarianism, or O Felix Culpa," which appeared in *Christian Faith and the Problem of Evil* (Peter van Inwagen, ed., Eerdmans 2004), is probably best characterised as a theodicy.
26. Alvin Plantinga, "An Evolutionary Argument against Naturalism," *Logos* 12, pp. 29–49.
27. *Naturalism Defeated? Essays on Plantinga's Evolutionary Argument Against Naturalism*, James Beilby (ed.), 2002, Ithaca, NY, and London: Cornell University Press.
28. The first being his contribution to the Beilby volume (see note 27), "Plantinga's Evolutionary Meditations," pp. 91–102.

1 | Natural Theology
GRAHAM OPPY

In this chapter, I provide a chronological survey of Plantinga's changing conceptions of the project of natural theology, and of the ways in which those conceptions of the project of natural theology interact with his major philosophical concerns. In his earliest works, Plantinga has a very clear and strict conception of the project of natural theology, and he argues very clearly (and correctly) that that project fails. In his middle works, he has a tolerably clear and slightly less strict conception of the project of natural theology, and he argues – in my view unsuccessfully – that this project succeeds. In his later works, he has a much less clear and less strict conception of the project of natural theology, and it is much harder to determine whether there is any merit in the claims that he makes for natural theology as thus conceived.

GOD AND OTHER MINDS (1967)

The central question that Plantinga seeks to answer in *God and Other Minds*[1] is whether it is rational to believe that the God of the Judaeo-Christian tradition exists. At least prima facie, it seems that there are two ways of understanding this question. On the one hand, the question might be whether reason *requires* belief in the God of the Judaeo-Christian tradition; on the other hand, the question might be whether reason *permits* belief in that God. It is not entirely clear how this question is meant to be interpreted in this work (though, in the light of Plantinga's subsequent publications, I think that the best guess is that the key question is whether reason *permits* belief in God).

In *God and Other Minds*, Plantinga claims that the aim of natural theology is to show that the claim that the God of the Judaeo-Christian tradition exists "follows deductively or inductively from propositions that are obviously true and accepted by nearly every sane man . . . together with propositions that are self-evident or necessarily true."[2] Moreover, he goes on to say that "it is evident that if [the natural theologian] succeeds in showing that these beliefs do indeed follow from those propositions, he succeeds in showing that these beliefs are rational."[3] Consequently, on Plantinga's account of natural theology, it seems that the aim of natural theology must be something very close to establishing that reason *requires* belief in God: for it seems that if the natural theologian can succeed in carrying out the project that Plantinga sets for him, then almost any sane man is rationally required to believe that God exists (at least once he is apprised of the relevant chains of reasoning). However, it is worth noting that while it might in some sense be overkill, the success of natural theology would also establish that reason *permits* the belief that the God of the Judaeo-Christian tradition exists: so we should not leap too quickly to the conclusion that the central question to which Plantinga seeks an answer is whether belief in God is rationally required.

In *God and Other Minds*, Plantinga argues that there are no successful pieces of natural theology: There is no known argument that establishes that the claim that God exists follows deductively or inductively from propositions that are obviously true and accepted by nearly every sane man, together with propositions that are self-evident or necessarily true. His argument for this conclusion has the following form: The most plausible candidates for successful pieces of natural theology are arguments X, Y, and Z; but, upon examination, we see that arguments X, Y, and Z are not successful. So "it is hard to avoid the conclusion that natural theology does not provide a satisfactory answer to the question [of whether it is] rational to believe in God."[4] I shall return to say more about the details of this argument in a moment.

Similarly, in the same work, Plantinga characterises natural atheology as "the attempt, roughly, to show that, given what we know, it is impossible or unlikely that God exists." More exactly, it seems that natural atheology should be the project of showing that the claim that the God of the Judaeo-Christian tradition does not exist follows deductively or inductively from propositions that are obviously true and accepted by nearly every sane man, together with propositions that are self-evident or necessarily true. But again Plantinga argues that there are no successful arguments of this kind. No doubt unsurprisingly, his argument for this conclusion has the following form: The most plausible candidates for successful pieces of natural atheology are arguments X, Y, and Z; but, upon examination, we see that arguments X, Y, and Z are not successful. So "natural atheology seems no better than natural theology as an answer to the question [whether religious beliefs are] rationally justified."[5] (Indeed, Plantinga adds that "if the answer of the natural theologian does not carry conviction, that of the natural atheologian is even less satisfactory."[6] But it seems to me to be highly doubtful that there is anything in his text that justifies this further claim.)

In the face of the (supposed) failure of both natural theology and natural atheology, Plantinga proposes to try "a different approach"[7] to the question of whether belief in God is rational. Consider the perennial philosophical problem of 'other minds', the problem of whether and how we know the thoughts and feelings of other people, or, more radically, how we know whether other people have minds at all. There is no doubt that the beliefs that other people have minds, and that one does – at least some of the time – know the thoughts and feelings of other people, are rational (i.e., both rationally permitted and rationally required). However, according to Plantinga, there is no satisfactory answer to the question of whether and how we know the thoughts and feelings of other people: The best argument that we can construct for the existence of other minds is the analogical argument, but this argument fails (in just the same way that the best argument for the existence of God fails). Since rational belief in other minds does not require an answer to the question of whether and how we know the thoughts and feelings of other people, it seems not unreasonable to suppose that rational belief in God does not require an answer to the question of why and how we know of the existence of God. "Hence my tentative conclusion: if my belief in other minds is rational, so is my belief in God. But obviously the former is rational; so, therefore, is the latter."[8]

There is much that I find elusive in this 'different approach'. In particular, it is quite unclear why one should think that the considerations that Plantinga advances support the claim that if belief in other minds is rationally permissible, then belief in God is rationally permissible, even if those considerations are independently plausible. On the one hand, there just is no intellectually serious dispute about the truth of the claim that if there is at least one mind, then there are many minds. On the other hand, there is intellectually serious dispute about the claim that God exists. While we all agree that it is a Moorean fact – a commonsense claim that is beyond serious dispute – that if there is at least one mind, then there are many minds, we do not all agree that it is a Moorean fact that God exists. Consequently, there is a good prima facie reason to suppose that the claim that belief in other minds is rationally permissible – and, indeed, arguably, rationally required – lends no significant support to the claim that it is rationally permissible, let alone rationally required, that one believe in God. Of course, one might also well wish to take issue with the claim that there is no satisfactory answer to the question of whether and how we know the thoughts and feelings of other people: but it would take us far beyond our current brief to try to explore *that* suggestion here.

If we agree that Plantinga's different approach fails to provide a satisfactory answer to the question of the rationality of belief in God, then there are two courses of response that seem indicated. On the one hand, we might wish to look more closely at Plantinga's treatment of what he calls 'natural theology' and 'natural atheology', to see whether his assessment of these projects is accurate; on the other hand, we might cast around for other ways in which that question might be answered (and, in so doing, we might consider the question whether he provides an appropriate characterisation of natural theology and natural atheology). In the rest of this section, we shall focus on the first of these possible responses.

As I noted earlier, Plantinga's critique of natural theology in *God and Other Minds* proceeds by examining what he takes to be the most plausible arguments for the existence of God and showing that these arguments fail. There are thus two ways in which his critique could fail: He could be wrong in his assessment of the arguments that he chooses to examine, and he could be wrong in his assumption that he has examined the most plausible arguments that are available to us.

The first argument that Plantinga examines – 'the cosmological argument' – is Aquinas's third way. Plantinga's analysis of this argument is exemplary; I doubt that there are any people who would seriously defend the claim that Aquinas's third way is a successful piece of natural theology, given the criteria for success that are currently in play. However, there are other arguments that have come to prominence in more recent philosophical discussion, and it would be interesting to know whether Plantinga is now disposed to see any kind of merit in those other arguments.[9]

The second argument that Plantinga examines – 'the ontological argument' – is presented in two forms: Anselm's famous *Proslogion II* argument, and Malcolm's very well known *Proslogion III* argument. Once again, Plantinga's discussion of these arguments is exemplary; once again, I doubt that there are any people who would seriously defend the claim that Malcolm's argument is a successful piece of natural theology. It is interesting that Plantinga's criticism of Anselm is tempered: While he maintains that the argument is unsuccessful, he allows for the possibility that there might be an interpretation of the argument upon which it succeeds. Moreover, he makes a strong case for the claim that no one has produced a compelling *general* argument against the possibility of successful ontological arguments – and, in particular, he provides very effective criticisms of Kant's claim that ontological arguments fail because they rely upon the misguided assumption that existence is a predicate.

The third and final argument that Plantinga examines – 'the teleological argument' – is cast in the following form:

1. Everything that exhibits curious adaptation of means to ends, and is such that we know whether or not it is the product of intelligent design, is in fact the product of intelligent design.

2. The universe exhibits curious adaptation of means to ends.

3. (Therefore) The universe is probably the product of intelligent design.

About this argument, Plantinga says that Hume identified the fatal flaw: While the premises of this argument may provide some – "not very strong, perhaps, but not completely negligible"[10] – support for the claim that the universe is designed, they provide no support at all for the claim that the universe is designed by exactly one person, or the claim that the universe is created ex nihilo, or the claim that the universe is created by the person who designed it, or the claim that the creator of the universe is omniscient, omnipotent and perfectly good, or the claim that the creator of the universe is an eternal spirit, without body, and in no way dependent upon physical objects. Given that the aim of natural theology is to prove the existence of the Judaeo-Christian God, it is plain – according to Plantinga – that this teleological argument is unsuccessful. One is left wondering whether we should suppose that the premises of the argument provide *enough* support for the conclusion to license the claim that it is rational to believe that the universe is probably the product of intelligent design. Alas, Plantinga did not take up this question in *God and Other Minds*. It is also a nice question whether he continues to suppose that the foregoing is the strongest type of argument for design; we shall have reason to return to this question later.

At the end of his discussion of these arguments, Plantinga adds: "Now of course these three are not the only arguments of their kind; there are also, for example, the various sorts of moral arguments for God's existence. But these are not initially very plausible and do not become more so under close scrutiny."[11] As we shall see, there are various moral arguments mentioned in "Two dozen (or so) Theistic Arguments," along with a slew of arguments that are plainly distinct from the teleological argument previously discussed. Again, one wonders whether any of these arguments can be considered to be successful, given the criteria for success that are in play in *God and Other Minds*.

The considerations that we have noted in connection with the arguments attributed to the natural theologian in *God and Other Minds* apply equally to the arguments attributed to the natural atheologian in that work. Plantinga considers only the standard (Mackie/McCloskey) logical arguments from evil, Mackie's argument that the concept of omnipotence is incoherent, Findlay's ontological argument for the nonexistence of God, and critiques of religious belief founded in verificationist considerations. While Plantinga's critiques of these arguments are compelling – particularly given the criteria for success that are in play – it is a nice question whether there are more successful atheological arguments that have appeared on the scene since the publication of *God and Other Minds*.

GOD, FREEDOM, AND EVIL (1974) AND *THE NATURE OF NECESSITY* (1974)

In *God, Freedom, and Evil*[12] – and in the relevant parts of *The Nature of Necessity*[13] – the central topic of inquiry is, once again, the rationality of belief that the God of the Judaeo-Christian tradition exists. However, in these works, it seems that the conception of natural theology and natural atheology changes dramatically, in line with a corresponding change in the assessment of the success of the arguments under consideration.

In *God, Freedom, and Evil*, Plantinga claims that natural theology is a response to the rejection of the belief that God exists, both by those who claim that the belief is false and those who claim that the belief is irrational. While a natural theologian "tries to give successful arguments or proofs for the existence of God . . . [he does not] typically offer his arguments in order to convince people of God's existence; and in fact few who accept theistic belief do so because they find such an argument compelling. Instead the typical function of natural theology has been to show that religious belief is rationally acceptable."[14]

This characterisation of natural theology is very interestingly different from the characterisation of natural theology in *God and Other Minds*. In particular, on this characterisation of natural theology, it seems that the 'different approach' that Plantinga adopts in the last part of *God and Other Minds* is, after all, a piece of natural theology. For, plainly enough, the argument of the different approach is intended to establish the conclusion that it is rationally permissible to believe that God exists – and, on the new account before us, *that* is the typical function of natural theology. What is unclear is whether Plantinga now supposes that the natural theologian offers his arguments in order to *convince* people of the rationality of the belief that God exists; talk of '*showing* that religious belief is rationally acceptable' neatly avoids any commitment on this point.

There is also a different characterisation of natural atheology in *God, Freedom, and Evil*. "Some philosophers . . . have presented arguments for the falsehood of theistic beliefs; these philosophers conclude that belief in God is demonstrably irrational or unreasonable. We might call this enterprise *natural atheology*."[15] There is now a curious asymmetry between the definition of 'natural theology' and the definition of 'natural atheology'. Given that natural theology has the aim of showing that religious belief is rationally acceptable, it ought surely to be the case that natural atheology has the aim of showing that nonreligious belief is rationally acceptable. Of course, one way of carrying out the aim of the natural atheologian would be to show that it is irrational to believe that God exists; but that is not the only way in which the project of the natural atheologian can be carried out. Moreover, when we come to consider the arguments of a natural atheologian, we should make sure that we evaluate them by the same standards that we apply when we are evaluating the arguments of the natural theologian. We can ask whether a given argument proves that God exists, and we can ask whether that same argument establishes that it is rationally acceptable to believe that God exists; equally, we can ask whether a given argument proves that God does not exist, and we can ask whether that same argument establishes that it is rationally acceptable to believe that God does not exist.

In *God, Freedom, and Evil*, under the heading of 'natural atheology', Plantinga considers various arguments from evil, an argument for the incompatibility of divine omniscience with human freedom, and the highlights of the discussion of verificationist arguments in *God and Other Minds*. His conclusion is this: "There are arguments we haven't considered, of course; but so far the indicated conclusion is that natural atheology doesn't work. Natural atheology, therefore, is something of a flop."[16] And, of course, what Plantinga means here is that these arguments do not establish that it is rationally impermissible to believe that God exists. But that does not rule out the possibility that these or related arguments do establish that it is rationally permissible to believe that God does not exist.

Under the heading of 'natural theology', Plantinga briefly rehashes the treatment of cosmological and teleological arguments from *God and Other Minds*, and then devotes considerable space to the discussion of ontological arguments and, in particular, to the development of a 'triumphant' modal ontological argument. This argument goes as follows:

1. It is possible that there is a maximally great being, that is, a being that is omniscient, omnipotent, and perfectly good in every possible world.

2. (Therefore) There is an omniscient, omnipotent, and perfectly good being.

About this argument, Plantinga says: "It must be conceded that not everyone who understands and reflects on its premise ... will accept it. Still, it is evident, I think, that there is nothing contrary to reason or irrational in accepting this premise. What I claim for this argument, therefore, is that it establishes, not the truth of theism, but its rational acceptability. And hence it accomplishes at least one of the aims of the tradition of natural theology."[17]

If we agree with Plantinga that this argument 'establishes the rational acceptability of theism', then, it seems to me, we have no choice but to agree that the following argument establishes the rational acceptability of atheism:

1. It is possible that there is no world that contains the amounts and kinds of evils that are present in our world and in which there is an omniscient, omnipotent, and perfectly good being.

2. (Therefore) There is no omniscient, omnipotent, and perfectly good being.

Of course, it must be conceded that not everyone who understands and reflects on its premise will accept it. Still, it is evident, I think, that there is nothing contrary to reason or irrational in accepting this premise. So, if I follow Plantinga, I can claim for this argument that it establishes the rational acceptability of atheism – and hence accomplishes what ought to be one of the aims of natural atheology.

In his discussion of his 'triumphant' modal ontological argument, Plantinga makes the point that even though theists are bound to suppose that the following argument is sound:

1. Either God exists, or $7 + 5 = 14$

2. It is false that $7 + 5 = 14$

3. (Therefore) God exists,

it is obvious that this argument fails to prove that God exists: "no one who didn't already accept the conclusion would accept the first premise."[18]

However, it seems to me that it is equally obvious that this argument fails to prove that the claim that God exists is rationally acceptable: for no one who didn't already accept this conclusion would accept that the first premise is rationally acceptable. But exactly the same point can be made about Plantinga's 'victorious' modal ontological argument: Since no (reasonable) person who doesn't already accept that the claim that God exists is rationally acceptable will accept the claim that the premise in Plantinga's argument is rationally acceptable, that argument fails to prove that the claim that God exists is rationally acceptable. Of course, all theists suppose that the claim that either God exists or $7 + 5 = 14$ is rationally acceptable – and many theists suppose that the premise in Plantinga's argument is rationally acceptable – but no one who denies (or doubts) that the claim that God exists is rationally acceptable will agree with theists in their assessment of these claims. Consequently, if the project of natural theology is to *convince* people of the rationality of the belief that God exists, then it seems that we are bound to conclude that Plantinga's 'victorious' modal ontological argument is not a successful piece of natural theology.

Suppose we take seriously the idea that it is not part of the project of natural theology to *convince* people of the rationality of the belief that God exists, and insist that all that natural theology aims to do is to *show* that it is rational to believe that God exists. In that case, even if the foregoing remarks are correct, we might still claim that there is nothing partisan about Plantinga's assessment of natural theology and natural atheology in *God, Freedom, and Evil*. For, we might say, while the 'victorious' modal ontological argument really does *show* that it is rational to believe that God exists, neither the corresponding atheological modal ontological argument nor any of the other atheological arguments *shows* that it is rational to believe that God does not exist. However, at the very least, one would like to have an account of *showing* that bears out the mooted differential treatment: If, for example, we hold that the 'victorious' modal ontological arguments show *to theists* that it is rational *for theists* to believe that God exists, why shouldn't we also say that the corresponding 'victorious' atheological modal ontological arguments show *to atheists* that it is rational *for atheists* to believe that God does not exist?

"REASON AND BELIEF IN GOD" (1983)

In "Reason and Belief in God,"[19] Plantinga takes up a set of questions about the connections between faith and reason: Do believers accept the existence of God as a matter of faith? Is belief in God irrational, unreasonable, or otherwise contrary to reason? Must one have evidence in order to have reasonable or rational belief in God? Are there proofs of the existence of God? Why are Reformed and Calvinist thinkers hostile to the project of natural theology? Are Reformed and Calvinist thinkers right to take a jaundiced view of natural theology? In answer to these questions, Plantinga defends the view that the Reformed objection to natural theology "is best understood as an implicit rejection of classical foundationalism in favor of the view that belief in God is properly basic."[20] According to Reformed and Calvinist thinkers, "it is entirely right, rational, reasonable, and proper to believe in God without any evidence or argument at all; in this respect belief in God resembles belief in the past, in the existence of other persons, and in the existence of material objects."[21] Moreover, says Plantinga, the 'fundamental insights' of the Reformed and Calvinist thinkers are correct: Classical foundationalism is "both false and self-referentially incoherent,"[22] and belief in God can be *properly basic*, that is such that the proposition that God exists is properly believed even though it is not believed "on the basis of other propositions."[23]

Much of "Reason and Belief in God" is taken up with the character-isation of classical foundationalism. In short, the classical foundationalist claims 1) that in a rational noetic structure the believed-on-the-basis-of relation is asymmetric and irreflexive, 2) that a rational noetic structure has a foundation, 3) that in a rational noetic structure belief is proportional in strength to support from the foundations, and 4) that a proposition p is properly basic for a person S if p is either self-evident to S, or incorrigible for S, or evident to the senses for S.[24]

The core of the argument that Plantinga mounts against classical foun-dationalism concerns the standing of claim 4:

> If the classical foundationalist knows of some support for (4) from proposi-tions that are self-evident, or evident to the senses, or incorrigible, he will be able to provide a good argument...whose premises are self-evident, or evident to the senses, or incorrigible, and whose conclusion is (4). So far as I know, no classical foundationalist has provided such an argument. It therefore appears that the classical foundationalist does not know of any support for (4) from propositions that are (on his account) properly basic. So if he is to be rational in accepting (4), he must (on his own account) accept it as basic. But according to (4) itself, (4) is properly basic for the classical foundationalist only if (4) is self-evident or incorrigible or evident to the senses for the classical foundationalist. Clearly, (4) meets

none of these conditions. . . . But then the classical foundationalist is self-referentially inconsistent in accepting (4).[25]

While it seems to me that there is some wiggle room here for the classical foundationalist – in particular, with respect to the assumption that if epistemic relations hold within a rational noetic structure, then those relations are *available* as items of knowledge to the person who possesses that rational noetic structure – it is not clear that there is much harm in the concession that Plantinga's argument inflicts mortal harm on classical foundationalism. For if we allow that a classical foundationalist can claim that knowledge of the relevant epistemic relations need not be available to the person who possesses a rational noetic structure, then we block any straightforward argument from classical foundationalism to the irrationality of theistic belief amongst those who are unable to offer good arguments on behalf of the claim that God exists.

Of course, as Plantinga himself acknowledges, it is a very long step from the rejection of classical foundationalism to the rejection of the evidentialist critique of theism, that is, to the rejection of the claim that 1) it is irrational or unreasonable to accept theistic belief in the absence of sufficient evidence or reasons, and 2) there is no evidence or at any rate not sufficient evidence for the proposition that God exists. However, for our purposes, it is more important to focus on the alternative viewpoint defended by those Reformed thinkers who deny the claim that, in a rational noetic structure, basic beliefs are either self-evident, or incorrigible, or evident to the senses. According to the view that Plantinga claims to endorse: a) Arguments or proofs are not, in general, the source of a believer's confidence in God; b) arguments or proofs are not needed for rational justification: a believer is entirely within his or her epistemic rights in believing, even if he or she has no argument at all for the conclusion that God exists; and c) the believer does not need natural theology in order to achieve rationality or epistemic propriety: the believer's belief in God can be perfectly rational even if the believer knows no cogent argument, and even if there *is* no cogent argument, for the existence of God. More strongly, some of the Reformed thinkers also maintain d) that we cannot come to knowledge of God on the basis of argument because the arguments of natural theology simply do not work; e) that Christian believers should start from belief in God rather than from the premises of an argument whose conclusion is that God exists; f) that God has created us in such a way that we have a strong tendency or inclination towards belief, albeit one that is often overlaid or suppressed by sin; and g) that belief in God relevantly resembles belief in the existence of the self, or the past, or other minds, in that in none of these cases do we have, or have need of, proofs or arguments.

While Plantinga maintains, at least loosely speaking, that belief in God is properly basic, he does not maintain that it is *groundless*. In general, those beliefs that are properly basic – perceptual beliefs, memory beliefs, beliefs about occurrent mental states, and the like – are so only in certain conditions that are the grounds for the justification of those beliefs. Similarly, he claims, there are conditions under which such beliefs as that God is speaking to me, or that God has created all this, or that God disapproves of what I have done, or that God forgives me, or that God is to be thanked or praised are properly basic: There are circumstances that properly "call forth"[26] these beliefs. Strictly speaking, then, it is *these* kinds of beliefs that are properly basic; but it is a short inference from the content of any of these beliefs to the claim that God exists. Consequently, then, the belief that God exists is shown to be neither gratuitous nor groundless on the Reformed view: There are conditions that are grounds for the justification of particular beliefs whose truth entails that God exists.

Given the foregoing considerations, one might suspect that, on the Reformed view, there is no role left for the arguments of either natural theology or natural atheology. However, at the end of "Reason and Belief in God," Plantinga does note that argument is not entirely *irrelevant* to basic belief in God. First, someone whose belief in God is properly basic may also have other more strongly held properly basic beliefs that entail that there is no God; when apprised of this fact – for example, by way of an argument that takes those other beliefs as premises – that person might give up the properly basic belief in God. Second, someone who believes that there is no God might be brought to believe that God exists by an argument that appeals to other beliefs that are more strongly held, and which jointly entail that God exists. Third, as Plantinga emphasises, the justification conditions for properly basic beliefs can only be taken to confer prima facie justification (rather than *ultima facie*, or all-things-considered, justification). Consequently, a person who holds a properly basic belief that God exists can be confronted by circumstances in which there is a potential defeater for this belief, for example, presentation of an atheological argument from evil, or presentation of a Freudian account of the origins of religious belief, or the like: "If the believer is to remain justified, something further is called for – something that *prima facie* defeats the defeaters."[27] Perhaps, for example, one might discover a flaw in the presented atheological argument, or have it on reliable authority that someone else has discovered a flaw in that argument, or whatever. So, at the very least, the Reformed view that

Plantinga defends leaves room for the suggestion that believers need to find 'defeaters' for the arguments of the natural atheologian (at least if they are placed in circumstances in which they encounter those arguments).

In closing this section, it is important to emphasise that in "Reason and Belief in God," Plantinga's primary objective is to defend the claim that the success of the arguments of natural theology is not *necessary* for rational belief that God exists. While I have noted that Plantinga seems to quote with approval the view of the Reformed thinkers that we cannot come to knowledge of God on the basis of argument – "the arguments of natural theology just do not work"[28] – it is not clear that this entails a negative verdict on the suitability of those arguments for other purposes. In particular, it is worth noting the following passage:

[That there is no evidence or at any rate not sufficient evidence for the proposition that God exists] is a strong claim. What about the various arguments that have been proposed for the existence of God – the traditional cosmological and teleological arguments for example? What about the versions of the moral argument as developed, for example, by A. E. Taylor and more recently by Robert Adams? What about the broadly inductive or probabilistic arguments developed by F. R. Tennant, C. S. Lewis, E. L. Mascall, Basil Mitchell, Richard Swinburne, and others? What about the ontological argument in its contemporary versions? Do none of these provide evidence? Notice: the question is not whether these arguments, taken singly or in combination, constitute proofs of God's existence; no doubt they do not. The question is only whether someone might be rationally justified in believing in the existence of God on the basis of the alleged evidence offered by them; and that is a radically different question.[29]

If we follow Plantinga in thinking that "natural theology is the attempt to prove or demonstrate the existence of God,"[30] then it seems entirely reasonable to claim that the project of natural theology is a failure. Nonetheless, it can still be supposed that this does not settle the question whether the arguments of natural theology can be well used to some other end. Suppose that 'the alleged evidence' offered by the arguments of natural theology is all propositional in form; suppose, in particular, that $\{p_1, \ldots, p_n\}$ are the propositions offered by all of the arguments of natural theology – or, at any rate, that $\{p_1, \ldots, p_n\}$ is a maximal consistent set of such propositions. If someone is rationally justified in believing that God exists on the basis of $\{p_1, \ldots, p_n\}$, then won't it be the case that '$p_1, \ldots, p_n \square$God exists' is a *proof* for that person of the claim that God exists? If other reasonable people can be reasonably brought to the belief that God exists by presenting them with the argument '$p_1, \ldots, p_n$ □God exists', then why shouldn't we suppose that that constitutes a success for the arguments of traditional natural theology?

"THE PROSPECTS FOR NATURAL THEOLOGY" (1991)

In "The Prospects for Natural Theology,"[31] Plantinga considers the uses or functions that natural theology might have. Taking it that natural theology is "the attempt to provide proofs or arguments for the existence of God,"[32] he approves of some potential uses of natural theology and disapproves of others.

If we suppose that the aim of natural theology is to show that the proposition that God exists follows from propositions that are self-evident to us, by way of arguments whose validity is self-evident for us,[33] then according to Plantinga, "it seems unlikely that natural theology can serve this function."[34] However, according to Plantinga, it should not be thought that this is to say anything against the traditional arguments of natural theology, since "no philosophical argument of any significance measures up to those standards."[35]

If we suppose that the aim of natural theology is to provide justification for theistic beliefs – that is, to show that the belief that God exists is not "somehow intellectually second-rate, intellectually improper, unjustified, out of order ... [or otherwise the cause of] big doxastic trouble"[36] – then, according to Plantinga, this is not a task that *needs* to be undertaken. As we have already seen – in our discussion of "Reason and Belief in God" – Plantinga does not accept that there is any good reason to suppose that someone who believes that God exists, but who fails to have any propositional evidence for that belief, is somehow going contrary to his or her epistemic duty. Of course, that's not to say that natural theology is not equal to the task of providing justification for theistic beliefs; the point here is only that those beliefs *may* be perfectly in order even if natural theology is not equal to the task. Consequently, we should not be too quick in supposing that the claims currently under consideration from "The Prospects for Natural Theology" are at odds with the claim – defended in *God, Freedom, and Evil* and *The Nature of Necessity* – that Plantinga's 'victorious' modal ontological argument accomplishes the task of establishing the 'rational acceptability' – the intellectual propriety – of the belief that God exists.

If we suppose that the aim of natural theology is to "transform belief into knowledge"[37] by providing *warrant* for belief in God – that is, by adding to belief "that quality, whatever exactly it is, that distinguishes knowledge from mere true belief"[38] – then, according to Plantinga, whether you accept that the arguments of natural theology are needed in order for the belief that God exists to have warrant depends upon whether or not you think that God exists. On the one hand, "from a non-theistic perspective . . . it will be natural to think that the arguments of natural theology [are] indeed needed for belief in God to have warrant."[39] On the other hand, from a theistic perspective, natural theology is not required in order for the belief that God exists to have warrant: Since properly functioning human cognitive capacities produce belief in God, and since the modules of the design plan governing the production of these beliefs are indeed aimed at truth, the natural view from the theistic perspective is that many people know that there is such a person as God without believing on the basis of the arguments of natural theology.

Even if we were to accept that natural theology is unable to show that the proposition that God exists follows from propositions that are self-evident to us, by way of arguments whose validity is self-evident for us, and that natural theology is not required either to provide justification for theistic beliefs or to provide warrant for theistic beliefs, it would not follow that there is nothing that natural theology can do. According to Plantinga, even if the arguments of natural theology are not the sole source of warrant for theistic beliefs, they may nonetheless "play the role of increasing warrant, and significantly increasing warrant."[40] In particular, good theistic arguments might play the role of "confirming and strengthening"[41] the belief that God exists when that belief is otherwise infirm and wavering.[42]

Even if it is conceded that good theistic arguments might play the role of confirming and strengthening the belief that God exists, it might be denied that there are any good theistic arguments. However, Plantinga claims that if theistic arguments are judged by reasonable standards, then there are many good theistic arguments, that is, arguments that are 'good' in the same sense as "Quine's argument for the indeterminacy of translation, or Kripke's argument against the Russell-Frege account of proper names, or Searle's oriental argument against functionalism."[43] That is, Plantinga claims that there are good arguments "from the nature of sets, of propositions, of numbers, of properties, of counterfactual propositions, . . . from the nature of knowledge, from the nature of proper function, from the confluence of proper function with reliability, from simplicity, from induction . . . good moral arguments; good arguments from the nature of evil; from play, enjoyment, love, nostalgia; and perhaps from colors and flavors,"[44] all of which can play the role of 'confirming and strengthening' theistic belief.

There are many questions that might be asked about the claims defended in "The Prospects for Natural Theology." In particular, there are questions to ask about the connections or relations that hold between the 'good arguments' for the existence of God that Plantinga mentions here and the traditional arguments of natural theology. It is interesting to note that the list of arguments given in "The Prospects for Natural Theology" does not appear to mention any of the traditional arguments of natural theology (though, of course, moral arguments have always been one of the mainstays of natural theology, and, as we shall see in a moment, 'the argument from the nature of proper function' might plausibly be taken to be one of Aquinas's five ways). By contrast, the list of arguments given in "Reason and Belief in God" that was mentioned earlier explicitly appeals to the traditional arguments of natural theology – cosmological arguments, teleological arguments, ontological arguments, and the like.

It is also worth asking questions about the alleged parallel to be found between, for example, Kripke's argument against the Russell-Frege account of proper names and, say, the argument from the nature of numbers to the existence of God. There is a sense in which more or less everyone recognises that Kripke's argument against the Russell-Frege account of proper names is good: Kripke raises a series of objections to the Russell-Frege account of proper names that are widely acknowledged to be both clever and difficult to defeat. However, it is, I think, hardly any less widely recognised that Kripke's objections to the Russell-Frege account of proper names can be overcome: There are descriptivist theories of names that avoid all of the legitimate objections that Kripke raises in the course of his discussion of the Russell-Frege account of proper names. Moreover, this is not an isolated case. Many of those well-known philosophical arguments of which we are inclined to speak approvingly are arguments that we know how to evade. Of course, there are *some* arguments that are successful and nothing more; in particular, there are reductio arguments that succeed in showing that certain philosophical theories are simply inconsistent.[45] However, when it comes to arguments that have as their conclusions claims about perennially controversial philosophical matters, I do not believe that it is particularly sceptical to claim that there are very few successful philosophical arguments. We might say that Quine's argument for the indeterminacy of translation, or Searle's oriental argument against functionalism is good; but, when we do so,

I think that we most likely mean that those arguments are interesting, and original, and insightful, and thought-provoking, and so forth . . . without in any way committing ourselves to the claim that those arguments are successful.

Moreover, even if we do suppose that there are successful philosophical arguments – say, for example, Kripke's arguments against the Frege-Russell theory of proper names – it is not clear that we should be prepared to allow that the various arguments for the existence of God to which Plantinga adverts should be placed in the same category as those successful philosophical arguments. If there are successful philosophical arguments, then those arguments are complicated and sophisticated; they involve long chains of reasoning, careful drawing of distinctions, and so forth. But the arguments of traditional natural theology – and, one might suspect, the arguments to which Plantinga adverts in "The Prospects for Natural Theology" – are not obviously of this kind. Very often, arguments for the existence of God have a couple of premises and involve a couple of inferential steps. It is, I think, very hard to believe that *those* kinds of arguments can be usefully or reasonably compared to 'Quine's argument for the indeterminacy of translation' or 'Kripke's argument against the Frege-Russell account of proper names'.

Finally, before we move on, it is worth noting that there are questions to ask about the very suggestion that good theistic *arguments* could play the role of 'confirming and strengthening' belief in God. Suppose that we accept – as least for present purposes – that belief in God can be strengthened by both testimonial and nontestimonial evidence. Then, of course, the propounding of an argument can confirm and strengthen belief in God in the case in which the propounding of the argument provides either testimonial or nontestimonial evidence that God exists to those to whom the argument is propounded. But in this case, it is highly implausible to suppose that it is the *argumentative virtues* of the argument that are doing the important work; assertions in nonargumentative dress would surely do just as well. However, once we set this kind of case aside, it is much less clear that it is plausible to suppose that there are good theistic arguments that can play the role of 'confirming and strengthening' belief in God, that is, cases in which it is the argumentative virtues of the argument that play the crucial role in the confirming and strengthening.[46] At the very least, one would like to see a more clearly worked out account of exactly how it is that the argumentative virtues of the arguments to which Plantinga adverts can have a significant role in confirming and strengthening theistic belief.

WARRANT AND PROPER FUNCTION (1993)

In the last two chapters of *Warrant and Proper Function*,[47] Plantinga provides two arguments against naturalism, one of which, at least loosely speaking, is intended to show that naturalism is false, and the other of which, at least loosely speaking, is intended to show that naturalism is irrational. Before I can say what these arguments are, I need to fill in some background.

Very roughly, Plantinga defends the view that a belief has warrant for a person only if 1) the belief has been produced in that person by cognitive faculties that are working properly – functioning as they ought to, subject to no cognitive dysfunction – in a cognitive environment that is appropriate for that person's kinds of cognitive faculties; 2) the segment of the design plan governing the production of that belief is aimed at the production of true beliefs; and 3) there is a high statistical probability that a belief produced under those conditions will be true.[48] He claims that this account of warrant is 'naturalistic' because "it invokes no kind of normativity not found in the natural sciences; the only kind of normativity that it invokes figures in such sciences as biology and psychology."[49] Moreover – and more importantly – he holds that "naturalism in epistemology can flourish only in the context of supernaturalism in metaphysics":[50] The correct theory of warrant must be "set in the context of a broadly theistic view of the nature of human beings."[51]

Plantinga's argument for the falsity of naturalism in metaphysics turns on his claim that there is no acceptable naturalistic explanation or analysis of proper function. This claim, in turn, is "supported by a consideration of the main attempts to produce such an analysis"[52] in the work of Hempel, Nagel, Wright, Boorse, Pollock, Millikan, Bigelow and Pargetter, and Neander and Griffiths. In the face of the failure to find an acceptable naturalistic explanation or analysis of proper function, one might consider retreat to a position that treats talk of 'proper function' as a convenient explanatory fiction; but Plantinga suggests that any such retreat must involve "doublethink" and cannot aid in the achievement of "straightforward understanding."[53]

So if you are a metaphysical naturalist, and if you are convinced that there is no way to make sense of the notion of proper function from a metaphysically naturalistic perspective, and if you are unwilling to countenance a fictionalist interpretation of talk of 'proper function', then it seems that you must reject the very idea of proper function and (in consequence) the analysis of warrant that Plantinga defends: "A high price, no doubt – but no more than what a serious naturalism exacts."[54] On the other hand, if you are convinced that there really are such things as warrant and proper function, and if you are convinced that there is no way to make sense of the notion of proper function from a metaphysically naturalistic perspective, and if you are unwilling to countenance a fictionalist interpretation of talk of proper function, then it seems that "what you have is a powerful argument against naturalism."[55] Indeed, says Plantinga, given the plausible alternatives, what you have, more specifically, is a powerful theistic argument, a version of Aquinas's fifth way. For, according to Plantinga, when Aquinas says that 'whatever lacks knowledge cannot move towards an end, unless it be directed by some being endowed with knowledge and intelligence', we may interpret this as the claim that there is no naturalistic explanation or analysis of proper function.

In what sense does Plantinga suppose that this argument from the nature of warrant and proper function is 'a powerful theistic argument'? Is he merely claiming that this argument could play some role in 'confirming and strengthening' belief in God – that is, is he merely claiming that this is a 'good theistic argument' in the sense of "The Prospects for Natural Theology"? If so, why does he use the term 'powerful' in describing what he takes to be the standing of this argument? Is the thought, perhaps, that more or less anyone whose properly basic belief that God exists is neither firm nor unwavering should be able to shore up that belief by appeal to this argument from the nature of warrant and proper function? Or is Plantinga suggesting that this argument goes much further down the path of accomplishing the traditional aims of natural theology?

In his discussion, Plantinga says that *if one satisfies certain conditions*, then one has a powerful argument against naturalism, where the conditions to be satisfied are that one accepts the various premises of the argument in question. This is a very curious way of characterising the virtues of an argument: Why shouldn't the defender of, say, an evidential argument from evil take exactly the same kind of line? If you accept the premises of Rowe's evidential argument from evil, then why don't you have a very powerful argument against classical theism? Perhaps Plantinga might say that the key point is that the cost of rejecting the very notion of proper function and the analysis of warrant upon which it depends is so high: Given that one accepts the premises of the argument from the nature of warrant and proper function, the price of denying his supernaturalist conclusion is very high. But surely the proponent of Rowe's evidential argument from evil is in an even stronger position here: Given that one continues to accept the premises of that argument, one will be positively irrational if one does not go on to accept its conclusion. Perhaps, then, Plantinga might say that the cases differ because theists can reasonably reject one or both of the premises in Rowe's argument, whereas naturalists cannot reasonably reject the premises in the argument from the nature of warrant and proper function. But this contention is manifestly false (or so it seems to me). If one is strongly committed to naturalism, then the most that Plantinga's argument establishes is that either there is a naturalistic explanation or analysis of proper function that has not yet been found, or else there is an acceptable fictionalist treatment of proper function, or else the notion of proper function has no respectable role to play in serious naturalistic theorising.

Those naturalists who think that the notion of proper function has a respectable, realist role to play in serious naturalistic theorising, and who are persuaded by Plantinga's critiques of Hempel, Nagel, Wright, Boorse, Pollock, Millikan, Bigelow and Pargetter, and Neander and Griffiths, can quite reasonably suppose that there is a naturalistic explanation or analysis of proper function that awaits discovery. Most philosophers accept that there are no fully satisfactory explanations or analysis of important philosophical concepts: No one has a *really* satisfying analysis of causation, or explanation, or dispositions, or artworks, or goodness, or rightness, or emotion, or belief, or truth, and so on. The 'puncture and patch' industry that has been engaged in during the past half century or so of analytic philosophy provides good grounds for supposing that new candidate naturalistic analyses or explanations of warrant and proper function will emerge. (Of course, some naturalists will dispute Plantinga's critiques of extant naturalist accounts of warrant and proper function; those naturalists can mount a far more straightforward response to his argument from the nature of warrant and proper function.)

Plantinga's argument for the irrationality of naturalism in metaphysics goes roughly like this. Let R be the claim that our cognitive faculties are reliable, in the sense that they produce mostly true beliefs in the sorts of environments that are normal for them; let E be the claim that human cognitive faculties arose by way of the mechanisms to which contemporary evolutionary thought directs our attention; let C be the proposition that states what cognitive faculties we have – memory, perception, reason, and so forth – and what sorts of beliefs they produce; and let N be the claim that metaphysical naturalism is true. Then, says Plantinga, it is plausible to suppose either that $Pr(R/N\&E\&C)$ is low or that no value can be assigned to $Pr(R/N\&E\&C)$. But, in that case, anyone who accepts N&E has an 'undercutting defeater' for any belief held, that is, a reason to doubt or to reserve judgment about that belief. In particular, then, anyone who accepts N&E has a reason to doubt or to reserve judgment about the acceptance of N&E.

Moreover, this reason to doubt or reserve judgment about the acceptance of N&E cannot itself be ultimately defeated; that is, if you accept N&E, then you have an ultimately undefeated reason to reject N&E. So the rational thing to do is to reject N&E. Furthermore, if you also accept that if N then E, then you have an ultimately undefeated reason to reject N. The rational thing to do is to reject N: "The conclusion to be drawn, therefore, is that the conjunction of naturalism with evolutionary theory is self-defeating: it provides for itself an undefeated defeater. Evolution, therefore, presents naturalism with an undefeated defeater. But if naturalism is true, then, surely, so is evolution. Naturalism, therefore, is unacceptable."[56]

If this argument is intended to persuade naturalists to give up their naturalism, then there are various criticisms that can be made of it. However, if this argument were intended to persuade naturalists to give up their naturalism, then one might think that, by Plantinga's lights, this argument must be a successful piece of natural theology, in something like the sense of success set out in *God and Other Minds*, "Reason and Belief in God," and "The Prospects for Natural Theology." For given the assumption that Pr(R/N&E&C) is either low or undefined, it is plausibly a straightforward matter of fact whether it follows – either deductively or inductively – that it is rationally required to reject N. If it does not follow, from the premise that Pr(R/N&E&C) is either low or undefined, that it is rationally required to reject N, then the argument is entirely without merit (and shows nothing to anyone). If, on the other hand, it does follow, from the premise that Pr(R/N&E&C) is either low or undefined, that it is rationally required to reject N, then the only remaining question is whether Pr(R/N&E&C) *is* either low or undefined. But now, if we suppose that it is not obvious, nor necessary, nor self-evident, nor believed by every sane person that Pr(R/N&E&C) is low or undefined – and, indeed, if we suppose that there is some sense in which reasonable naturalists can hold that Pr(R/N&E&C) is high – then we have no reason at all for thinking that this argument is capable of rationally persuading rational naturalists to give up on their naturalism.

Given that the argument is not intended to persuade naturalists to give up on their naturalism, then what purpose should we suppose it to have? Is it intended to show to theists that theists can reasonably believe that naturalists are irrational? I don't think so. Plantinga does not argue that one cannot reasonably suppose that Pr(R/N&E&C) is high; rather, what he argues is that it is plausible – that is, I take it, plausible *by his lights* – that Pr(R/N&E&C) is either low or undefined. But then, plainly, the argument does not show *anyone* that naturalists are irrational, even if it shows *everyone* that any naturalists who accept that Pr(R/N&E&C) is either low or undefined are irrational.

Is it rather that this argument can play some role in 'confirming and strengthening' belief in God, and in 'increasing the degree of warrant' that belief in God has for given theists? Let's see. Suppose that you are a theist, and that you find yourself wavering on the question of the existence of God. You refer to Plantinga's argument, and note that if you hold that Pr(R/N&E&C) is either low or undefined, then it would be irrational for you to be a naturalist. Even if you suppose that belief in the existence of God is the only serious alternative to naturalism, and even if you do hold that Pr(R/N&E&C) is either low or undefined, it seems – in light of these considerations – that if you have good reason to be wavering on the question of the existence of God, then you have good reason to be wavering on the question whether Pr(R/N&E&C) is either low or undefined. Indeed, given that you are wavering on the question of the existence of God – and given that you hold that naturalism is the only serious alternative to belief in the existence of God – it seems that you *ought* to be wavering on the question of the truth of naturalism, and moreover, if Plantinga's argument is any good, that you *ought* to be wavering on the question whether Pr(R/N&E&C) is either low or undefined. But, if that's right, then it isn't entirely clear how Plantinga's argument *could* play the role of confirming and strengthening belief in God in reasonable believers. (Here, we return to the kinds of questions that were raised at the end of the last section.)

"TWO DOZEN (OR SO) THEISTIC ARGUMENTS" (1986)

Before we turn to an examination of Plantinga's most recent pronounce-ments about natural theology, it will be worthwhile to have a look at some more of the arguments that he claims are 'good theistic arguments,' and to see what else Plantinga says on behalf of those arguments, in "Two Dozen (or so) Theistic Arguments."[57] Plantinga has very similar things to say on behalf of these arguments in "Augustinian Christian Philosophy"[58] and "Rationality and Public Evidence: A Reply to Richard Swinburne."[59] I do not know of any more detailed discussion of these arguments than the one provided in "Two Dozen (or so) Theistic Arguments." Though Plantinga averts to this set of lectures in many places in his published work, until now "Two Dozen (or so) Theistic Arguments" has not been officially published. It is one of the contributions of this volume that this impor-tant phase of Plantinga's work is now published (see the Appendix). In introducing the two dozen (or so) theistic arguments, Plantinga says that they are "not coercive in the sense that every person is obliged to accept their premises on pain of irrationality. It may be just that some or many sensible people do accept their premises." Moreover, he notes that these arguments are 'probabilistic', and that "they can serve to bolster and confirm, and perhaps to convince." Finally, he notes that "you or someone else might just find yourself with these beliefs; so using them as premises gets an effective theistic argument for the person in question," and that "perhaps in at least some of the cases if our faculties are functioning properly and we consider the premises we are inclined to accept them, and, under those conditions, the conclusion has considerable warrant on the premises."

Given the availability of "Two Dozen (or so) Theistic Arguments" in this volume, I will not rehash the arguments here. In response, I take it that there are many atheological arguments of which it is true that some or many sensible people do accept their premises. Moreover, I take it that if theistic arguments can serve to bolster and confirm and perhaps to convince, then so too can atheological arguments. Finally, I take it that people do just find themselves believing the premises of certain atheological arguments. So I take it that in whatever sense Plantinga supposes that there are good theistic arguments, he ought to be prepared to allow that there are also good atheological arguments. Of course, as I have already indicated, I'm sceptical of the claim that the aforementioned properties really do suffice to warrant the claim that an argument is good; but perhaps we do not need to go over that ground again.

As I mentioned initially, all of these arguments are meant to be interpreted as probabilistic arguments: Either the premises are likely to be true, or the probability of the conclusion on the premises is high, or both. And, of course, as I said before, Plantinga does not deny that reasonable atheists can have reasons to resist these arguments. However, it is very hard to know how to go on to discuss these arguments, particularly since Plantinga insists that they are no more than brief encapsulations of arguments that must properly be developed at much greater length. It is very hard to believe that the arguments articulated by Plantinga in "Two Dozen (or so) Theistic Arguments" could play any serious role in confirming and supporting Christian belief, or in 'moving [reasonable and thoughtful] fence-sitters', or in defeating potential defeaters for Christian belief. But as things stand, we have nothing more than Plantinga's confident assertion that these argument sketches can be developed into fully fledged arguments that are capable of playing these roles. At the very least, it seems clear that no good reason has been provided to move atheists to allow that there are any good arguments of the kind to which Plantinga here adverts.

More strongly, one might suspect that there are reasons for doubting that *these* 'argument sketches' are susceptible of development into fully fledged arguments that are capable of playing the roles to which Plantinga appeals. Consider, for example, the Argument from Natural Numbers, which clearly builds upon the discussion of numbers in the concluding pages of *Does God Have a Nature?* The view that Plantinga defends is that numbers are ideas in the mind of God, and that the possession of these ideas is part of God's nature, that is, something that God has in every possible world. Even if we suppose that this is a defensible Christian account of the nature of numbers, it seems to me doubtful to think that this kind of consideration is really well suited to the task of confirming and supporting Christian belief, or of moving reasonable and thoughtful fence-sitters, or of defeating potential defeaters for Christian belief. For instance, I do not think that if I were a fence-sitter, I would suppose that this Christian account of the natural numbers carries any significant weight; I do not think that if I were a wavering Christian, I would suppose that this Christian account of the natural numbers is apt to bolster, or confirm, or support, my declining faith. At the very least, there is a large promissory note here on which payment remains to be made.

Even if – most implausibly – Plantinga were to agree that some – or many, or most, or all – of the two dozen (or so) theistic arguments are not fit for reasonable "bolstering", or "confirming", or "convincing", and so forth, it does not follow that he would need to concede that there are no other arguments that are fit for reasonable bolstering, or confirming, or convincing, and so forth, with respect to the claim that God exists. If theism is true, it seems not outrageous to suppose that there are arguments – or chains of reasoning, or accessible propositions – that are fit to play these roles. Even if theism is false, it seems not outrageous to suppose that there are arguments – or chains of reasoning, or accessible propositions – that are fit to play these roles; indeed, it seems to me that even if theism is false, there is probably good reason to suppose that there are arguments – or chains of reasoning, or accessible propositions – that can serve to bolster or confirm the beliefs of reasonable but wavering theists, and so forth (though I admit to some uncertainty about how exactly to conceive of the mental state of someone who is 'wavering' on the truth of a given proposition, and to holding serious doubts about the idea that *arguments* are the right kinds of entities to appeal to at this point).

WARRANTED CHRISTIAN BELIEF (2000)

Warranted Christian Belief[60] is the most recent extended discussion of Plantinga's views on most of the topics that have been mentioned in the foregoing discussion. The question that he seeks to answer in that book is whether "it is rational, reasonable, justifiable, warranted to accept Christian belief" and whether "there is something... foolish, or silly, or foolhardy, or stupid, or unjustified, or unreasonable" in so doing.[61] And the answer that he provides is that there need be nothing irrational, or unreasonable, or unjustifiable, or unwarranted, or foolish, or silly, or foolhardy, or stupid, or unjustified in the acceptance of Christian belief.

A (very) basic outline of the structure of *Warranted Christian Belief* is as follows. First, Plantinga discusses the suggestion that Christian belief is impossible because there is no way that our concepts could apply to God. Against Kant, Kaufman, and Hick, Plantinga argues that no one has ever provided the slightest reason to think that it is impossible that our concepts apply to God; and, in particular, that Kant, Kaufman, and Hick provide no reason at all to suppose that this is so.[62]

Second, Plantinga considers several different ways in which his question might be understood. If the question is understood to concern justification and doxastic propriety, then, according to Plantinga, it is entirely obvious that Christian belief can be justified and held with proper doxastic propriety. If the question is understood to concern rationality, then on any of the various ways in which 'rationality' might be understood it is entirely obvious that Christian belief can be rational. If the question is understood to concern warrant – that is, that quality or quantity enough of which suffices to make true belief knowledge – then there is a genuine question to be addressed, and one which is plausibly taken to be raised in naturalistic challenges to Christian belief of the kind advanced by Marx, Nietzsche, and Freud.

Third, Plantinga provides a 'model' – or, more exactly, a series of refinements of a 'model' – that is intended to establish that if Christian belief is true, then it is highly likely that Christian belief is warranted. According to this 'model', a person with proper cognitive function has a *sensus divinitatis*, that is, a set of dispositions to form various theistic beliefs in various kinds of circumstances. While the operation of the *sensus divinitatis* is impaired by the consequences of sin, this shortcoming can be – and in the case of the Christian believer is – remedied by the inward instigation of the Holy Spirit. Moreover, according to the model, this inward instigation of the Holy Spirit explains how belief in the divine teachings of Scripture – and, hence, belief in the particular Christian doctrines of the trinity, incarnation, resurrection, atonement, forgiveness of sins, eternal life, and so forth – can be warranted.

Finally, Plantinga replies to various arguments for the conclusion that, while it is indeed possible that Christian belief has warrant, given that the model that he presents is true, there are various reasons for supposing that Christian belief is 'defeated' by countervailing considerations. (Roughly speaking, a person acquires a 'defeater' for a belief B if he or she takes on a belief D that rationally requires rejection of B, or, at any rate, holding B less firmly.)[63] Plantinga assesses Scripture scholarship, postmodernism, religious pluralism, and the amounts and kinds of evils in the world as potential – but rationally rejectable – defeaters for warranted Christian belief.

While there is no systematic discussion of natural theology and natural atheology in *Warranted Christian Belief*, there are various points in this rich and lengthy work at which relevant considerations are advanced. In the remainder of this section, I shall point to some of the relevant material (without pretending that this treatment is in any way comprehensive).

In the course of his discussion of 'justification', Plantinga provides an interesting reassessment of the central arguments of *God and Other Minds*. He claims that early in his career, he took it for granted that the right way to approach the question of the rational justification of theistic beliefs was to think in terms of evidence, or proofs, or good arguments: for example, does the evidence support Christian belief? (I think that it is one question whether the balance of *evidence* comes down in favour of Christian belief, and quite another question whether the balance of *argumentation* comes down in favour of Christian belief. However, it seems that Plantinga still sees no need for any distinction of this kind.) Moreover, he claims that when he assessed "the theistic proofs and arguments" in *God and Other Minds*, he employed a "traditional but wholly improper standard," failing to note that "no philosophical arguments of any consequence" live up to the standards in question.[64] These observations plainly clear the ground for subsequent declarations about the utility and success of 'the theistic proofs and arguments'.

There are various places where Plantinga's remarks suggest that he continues to hold an asymmetric conception of natural theology and natural atheology. On the one hand, natural atheology is in the business of "attacking theistic belief."[65] In order to succeed, natural atheology has to convince Christian believers that Christian belief is false, or unwarranted, or irrational, or unjustified. On the other hand, "Christian philosophers have been for the most part responding to various kinds of attacks on the rational justifiability of religious belief."[66] In order to be successful, natural theology has only to produce arguments that can play some role in defeating potential defeaters of Christian belief, or in confirming and strengthening Christian belief, or in moving fence-sitters to adopt Christian belief, or the like.

I'm inclined to think that as a matter of historical fact, there are many more works that seek to show that atheism is irrational than there are works that seek to show that theism is irrational. Consequently, I doubt that there is any good de facto reason for holding this asymmetrical conception of natural theology and natural atheology. On the other hand, Plantinga might insist that he has a good de jure reason for thinking of the terrain in the way that he does: Because Christian belief seems to him to be true, and, indeed, to be "maximally important truth,"[67] he isn't interested in the other uses to which the arguments of natural atheology might be put by atheists and agnostics. Even if atheists and agnostics can use considerations about evil to confirm and bolster naturalistic beliefs, or to defeat potential defeaters to naturalistic belief, this is of no consequence to Christians.[68]

Perhaps it might be objected here that Plantinga supposes that theism differs importantly from naturalism (at least) in that it is not subject to an undefeated defeater. At one point, he says that "the extended Aquinas/Calvin model... enables us to see what is most important about ourselves, and in so doing removes the defeater that is the Achilles' heel of naturalism."[69] His remark might be taken to suggest that he argues for the claim that belief in naturalism is, at the very least, unwarranted (if not unjustified or irrational). But I take it that all that Plantinga is claiming here is that if theism is true, then naturalism is unwarranted. After all, if naturalism is true, and if you are a naturalist who rejects Plantinga's arguments on behalf of the claim that $Pr(R/N\&E\&C)$ is not high, then – by Plantinga's lights – it's hard to see why it should be denied that your belief in naturalism could be warranted, and justified, and rational.

CONCLUDING REMARKS

As we have seen, Plantinga himself has given different accounts of 'natural theology' at different points in his career. When he supposes that natural theology is the project of showing that the claim that the God of the Judaeo-Christian tradition exists follows deductively or inductively from propositions that are obviously true and accepted by nearly every sane man, together with propositions that are self-evident or necessarily true, he consistently takes the view that natural theology is a failure, and he also consistently takes the view that the reasonableness of belief in God is quite independent of the success or failure of natural theology. When he supposes that natural theology is the project of showing that religious belief is rationally acceptable, his thought moves in two different directions. On the one hand, there are various places where he has given arguments whose conclusion *seems* to be that religious belief is rationally acceptable *tout court* – for example, in the 'different approach' of *God and Other Minds*, and in the 'victorious' modal ontological argument of *God, Freedom, and Evil* and *The Nature of Necessity*; on the other hand, there are places where he argues that religious belief is rationally acceptable *provided* that theism is true – for example, in "Reason and Belief in God" and in *Warranted Christian Belief*. When he supposes that natural theology is the project of providing arguments for the existence of God, then his view seems quite consistently to be that there are various senses in which there are numerous good arguments for the existence of God, that is, arguments that can serve to 'bolster' or 'confirm' the beliefs of reasonable but wavering theists (and perhaps do other things as well).

By my reckoning, Plantinga is entirely right in his assessment of natural theology on its strongest interpretation: There is no prospect of anyone's showing that the claim that the God of the Judaeo-Christian tradition exists follows deductively or inductively from propositions that are obviously true and accepted by nearly every sane man, together with propositions that are self-evident or necessarily true. Moreover, Plantinga's analyses of the arguments of natural theology thus understood are models to be emulated, as are his analyses of the arguments of natural atheology when analogously understood.

It is, however, my view that the arguments Plantinga advances that seem intended to establish that belief in the existence of God is rationally acceptable and nothing more are not successful (for reasons that I have given here). Perhaps it might be suggested that a suitable modification of the synoptic argument ought to suffice to establish this conclusion, but it is not clear to me that this is so. In any case, *I'm* inclined to grant from the outset that belief in the existence of God is rationally permissible: Some – but only some – of the smartest, most thoughtful, and most well informed people that I know are theists. On the other hand, the arguments that Plantinga advances on behalf of the claim that belief in the existence of God is rationally acceptable if theism is true seem to me to be plausible (though perhaps controversial from some *theistic* standpoints). But it seems unlikely that these arguments should cut any ice with those who are not disposed to grant that belief in the existence of God is rationally permissible – for, of course, not one of those people is going to allow that theism is true.

It is also my view that Plantinga's assessment of natural theology on its weakest interpretation is seriously underdeveloped, at least in the materials that I have examined here. I think that we need to look much more closely at the theory of arguments and the theory of rational belief revision before we are in a good position to say whether there are arguments that can serve to bolster or confirm the beliefs of reasonable but wavering theists. When Plantinga analysed some of the traditional arguments under the strongest construal of 'natural theology', it was tolerably clear to what kinds of considerations one could appeal in arguing that a given argument is unsuccessful. But when we turn to those same arguments under the weakest construal of 'natural theology', it is much less clear how we go about scrutinising and discussing the claim that a given argument is successful.[70]

Apart from consideration of Plantinga's views about natural theology, I have also had occasion to make some remarks about his views on natural atheology and naturalism. While Plantinga's conception of natural theology has changed over time, his conception of natural atheology has not visibly altered (though, it must be said, he has less and less to say on this topic in his later works). I take it that this is a weakness in his discussion of natural theology, though I suspect that Plantinga may not see matters in this light. In "Reason and Belief in God," he writes:

> The Christian will of course suppose that belief in God is entirely proper and rational; if he does not accept his belief on the basis of other propositions, he will conclude that it is basic for him and quite properly so. Followers of Bertrand Russell and Madelyn Murray O'Hare may disagree; but how is that relevant? Must my criteria, or those of the Christian community, conform to their examples? Surely not. The Christian community is responsible to *its* set of examples, not theirs.[71]

Perhaps we might think that this attitude applies more generally: What matters to Plantinga is how things are for the theist, and nontheists can look after themselves. If this is right, then it does raise an interesting question about the audience for whom Plantinga is writing. There are pragmatic reasons for supposing that his books are addressed to philosophers in general, that is, that he hopes that his books will be read by theist and atheist alike. The books do not come with warnings to prospective atheist readers; indeed, in *Warranted Christian Belief*, he says that one of the two central projects of the book is addressed "to everyone, believer and non-believer alike."[72] But, if you're genuinely interested in the various disagreements between theists and atheists, then it seems to me that you should be prepared to try to understand how things look from the different sides of the fence.[73] That said, it is worth repeating that Plantinga's analyses of the traditional arguments of natural atheology, on its strongest construal, are also models to be emulated.

As my earlier remarks about Plantinga's arguments against naturalism indicate, it is not entirely clear how these arguments stand in relation to his views about natural theology and natural atheology. While there is some temptation to think that an argument for the conclusion that naturalism is irrational must go most of the way towards establishing that theism is rationally required, it seems to me that it is more accurate to take Plantinga to be claiming that his arguments against naturalism can contribute to the task of bolstering or confirming the beliefs of reasonable but wavering theists. However, it is perhaps safer simply to conclude that he might have done more by way of making clear the connections that he sees between natural theology (on any of its construals) and his arguments against naturalism.

Notes

1. Alvin Plantinga, *God and Other Minds: A Study of the Rational Justification of Belief in God*, Ithaca, NY: Cornell University Press, 1967.
2. Ibid., p. 4.
3. Ibid.
4. Ibid., p. 111.
5. Ibid., p. 183.
6. Ibid., p. 268.
7. Ibid., p. 183.
8. Ibid., p. 271.
9. In particular, it is interesting that only one of the arguments presented in Plantinga's much more recent "Two Dozen (or so) Theistic Arguments" is a cosmological argument; it is also interesting to note that this argument is, at best, a *very* distant cousin of Aquinas's third way.
10. Plantinga, *God and Other Minds*, p. 109.
11. Ibid., p. 111.
12. Alvin Plantinga, *God, Freedom, and Evil*, Grand Rapids, MI: Eerdmans, 1974.
13. Alvin Plantinga, *The Nature of Necessity*, Oxford: Clarendon, 1974.
14. Plantinga, *God, Freedom, and Evil*, p. 2.
15. Ibid., p. 3. Also: "Natural atheology – the attempt to prove that God does not exist or that at any rate it is unreasonable or irrational to believe that He does" (7).

16. Ibid., pp. 73–74.
17. Ibid., p. 112.
18. Ibid.
19. Alvin Plantinga, "Reason and Belief in God," in *Faith and Rationality*, ed. Alvin Plantinga and Nicholas Wolterstorff, Notre Dame, IN, and London: University of Notre Dame Press, 1983, pp. 16–93.
20. Ibid., p. 17.
21. Ibid.
22. Ibid.
23. Ibid., p. 46.
24. A person's noetic structure is the set of propositions that person believes, together with certain epistemic relations that hold between that person and these propositions. An account of a person's noetic structure specifies a) which of that person's beliefs are basic and which are nonbasic; b) an index of the degree of belief, i.e., an indication of how firmly each belief is held; and c) an index of depth of ingression, i.e., an indication of how much the giving up of a particular belief would reverberate through the rest of that person's noetic structure. A noetic structure is rational if it could be the noetic structure of a completely rational person.
25. Plantinga, "Reason and Belief in God," p. 60.
26. Ibid., p. 81.
27. Ibid., p. 84.
28. Ibid., p. 65.
29. Ibid., p. 30.
30. Ibid., p. 63.
31. Alvin Plantinga, "The Prospects for Natural Theology" in *Philosophical Perspectives* 5: *Philosophy of Religion*, ed. James Tomberlin, Atascadero, CA: Ridgeview Press, 1991, pp. 287–316.
32. Ibid., p. 287.
33. Cf. the characterisation of natural theology that Plantinga adopted in *God and Other Minds* and in "Reason and Belief in God."
34. Plantinga, "The Prospects for Natural Theology," p. 289.
35. Perhaps Plantinga overstates matters slightly here. I think that Gödel's argument against the project of Russell and Whitehead's *Principia* does plausibly measure up to the standards in question; however, even if this is so, we can surely agree that it is *very rare* to find significant philosophical arguments that measure up to the standard in question.
36. Plantinga, "The Prospects for Natural Theology," p. 290.
37. Ibid., p. 294.
38. Ibid.
39. Ibid., p. 311.
40. Ibid.
41. Ibid., p. 312.

42. It is interesting to note that in his discussion of this point, Plantinga observes that it is unlikely that arguments for other minds can 'confirm and strengthen' belief in the existence of other minds. This is the kind of disanalogy between the case of belief in the existence of God and belief in the existence of other minds to which I adverted earlier, and which I think serves to disarm the 'different approach' of *God and other Minds*.

43. Plantinga, "The Prospects for Natural Theology," p. 312.

44. Ibid.

45. Perhaps, as I suggested earlier, Gödel's critique of Russell and Whitehead provides an example of this.

46. In the case of Gödel's objection to Russell and Whitehead, ordinary people would not discover the chain of reasoning for themselves, even if apprised of the premises and the conclusion. So, in this case, the argumentative virtues of Gödel's argument do have a significant role to play. Perhaps the same is true in the case of Kripke's objections to the Frege-Russell theory of proper names, or in the case of Kripkenstein's private language argument – though here I think that matters are less clear-cut. But, as I noted above, in the vast majority of cases, theistic arguments are much simpler than the arguments just mentioned.

47. Alvin Plantinga, *Warrant and Proper Function*, New York and Oxford: Oxford University Press, 1993.

48. Ibid., p. 46.

49. Ibid., p. 194.

50. Ibid.

51. Alvin Plantinga, *Warrant: The Current Debate*, New York and Oxford: Oxford University Press, 1993, p. viii.

52. Plantinga, *Warrant and Proper Function*, p. 215.

53. Ibid., p. 214.

54. Ibid.

55. Ibid.

56. Ibid., p. 235.

57. Previously unpublished, now published as an appendix to this volume.

58. Alvin Plantinga. "Augustinian Christian Philosophy," *Monist* 75 (3), 1992, p. 294.

59. Alvin Plantinga, "Rationality and Public Evidence: A Reply to Richard Swinburne," *Religious Studies* 37 (2), 2001, pp. 215–222.

60. Alvin Plantinga, *Warranted Christian Belief*, New York and Oxford: Oxford University Press, 2000.

61. Ibid., p. 3.

62. These animadversions draw on earlier discussions in *Does God Have a Nature?* and elsewhere.

63. Plantinga, *Warranted Christian Belief*, p. 366.

64. Ibid., p. 69.

65. Ibid., p. 191.

66. Ibid., p. 200.
67. Ibid, p. 499.
68. Plantinga does say, for example, that new arguments from evil by Rowe and Draper "give the person on the fence little if any reason to prefer atheism over theism" (*Warranted Christian Belief*, p. 481); but I don't see that he gives any reason at all to suppose that these arguments are, in this respect, any worse than the arguments of natural theology of which he approves.
69. Plantinga, *Warranted Christian Belief*, p. 281.
70. If we take seriously the idea that properly functioning human cognitive mechanisms automatically deliver the belief that God exists, then we might wonder how there could really be any point to the enterprise of 'bolstering' or 'confirming' the beliefs of wavering theists. Given, on this view, that 'wavering' in belief points to mechanical failure – breakdown in proper cognitive functioning – there is no evident reason at all to suppose that adopting the belief that God exists on the basis of argumentation is going to help fix the broken mechanism. So the difficulties here don't just belong to the theory of successful argumentation; there are also difficulties that arise on the side of Plantinga's version of Reformed epistemology.
71. Plantinga, "Reason and Belief in God," p. 77.
72. Plantinga, *Warranted Christian Belief*, p. xiii.
73. Of course, it's not really a fence; there are many importantly different kinds of theists, and many importantly different kinds of atheists. But let's not worry about this point.

2 | Evil and Alvin Plantinga
RICHARD M. GALE

Among Alvin Plantinga's many outstanding contributions is his career-long attempt to neutralize the challenge that evil presents for theism.[1] This challenge takes both a logical and an evidential form. The former attempts to deduce an explicit contradiction from the existence of both God and evil, whereas the latter argues that the known evils of the world, if not rendering it improbable that God exists, at least lower the probability that he does. Plantinga meets the logical challenge with his famed free will defense and the evidential one based on the doctrine of theistic skepticism, according to which our epistemic limitations preclude our being able to determine whether these known evils are justified. Each of these responses will now be considered.

THE FREE WILL DEFENSE

The free will defense[2] (hereafter FWD) attempts to show how it is possible for God to coexist with moral evil – evil that results from the improper use of free will by finite beings – by describing a possible world in which God is morally justified or exonerated for creating beings who freely go wrong. In response to the charge that the FWD does not go far enough because it leaves natural evil – evil that does not result from the improper use of free will by finite beings – unaccounted for, Plantinga claims that it is possible that all of the *apparent* natural evils of the world result from the mischief freely wrought by very powerful but finite nonhuman persons, such as wayward angels. This is true but does not spare theists from having to come up with a defense for natural evils; for, given that theists grant that it is at least logically or conceptually possible for God and natural evil to coexist, they must find some possible morally exonerating justification for God permitting natural evils, even if they do not actually exist. The proposition that God coexists with an evil for which he lacks such a justification is contradictory. Therefore, if God could not have a morally exonerating justification for permitting natural evil, then it is possible that this contradiction is true. But whatever entails that it is possible that some impossible proposition is true is impossible.

A crucial premise in every version of a FWD is the Libertarian theory of freedom, a tenet of which is

L: A free act is not sufficiently caused by anything external to the agent.

Without this premise, Plantinga would have no response to the objection of the causal or theological compatibilist, who contends that God could have determined that every created free person always freely goes right either, respectively, by a suitable determination of the initial state of the universe and the causal laws or by simply willing in his own inimitable supernatural way that the person does. Another crucial premise is that it is possible that God is unlucky in that any free person he might actualize is such that its instantiator would freely go wrong at least once. In such a circumstance, given the great value of free will, God is morally excused for creating free people who freely go wrong, provided that for the most part they freely go right, thus resulting in a favorable balance of moral good over moral evil.

Plantinga has a very ingenious story to tell about how God could be unlucky. We know from *L* that God cannot both create free beings and determine what they freely do. What he must do, therefore, is to create persons who are free with respect to certain actions and then leave it up to them what they freely do. God does not instantiate *a possible free person* but rather what I will call *a diminished possible free person*. The former is a maximal and compossible set of abstract properties that could be instantiated by a single person and contains the property of being free with respect to at least one morally significant action, *A*, that is, the property of either freely doing *A* or freely refraining from doing *A*. The set is compossible in that it admits of the logical possibility of coinstantiation by a single concrete individual, and it is maximal because for every property either it or its complement is included in the set. Each possible free person contains *a diminished possible free person* (*DP*), which is its largest proper subset of properties that is such that for any action *A* it neither includes or entails freely doing *A* nor includes or entails freely refraining from doing *A*, in which a property *H* includes or entails another property *G* just in case it is logically impossible that *H* be instantiated and *G* not be. A diminished possible free person is a "freedom-neutral" set of properties. Each property included in a set of properties could be freedom-neutral and yet the set as a whole not be, for the set could contain the properties (either freely doing A or freely refraining from doing A) and doing A.

For every possible free person containing the property of freely doing A there is a numerically distinct possible person that includes all of the same properties save for its including freely refraining from doing A instead. Let us call such a pair of possible free persons an "incompatible pair." Whenever you freely perform an action you instantiate one member of such a pair to the exclusion of the other. For any incompatible pair God will be contingently unable to actualize one person in the pair. Let our specimen incompatible pair be P and P_1, who include all of the same properties save for P's including freely doing A and P_1's instead including freely refraining from doing A. The question is what would result if God were to instantiate DP. Would the instantiator of this diminished person or set of freedom-neutral properties freely do A or freely refrain? Plainly, it must do one or the other, since it has the disjunctive property of either freely doing A or freely refraining from doing A. Thus, it is either true that

F: If DP were instantiated, the instantiator would freely do A.

or true that

F': If DP were instantiated, the instantiator would freely refrain from doing A.

Let us call a subjunctive conditional whose antecedent reports the instantiation of a diminished possible free person and consequent the performance of a free action by the instantiated person a "free will subjunctive conditional," for short an F-conditional. If F is true, then were God to instantiate DP, it would result in P being actualized; whereas if F' is true, were God to actualize DP, it would result in P_1 being actualized. Since F and F' are logically incompatible, it follows that if F is true God is unable to actualize P_1, and if F' is true God is unable to actualize P. But necessarily one of them is true and therefore necessarily true that God cannot actualize P or cannot actualize P_1.

This proof assumed that the law of the conditional excluded middle holds for F-conditionals. Herein the necessarily true disjunction is formed not from the disjunction of an F-conditional with its negation, as is the case when the weaker law of excluded middle is applied, but from the disjunction of an F-conditional with an F-conditional containing the same antecedent and the denial of the former's consequent, as is the case with the disjunction of F and F'. Plantinga gives an alternate proof that applies only the law of excluded middle to F-conditionals. It begins with what Plantinga calls "Lewis's lemma," which, when translated into my terminology, says that God can actualize a possible person P containing the property of freely doing A only if it is true that if God were to actualize its diminished person DP, the instantiator would freely do A. It next is claimed by appeal to the law of excluded middle that it is either true or false that F. If it is false, then, given Lewis's lemma, God cannot actualize P; and, if it is true, then he cannot actualize P_1.

At the outset let us confine ourselves to possible persons that include the property of being free with respect to only one action, such as the afore-mentioned persons P and P_1. What we establish then can be generalized to more complex possible persons. Any incompatible pair of such simplified persons is a Dr. Jeckyl and Mr. Hyde pair, the former being the one that contains the property of freely doing A (which we'll suppose is the morally right thing to do), the latter the property of freely refraining from doing A (which is the morally wrong thing to do). God might not be able to actualize P, the Dr. Jeckyl member of the pair, since F could be false. But what could be true for this particular Dr. Jeckyl and Mr. Hyde pair could be true for all of them. Every incompatible pair of this sort could be such that it is true that if God were to instantiate the diminished possible person common to both, the instantiator would freely do the morally wrong alternative. Under such unfortunate circumstances, God can actualize only Hydes, and therefore will not attempt to instantiate any of these simple possible free persons, assuming that his brand of benevolence requires that there be a favorable balance of moral good over moral evil.

The result can be generalized so as to apply to more rich possible persons that contain the property of being free in respect to more than one action. It could still be the case for every such person that it is true that if God were to actualize its diminished person, the instantiator would freely go wrong with respect to at least one of these actions, which shows that it is possible that God cannot actualize a possible world in which all free persons always freely go right.

At this point Plantinga can complete his FWD by claiming that in the possible world in which the truth-values of the F-conditionals preclude God from actualizing any Dr. Jeckyls or, more generally, possible persons containing the property of always freely doing what is right, he is excused for creating persons who sometimes freely go wrong but for the most part freely go right. This completes my rough sketch of Plantinga's FWD account of the possible world in which God is unlucky and thereby morally exonerated for allowing moral evil.

There are two salient theses in Plantinga's version of the FWD that must be stated explicitly, since they are challenged by other versions of the FWD, namely:

I. Every F-conditional has a contingent truth-value, that is, is contingently true or contingently false.

II. God knows the truth-value of all F-conditionals prior, either in the order of time or explanation, to his creative decision.

Theses I and II together comprise the doctrine of God's "middle knowledge." Tenet II is entailed by I because God's omniscience requires him to know every true proposition. Another way of formulating the doctrine of God's middle knowledge is that God foreknows for every diminished possible person what free actions would be performed if that person were to be instantiated. Robert M. Adams's version of the FWD[3] rejects I and thereby II as well, holding that every F-conditional is either necessarily false or neither true nor false, whereas Richard Swinburne's[4] accepts I but denies II. What they have in common is that they both render God blameless for moral evil because of excusable ignorance. Either there was nothing to be known prior to God's decision to actualize certain diminished possible free persons or there was something to be known but God was unable to access it. These alternatives to Plantinga's FWD will be motivated by considering some problems that beset it.

The first problem concerns how it is possible for an F-conditional to be true. Adams is unable to imagine what could be its truth-conditions, the things in reality that make it true; for not only does an F-conditional's antecedent not entail its consequent for the Libertarian, but an F-conditional can also be true (or false) even when counterfactual, thereby lacking anything in reality that could make it true (or false). We know that it cannot be God in Plantinga's FWD that determines the truth-values of F-conditional's truth-value, since that would violate L were he to actualize one of their antecedents. So what are these truth-conditions? The wrong answer is that an F-conditional is made true by the performance of a free action by the instantiator of the diminished possible person referred to in its antecedent. First, this account works only for F-conditionals that have their antecedent actualized, and thus leaves the truth-conditions of counterfactual F-conditionals unaccounted for. Second, as will shortly be shown, it leads to a vicious circularity in the order of explanation.

In an attempt to placate Adams, Plantinga tried in 1985 to show how his FWD need not assume that any F-conditional is true. Whereas his earlier version of the FWD requires, in virtue of its use of the law of conditional excluded middle, that some F-conditional proposition is true, his later version, although making use of F-conditionals because it requires that they have determinate truth-values (for it applies the law of excluded middle to them), does not make use of the law of conditional excluded middle and thereby permits them all to be false. It makes use, however, of Lewis's lemma, which holds that God can actualize a possible free person only if the relevant F-conditional about what its diminished possible free person would do if instantiated is true. Thus God can actualize $P(P')$ only if $F(F')$ is true. This, however, allows for the possibility that both F and F' are false and God thereby cannot actualize either P or P'. But even if this were the case, it suffices to show how it is possible that God would be unable to create a person who always freely goes right.

After pointing out that this new version of the FWD allows every F-conditional to be false, Plantinga rightly points out: "What follows from the premises of the argument is that if that were so, then no possible world containing free creatures is one that God could have weakly actualized."[5] God *strongly actualizes* a state of affairs if his action alone is sufficient to cause it and only *weakly actualizes* it if his action is a necessary but not sufficient cause of it since it requires the free, causally undetermined action of another agent to bring about this effect. Unfortunately, this concession to Adams is inconsistent with the key premise that specifies that God is omnipotent in the sense of being able to strongly actualize anything that it is consistent for him to actualize. This premise is needed to ward off the theological and causal compatibilist objection that God's omnipotence requires that he can bring it about that all persons always freely go right, since, given the Libertarian premise of the FWD, it is inconsistent for God to do this. But God's actualizing a diminished possible free person is a case of strong actualization, for there is no inconsistency in his doing so, since he does not thereby determine what the created person freely does. What God can strongly actualize, however, cannot vary across worlds in which he exists, but it is just such variance that is a consequence of Plantinga's concession to Adams.

There is no reason for Plantinga to make any such concession to Adams, however, for it seems clear that an F-conditional can be true. Contrary to Adams, if DP were to be instantiated and its instantiator were to do A, we would say that F was true. Moreover, if F were not true, it would not be possible for God to instantiate P, as Lewis's lemma states. It would be a mistake, however, to say that DP's instantiator doing A makes F true. For this makes it appear as if the instantiator's freely doing A is a sufficient *truth-condition* for *F*, being that thing in the world that makes *F* true, in answer to Adams's puzzlement about how an *F*-conditional could be true. The action of the instantiator of *DP* is only a *verifying-condition*, not a *truth-condition*, for *F*. A verifying-condition is what enables us to discover the truth of a proposition but need not coincide with what makes it true. Think in this connection of how you go about indirectly verifying a proposition about the past or about another mind. What makes a proposition about a past event (another person's conscious state) true is not the future effects of the past event (the person's overt behavior) by which we indirectly verife it but the past event (conscious state) itself.

This way of distinguishing between the truth-conditions and verifying-conditions for *F*-conditionals escapes an argument against Plantinga's FWD that attempts to unearth a vicious circularity in the order of explanation or causation in it. The argument goes as follows. Prior to God's decision to instantiate *DP*, be it in the order of time or that of explanation, God knows that *F* is true. That *F* is true is part of the explanation for his decision to instantiate *DP*, which in turn at least partly explains *DP*'s instantiator freely doing *A*, given that it is a necessary cause of *A* since it is the cause of the very existence of this instantiator. But *DP*'s instantiator freely doing *A* is the truth-condition for *F* and thereby explains why *F* is true, which completes the vicious circle in the order of explanation. This vicious circle is broken when *DP*'s instantiator freely doing *A* is downgraded to a verifying- but not a truth-condition for *F*, since *DP*'s instantiator freely doing *A* no longer explains why *F* is true, only how we come to know that *F* is true. God cannot know prior to his decision to instantiate *DP* that the worldly verifying-conditions for *F* obtain: For, necessarily, before an agent decides, that agent knows neither what he or she will decide nor of the occurrence of an event that is dependent on how he or she decides. Whether the verifying condition for *F* will occur depends upon whether God chooses to actualize *DP*.

But showing that *F*-conditionals must have contingent truth-values does not solve the problem of what could possibly be their truth-conditions. There is an answer to this that is implicit in the Platonic ontology employed in Plantinga's FWD that goes back to Suarez. Since possible free persons, including diminished possible free persons, are sets of abstract properties, they exist in every possible world. Abstract entities have both essential and accidental properties. The number two has the property of being even in every possible world but has the property of being Igor's favorite object in only some. Our old friend, diminished possible free person *DP*, being a set of properties, has the same essential properties in every possible world, such as containing the property of being free with respect to A. However, it also has some accidental properties, among which is the following property of being-such-that-if-it-were-instantiated-its-instantiator-would-freely-do-A. In some worlds it has it and in others not. In virtue of this, the F-conditional, that if DP were instantiated its instantiator would freely do A, is true in some worlds but not others. It is all right to call this funny property of DP a "dispositional property" provided we are clear that it is not a disposition of DP to freely perform A if instantiated (abstract entities, with the possible exception of God, cannot perform actions) but rather a disposition to have its instantiator freely do A.

But what, it will be asked, determines whether a diminished person has one of these funny dispositions? As they used to say in the Bronx, "Don't ask!" Here's where the regress of explanations hits the brick wall of brute, unexplainable contingency. There are no further elephants or tortoises upon whose back this contingency rests.

There are many other objections to Plantinga's FWD, most of them of the God-could-do-more-than-Plantinga-allows-to-ensure-that-there-is-moral-good-sans-moral-evil variety, but the really serious objection is of the God-cannot-consistently-do-as-much-as-Plantinga-requires. It arises from tenet II of God's middle knowledge, requiring him to know the truth-values of F-conditionals prior to his creation of free persons. It is argued that this gives God a freedom-canceling control over the actions of the persons he creates. If this objection has merit, it will provide a good reason to opt for one of the two excusable ignorance versions of the FWD.

The objection begins with the case of a stochastic machine. When its button is pressed, a stochastic process, such as the decay of a radioactive element or the spinning of a wheel of fortune, is triggered, the outcome of which determines whether a poisonous gas will be released into a crowded stadium that will result in the deaths of fifty thousand innocent people. When the button is pressed, either this outcome will ensue or it won't. Therefore, either it is true that if the button were to be pressed this horrendous outcome would ensue, or it is true that if the button were pressed this outcome would not ensue. Let us assume, furthermore, that we mortals cannot discover by any discursive methods which of these subjunctive conditional propositions is true, any more than we can for similarly matched F-conditionals.

Imagine the case in which I chance on the scene and inadvertently press the button, resulting in the horrendous outcome. Given that I did not have "middle knowledge" of what would result from pressing the button and did not intend to bring about or even risk bringing about this outcome, I am blameless for the resulting evils. Furthermore, I do not even cause these evils.

Let us change the circumstances so that I now have middle knowledge via some ESP faculty and press the button so as to bring about the deaths. In this case my action is a sufficient cause of the deaths, and is so in spite of the interposition of a stochastic process, which shows that causation can reach through an intervening stochastic process. Furthermore, I am blameworthy for the deaths, unless I have got a mighty good excuse, such as "They were not innocents but terrorists."

Although there is no doubt that this is what people on the street would say, it might be objected that their concept of causation is confused, for the only difference between the two cases is my psychological state, what I know and intend, and how can this determine whether or not I cause the deaths? If what was at issue was the physicist's concept of causation, this would be a powerful objection. But this is not the concept of causation in question. Rather, it is the forensic one that concerns moral and legal responsibility and blame, which is the very concept that figures in the FWD, since it is concerned with the assignment of responsibility and blame to God and man for moral evil. And given that God sufficiently causes the actions of the instantiators of diminished possible free persons he actualizes, these actions, according to L, are not done freely, thereby rendering Plantinga's FWD inconsistent. This inconsistency is not avoided by applying the doctrine of double effect to God's actualizing of diminished possible free persons who he foreknows will produce some moral evil. That he did not intend to bring about these collateral moral evils might concern whether he is to blame for them but not whether he causes them.

Plantinga's God has a freedom-canceling control over created persons even if the Libertarian tenet L is not accepted; and there are some grounds for not accepting it, since one person can cause another to act without thereby rendering the act unfree. As a rule, the more the external event only triggers a deep-seated character trait or natural disposition of the agent, the less difficulty there is in treating it as not abrogating the free will of the affected agent. When I induce a person of amorous nature to call Alice for a date by telling him that she is desirous of going out with him, I cause him to act but do not usurp his free will in doing so since prominent among the causes of his action are his own deep-seated character traits, which traits were not imposed on him by me. I didn't have to "work on him" – drug, hypnotize, or brainwash him – to call Alice. Unfortunately, God's way of causing created persons to act is not of this innocent sort. It is freedom-canceling.

There is a more plausible requirement than L that Plantinga's God fails to satisfy, namely,

C: For a person to act freely all of his or her actions must not be caused by another person.

First, it will be shown how C applies to man-man cases, and then it will be deployed to a God-man case. A theological compatibilist, such as Augustine or Leibniz, might object to reasoning in this anthropomorphic manner. But Plantinga is not in a position to make this objection, since his FWD is steeped in anthropomorphism.

Consider the case of The Evil Puppeteer. Stromboli has poor Pinocchio wired up in such a way that he controls his every movement. An observer who fails to notice the wires might falsely believe that Pinocchio's behavior was fully free and voluntary. Stromboli controls Pinocchio, not via having imposed on him an inner network of dispositions, motivations, intentions, and so on but by exerting a compulsive force over him that renders such inner factors irrelevant. There need not be actual wires connecting the controller with the "puppet." It could be a wireless radio hookup such as exists between a controller and a remote-control toy airplane or between the Horrible Dr. Input and a brain in a vat that in turn has a radio control hookup with a shell body.

By a coincidence that rivals that of the preestablished harmony, it could be the case that every time the external controller causes the "puppet" to perform some movement, the puppet endeavors on its own to perform this movement. This is a case of causal over determination in which there is more than one sufficient cause of a given occurrence. Although the puppet's action is unavoidable in that it would have made this movement even if it had not endeavored to, there are those, like Locke, who would still call it free. Locke's intuition in this matter is quite dubious.

What is it about these cases that makes us say that the controller, be it the Evil Puppeteer or the Horrible Dr. Input, has a freedom-canceling control? It is that most of the "victim's" behavior is caused by and subject to the whim of the controller, which is just what principle C rules out. The God-man relation in the FWD also satisfies C, for when God instantiates diminished possible persons or sets of freedom-neutral properties, he does have middle knowledge of what choices and actions will result, and thereby sufficiently causes them.

If the God-cannot-do-as-much objection is formidable, it gives one a good reason to opt for a version of the FWD that rejects tenet II of God's middle knowledge. For it was God's foreknowledge of F-conditionals that mucked things up by making him inconsistently be the cause of the actions performed by created free persons. The Adams version rejects tenet I; and since F-conditionals fail to be true, either because they lack truth-values or are necessarily false, there was nothing to be known in advance, not even by an omniscient God, as to what would result from the actualization of different diminished possible free persons. In the Swinburne version, F-conditionals do have contingent truth-values but God cannot know what they are prior to his creative decisions. By denying prior knowledge to God, both versions prevent God from being the cause of the actions performed by created free persons and, due to excusable ignorance, render him blameless for the moral evil they wrought. Created free persons can now serve as suitable scapegoats for moral evil, take "the fall" for it, so to speak. God winds up watching the unfolding of the history of the universe containing free persons in just the way parents watch their son play in a hockey game. In both cases, there are a lot of grimaces and groans as they observe unforeseen errors and transgressions.

The Adams version will not be discussed further, since it has already been argued that, contrary to Adams, F-conditionals do have contingent truth-values. Thus, the Swinburne version might be the only hope for finding a viable FWD. But in denying that God knows true F-conditionals, it violates the traditional definition of God's omniscience according to which God knows all and believes only true propositions. Swinburne espouses a new definition of God's omniscience that is modeled on the definition of his omnipotence. Just as God can bring about anything that it is consistent for him to bring about,

> K: God knows every true proposition that it is logically consistent that God knows.

Since it is an essential property of God that he is able to create free persons and he cannot do so if he knows the truth-values of the F-conditionals in advance of his creative choices, it is inconsistent for God to know their truth-values in advance.

This definition will not appear to be objectionably ad hocish once it is realized that it is an essential property of God that he is able to create free persons. Notice that the God of Swinburne's FWD must be temporal, for he changes over time; prior to his creative decision he does not know any F-conditional, but after he actualizes diminished possible free persons he comes to know some F-conditionals in virtue of coming to know their verifying-conditions. For those who think that God must be timelessly eternal, this will constitute a ground for rejecting the Swinburne version, but this is an issue that cannot be pursued here.

THE EVIDENTIALIST ARGUMENT FROM EVIL

In recent years, it is generally conceded that the logical challenge of evil has been successfully neutralized by Plantinga and his cohorts. In case you are not convinced of the viability of the FWD, there is always the compensation-in-an-afterlife defense for any type and/or amount of evil. In recognition of this fact, opponets of theism have developed many different versions of the evidential argument from evil. All of them have as a premise that

1. God cannot coexist with an *unjustified evil*.

The reason is that God is essentially omnibenevolent and such an evil is one for which there does not in fact exist a set of conditions that would morally exonerate God, were he to exist, for permitting it. The next premise is that

2. There are many known evils of the world for which we humans cannot discover any justification.

Among these evils are the horrendous suffering of young children and animals. None of the justificatory reasons that we can think of seem to apply to them: They are not due to a misuse of free will, required for soul building, merited as punishments, necessary for the realization of a greater good, or aids to our acquiring faith in God because of the realization that pointless evils can randomly happen to anybody, and so on for all the other morally exonerating excuses that we can think of. It is then inferred either that

3. It is improbable that God exists; or, more weakly, that
4. The probability that God exists (G) relative to these evils (E) and background knowledge (K) is less than the probability that God exists relative to this background knowledge alone, that is, $P(G/E \text{ and } K) < P(G/K)$.

Herein, it is not inferred from the fact that there are evils E that the probability of G is less than $1/2$, which is what 3 proclaims, only that the fact that there are evils E lowers the probability of G over what it is relative to K alone. Let us call this version of the probabilistic argument the "modest probabilistic argument" and the preceding one the "strong probabilistic argument."

There is an ablative or inference to the best explanation version of the evidential argument that goes back to Hume. Let O be a proposition that reports all of the goods and evils that are known to befall sentient beings. It is contended that O is better explained by HI – Neither the nature nor the condition of sentient beings on earth is the result of benevolent or malevolent actions performed by nonhuman persons – than it is by the incompatible theistic hypothesis (T). HI amounts to the anything-but-theism hypothesis, and it is preferable to T because O is more to be expected on HI than it is on T, that is, $P(O/HI) < P(O/T)$.

Plantinga has a three-pronged attack against all of these probabilistic arguments. The initial response, which is developed in great detail in "The Probabilistic Argument from Evil" (all fifty-three pages of it!), attempts to show that "none of the current conceptions of probability, so far as I can see, gives [an espouser of a probabilistic argument from evil] a polemical leg to stand on."[6] The *personalist* conception has no polemical teeth, because it is based on subjective estimates of probability. That an atheologian finds it improbable that there should be evils E in a world created by God is nothing more than an interesting autobiographical fact that cuts no ice with the theist. The *propensity* or *frequency* account does not seem applicable to determining probabilistic relations between the propositions that God exists and that there are evils E, since it comes to grief over the *problem of the single case*. Finally, there is the *logical* account with its a priori probabilities. For the theist who believes that it is necessary that God exists, this a priori probability is 1, but then the conditional probability that God exists on any evidence, including evils E, also is 1. Plantinga also presents a reductio ad absurdum argument against the logical account, but it is beyond the purview of this essay to go into its details.

Plantinga should not advance his attack on the extant accounts or theories of probability as a decisive refutation of probabilistic arguments from evil, for we are able to successfully employ a concept for which we cannot give an adequate analysis or definition in an argument. This is true of all philosophical arguments that employ such apparently indefinable concepts as causation, time, and the like. The reason for this is that we have a sufficient preanalytic grasp of the concept in virtue of which we can identify paradigm cases for the concept's application and for its being withheld. Plantinga recognizes that this is true of the concept of probability when he writes: "We do in fact have some idea of probability and some grasp of probabilities, halting and infirm though it be; and there are many clear cases of improbable propositions, and many clear cases of pairs of propositions one of which is improbable on the other."[7] And maybe the pair of propositions that it is probable that God exists relative to our background knowledge alone and that God exists relative to this background knowledge in conjunction with the known evils of the world is a case in point, the former being significantly more probable than the latter. This admission seems to allow probabilistic arguments from evil to have some force, though a limited one due to our inability to give a proper account of probability.

The second prong of Plantinga's attack on probabilistic arguments from evil is based on the fact that a proposition's probability can vary relative to different propositions. The probability that Feike can swim relative to the proposition that he is Swiss is quite low, say .1, but relative to the proposition that many have seen him swim quite high, near 1, given that seeing is believing. Similarly, the proposition that God exists relative to the conjunction of K and that there are evils E could be quite low but quite high when all of the arguments for the existence of God discussed in Graham Oppy's contribution to this volume are added to this conjunction. And if it is probable that God exists relative to the agglomeration of these arguments, then it also is probable that for each evil specified in E there is a God-justifying reason. In fact, if among them is a knock-down ontological argument, we can be certain that there is, and thus that there are evils E does not even lower the probability that God exists, as the modest probabilistic argument contends. It was because Leibniz thought he had such an argument that he confined himself in his misnamed book *Theodicy*[8] to sketching some possible *defenses* for God's allowing evil without making any effort to give evidence for their actually obtaining. Saint Augustine did likewise.

From his initial book on *God and Other Minds*[9] in 1967 to his monumental *Warranted Christian Belief*[10] in 2000, Alvin Plantinga has defended theism by lodging a circumstantial ad hominem objection against his nontheist opponents, in which it is argued that they uphold epistemic standards for theistic belief that their own nontheistic beliefs fail to satisfy. It is widely assumed, as part of our Lockean legacy, that a belief that God exists can be epistemically rational, justified, or warranted only if it has adequate evidential support from beliefs that are either self-evident or evident to our senses. Without suitable argumentative support, theistic belief fails to measure up to proper epistemic standards and thereby violates our epistemic duties. Plantinga, who accepted this evidentialist assumption in his writings prior to the early 1980s, mounts a vigorous attack on it in *Warranted Christian Belief*. He had argued with considerable force in *Warrant: The Current Debate*[11] and *Warrant and Proper Function*[12] that what warrants a "basic belief," a belief that is not based on or inferred from another belief, is that it results from the proper functioning of one's cognitive faculties in the right kind of epistemic environment according to a design plan successfully aimed at truth.

Plantinga begins with basic beliefs that arise from our senses, memory, introspection, sympathy, and a priori reason, which comprise the "standard package" of cognitive faculties. He makes out a powerful case in the two earlier *Warrant* books that such beliefs are warranted when the faculty that produces them is functioning properly in the right sort of epistemic environment according to a design plan aimed at seeking truth. Someone who seems to see a tomato and then believes that there is a tomato out there has a warranted belief and moreover knows that there is a tomato out there. The person's warrant for believing this, however, is subject to defeaters or overriders concerning something that is abnormal about his or her faculty of vision (having cataracts) or the epistemic circumstances (being in a factory that manufactures plastic tomatoes). For the sake of argument, this account of warrant will be accepted.

The next step in Plantinga's argument is to show that it is possible that theistic, and in particular Christian, beliefs have warrant in an analogous way to that in which sensory and memory beliefs and so on do. If theism is true, then God would want to reveal himself to created persons. Toward this end he implanted in them as part of their original cognitive equipment, along with the cognitive faculties in the standard package, a *sensus divinitatis* that would enable them to form true noninferential beliefs about God's presence, nature, and intentions upon having certain experiences, such as reading the Scriptures, hearing the choir sing, seeing a beautiful sunset, feeling guilt, and so on. Provided their *sensus divinitatis* is functioning properly on these occasions in accordance with its divinely determined design plan in the right sort of epistemic environment, their basic beliefs are warranted and constitute knowledge even if the subjects of the experiences are unable to offer any argument or justification for their beliefs. That they have such a noninferential warrant does not preclude their also having an evidentialist-based warrant: Plantinga is no fideist. He also introduces a special supernatural process involving the internal instigation of the Holy Spirit by which one is directly caused by God, without any intervening worldly causes, to believe the great things of the Gospel concerning the incarnation, resurrection, salvation, and the like.

If it is true that we possess a properly functioning God-implanted *sensus divinitatis* that supplies us with nonpropositional evidence for the existence of God that is analogous to the sort of nonpropositional evidence that our ordinary senses supply us with for the existence of material objects, then the challenge posed by probabilistic arguments is neutralized. For just as an ordinary sensory-based belief trumps almost any counterevidence, given that it has a probability of close to 1, so does a *sensus divinitatis*-based belief. Plantinga does not argue that we in fact possess warranted basic beliefs based on our *sensus divinitatis*, only that it is possible that we do. To do the former would require giving evidence or arguments that

God exists and has set things up the way in which Plantinga's so-called Aquinas/Calvin model (A/C for short) says that he has. Plantinga admits this when he writes: "To determine whether there is nonpropositional warrant for Christian and theistic belief, we have to determine whether Christian and theistic beliefs are true; the question whether there is nonpropositional evidence for these propositions is not theologically or religiously neutral."[13] He believes that we have a battery of theistic arguments that give some warrant for theistic belief, even though they will not convince the atheist. His ontological argument, for example, is claimed to be deductively valid and to have premises that are just as likely to be true as false, thereby giving some epistemic respectability to theistic belief.

The major problem with Plantinga's appeal to his Calvinist or Reformed epistemology is not that its contentions cannot be evidentially established but rather that it rests on an analogy between the *sensus divinitatis* and our standard-package cognitive faculties of sense and memory that limps on both legs. The heart of the analogy is that we can predicate of both types of experience the notion of being produced by a cognitive faculty that is "functioning properly," as contrasted with one that suffers from a "disease," "dysfunction," "malfunction," "pathology," or "disorder." A dilemma argument can be constructed in regard to the predication of these terms. Either they are supposed to be predicated in the same sense of both theistic and standard package beliefs or they are not. On both alternatives Plantinga's argument for the possibility of theistic and, in particular, Christian belief being warranted fares badly.

If Plantinga assumes that they are predicated in the same sense, he winds up with a false analogy. For there are agreed-upon objective tests for a cognitive faculty in the standard package being in a state of dysfunction, malfunction, pathology, or disorder. But it is obvious that there are no agreed-upon objective tests for a person's *sensus divinitatis* suffering from a dysfunction, malfunction, pathology, or disorder. It will not do to charge this objection with resting on an unacceptable verificationist requirement and then have verificationism die from Plantinga's favorite death of self-refutation when it is required that it be applied to itself. The point of the objection is not that every type of cognitive experience must admit of a distinction between proper and improper functioning that measures up to verificationist standards, only that Plantinga's analogically based argument commits him to this being so for his *sensus divinitatis* since it is true of the cognitive faculties in the standard package.

In regard to basic religious beliefs that are internally instigated by the Holy Spirit, it is obvious that the notion of proper functioning could have no application to them since they are supernaturally caused directly by God.

Such instigation, furthermore, is not a faculty but a process and thus cannot be said to have any function, and therefore cannot be said to malfunction or be subject to a pathology; for there is no correct way for God to supernaturally cause worldly occurrences. Plantinga recognizes this difficulty: "A *caveat*: as Andrew Dole points out in 'Cognitive Processes, Cognitive Faculties, and the Holy Spirit in Plantinga's Warrant Series' . . . , it is not obvious that one can directly transfer necessary and sufficient conditions for warrant from beliefs produced by *faculties* to beliefs produced by processes."[14] Plantinga gives no response to this caveat, nor do I think one can be given.

Plantinga continually talks about the *sensus divinitatis* in natural law terms; but whereas for Aristotelian natural law theorists, questions concerning an individual's nature and proper mode of functioning are to be answered, at least in part, by empirical inquiry, there is nothing analogous in regard to determining the nature and proper functioning of the *sensus divinitatis* or for what constitutes a proper way for the internal instigation of the Holy Spirit to occur.

There are further damaging disanalogies between Plantinga's A/C experiences and those in the standard package. Whereas there is universal participation in the very same doxastic practices based on the experiences in the standard package, this is not so 'for *sensus divinitatis*–based experiences. Plantinga has an explanation for this disanalogy based upon the serious damage that the *sensus divinitatis* suffered as a result of Original Sin, a damage that is repairable only by the supernatural intervention of the Holy Spirit. But to explain why there is this disanalogy does not explain it away.

Another disanalogy is that there is no standard-package analogue to religious diversity. There is widespread disagreement among persons of different religions in regard to how they respond to reading the New Testament in that only some find themselves suddenly believing that a triune God exists who has atoned for our sins. In contrast, persons have pretty much the same doxastic responses to their standard-package experiences.

The third prong in Plantinga's rebuttal, if successful, delivers a knockout blow against probabilistic arguments from evil. It consists in the doctrine of theistic skepticism, which has its roots in the *Book of Job* and finds favor among many able contemporary analytical philosophers of religion, such as William Alston, Peter van Inwagen, and Stephen Wykstra. There are two components to theistic skepticism. The first is based on radical limitations in our knowledge of history, especially in regard to the remote causes and distant consequences of an event, the second on our limited ability to conceive of morally exonerating justifications for permitting an evil. Let us call the former the "historical component" and the latter the "axiological component" of theistic skepticism.

The following quotations from Plantinga make it clear that he espouses both the historical and axiological component

> From the theistic perspective there is little or no reason to think that God would have a reason for a particular evil state of affairs only if we had a pretty good idea of what that reason might be. On the theistic conception, our cognitive powers, as opposed to God's, are a bit slim for that. God might have reasons we cannot so much as understand; he might have reasons involving other free creatures – angels, devils, the principalities and powers of which St. Paul speaks – of which we have no knowledge.
>
> But (granted that it is indeed possible that he has a reason) can we just *see* that he doesn't have a reason? Perhaps his reason lies in some transaction involving free creatures of sorts we have little conception of. Perhaps God's reason involves a good for other creatures, a good for some other creature such that God can't achieve that good without permitting the evil in question. Or perhaps his reason involves a good for the sufferer, a good that lies in a future life. It is a part of Christianity and many theistic religions to suppose that our earthly life is but a small initial segment of our total lives; there is life after death and indeed immortality.[15]
>
> Clearly, the crucial problem for the probabilistic argument from evil is just that nothing much follows from the fact that some evils are inscrutable; if theism is true we would expect that there would be inscrutable evil. Indeed, a little reflection shows there is no reason to think we could so much as grasp God's plans here, even if he proposed to divulge them to us. But then the fact that there is inscrutable evil does not make it improbable that God exists.[16]

The upshot of Plantinga's theistic skepticism is that it is not incumbent upon theists to construct theodicies for the known evils of the world, in which a theodicy is a defense (a description of a possible world in which God has a morally exonerating excuse for permitting the evil in question) plus an argument to show that it is likely, or, more weakly, at least not implausible, that the excusing condition described in the defense actually obtains. Would Plantinga go so far as to hold that it isn't even incumbent upon theists to produce defenses for these known evils? Does he think that these defenses, though having a pastoral value in helping people cope with the evils that befall them so that they will not lose their faith, are not epistemically required by theism? In other words, is the production of a defense an act of philosophical or religious supererogation?

Does Plantinga's theistic skepticism do the job of neutralizing the challenge that evil poses for theism? No doubt, there are some working theists, such as those who have an unshakable faith in God, who will find it completely satisfactory, but for many it will seem too quick and glib. I am in complete agreement with Robert M. Adams's remark that "theists have reason for a more extensive response to the problem of evil than Plantinga seems to have a use for."[17] The following are some problems that the theistic skeptic must address, and I am sure that Plantinga will be prepared to give forceful responses to all of them.

The axiological component of theistic skepticism contends that a universe created by God would likely have great moral depth in that many of the goods below its puzzling observable surface, many of the moral causes of God's current allowings and intervenings, would be "deep" moral goods. Alston develops an analogy between the physical world and morality in respect to their having a hidden nature that is gradually brought to light by painstaking investigation.

This analogy appears strained. To discover the hidden nature of gold, its molecular structure, required a long-term, sustained inquiry. But no analogous inquiry was required to unearth the hidden nature of morality, for a hidden morality is no morality. The "discovery" that love is better than hate because it is more affectionate is quite different from the discovery that gold has a certain atomic weight and number. To be sure, some of our primitive progenitors in the evolutionary process did not recognize any moral rules and principles, but that no more shows that we had to perform inquiries over a long period of time analogous to those employed by scientists to discover the inner nature of morality than does the fact that they blew their nose on the ground while we use Kleenex show that we had to inquire deeply into the nature of nose blowing. No doubt we have a heightened moral sensitivity relative to them but that is not due to our having unearthed the deep, hidden nature of morality.

That morality be on the surface, common knowledge of all, is an empirical presupposition for our engaging in our social moral practices, the purpose of which is to enable us to modify and control each other's conduct by the use of generally accepted rules and principles of moral evaluation, thereby effecting more satisfactory social interactions. It also is required for our entering into relationships of love and friendship with each other. Such relationships require significant commonality of purposes, values, sympathies, ways of thinking and acting, and the like.

Another objection to theistic skepticism is that it precludes the theist from employing teleological arguments, though not ontological and cosmological arguments; for if the bad things about the world should not be evidence against the existence of God, the good things should not count in favor of his existence. The teleological arguments turn into a two-edged sword. Maybe the good aspects of the world that these arguments appeal to are produced by a malevolent deity so as to highlight evil or because they are necessary for the realization of an outweighing evil, and so on for all the other demonodicies.

The most serious problem for theistic skepticism is that it seems to require that we become complete moral skeptics. Should we be horrified at the brutal rape and murder of a child? Should we have tried to prevent it or take steps to prevent similar incidents in the future? Who knows?! For all we can tell it might be a blessing in disguise or serve some God-justifying reason that is too "deep" for us to access: For example, it might be a merited Divine punishment for some misdeed that this child will commit in the afterlife. The result of this moral skepticism is paralysis of the will, since we can have no reason for acting, given that we are completely in the dark whether the consequences of our action is good or bad.

Another objection concerns whether theistic skepticism allows for there to be a meaningful personal love relation with God. The problem concerns whether we humans can have such a relation with a being whose mind so completely transcends ours, who is so inscrutable with respect to his values, reasons, and intentions. Not all kinds of moral inscrutability preclude a love relationship. It is important to distinguish between the moral rules and principles employed by a person and the manner in which he or she applies them to specific cases based on knowledge of the relevant circumstances, this being a casuistic issue. A distinction can be made between moral principle inscrutability and casuistic inscrutability. That another person is casuistically inscrutable to us need not prevent our entering into a communal love relationship with it, provided it is far more knowledgeable than us about relevant worldly conditions, such as God, an omniscient being, is supposed to be. But moral principle inscrutability of a certain sort does rule out such a relationship. While we need not understand all of the beloved's moral reasons for his or her behavior, it must be the case that, *for the most part*, we do in respect to behavior that vitally affects ourselves. One thing, and maybe the only thing, that can be said in favor of the theodicy favored by fundamentalists, according to which all the evils reported by E result from The Fall and are messages from God to show us how lost we are without him, is that it does not run afoul of this requirement. We can hardly love someone who intentionally hurts us and keeps his or her reasons a secret unless for the most part we know those reasons for affecting us as they do and moreover know that they are benevolent. The answer to Plantinga's rhetorical understatement that "there is no reason to think that if God *did* have a reason for permitting the evil in question we would be the first to know"[18] is that we should be for those that vitally concern us, at least for the most part. No doubt, the theistic skeptic will respond that this is being too anthropomorphic in its likening of a human-God personal relation to a human-human personal relation. There is considerable disagreement among philosophical defenders of theism, as well as among working theists, as to how anthropomorphic our concept of God should be.

Making God so inscrutable also raises a threat that theism thereby will turn out to be falsified or, if not falsified, rendered meaningless. Several atheists have used the hiddenness of God as the basis for an argument against his existence. There is, they say, a presumption of atheism so that no news is bad news. Numerous quotations can be given from the Bible to the effect that God's intention in creating men was so that they would come to know of his existence and worship, obey, and enter into a communal loving relation with him. Thus, if we do not have good evidence that God exists because he has chosen to remain hidden, this constitutes good evidence against his existence.

Swinburne has an answer to this atheistic argument that is based on God wanting created persons to come to know of his existence and enter into a communal relation with him of their own free will. If he were to make his existence too obvious, this would necessitate their doing so and thus be freedom-canceling. If God's existence, justice, and intentions became items of evident common knowledge, then man's freedom would in effect be vastly curtailed. An ontological argument would do even greater violence to the traditional Christian view of God as wanting men to come to know, love, and obey him of their own free will. If someone were to come up with a really convincing version of the ontological argument, Swinburne might not be crushed if we followed the example of the Pythagoreans, who set adrift sans supplies the person who demonstrated the existence of irrational numbers. Swinburne radically overestimates the value of free will. A consequence of his position is that we should not raise our children in a religion, since then their subsequent religious belief will not have been acquired freely. He has mislocated the point at which free will enters into the religious life. It is not in regard to one's believing that God exists but how one lives up to this belief in life.

By not allowing known evils E to count against God's existence, not even allowing it to lower the probability that he exists, the skeptical theist might be draining the theistic hypothesis of all meaning. E is itself a staggering array of evils, many of the most horrendous sorts. If E is not the least bit probability lowering, then it would appear that for theistic skeptics no amount of evil would be. Even if the world were a living hell in which each sentient being's life was one of unrelenting suffering of the worst sort, it would not count as evidence against God's existence, would not lower the probability of his existence one bit. This seems highly implausible and calls into question the very meaningfulness of their claim that God exists. And this is so whether or not we accept the notorious verifiability theory of meaningfulness, which Plantinga likes to have die the death of self-reference by pointedly asking whether it is applicable to itself. We can recognize that something has gone wrong even if we cannot come up with a good theoretical explanation of why it is wrong.

That E is not probability lowering will come as news to working theists who see the evils reported by E as counterevidence to God's existence that tries their faith. The response of defensive skeptics, such as Plantinga, is to make a distinction between the pastoral and epistemic problem of evil. What this amounts to, though they wouldn't want to put it this bluntly, is that the working theists whose faith is strained or endangered by the evils that directly confront them are emotionally overwrought and not able to take the cool stance of the epistemologist of religion and thereby see that these evils, however extensive and seemingly gratuitous, are really no challenge to their theistic beliefs. Since they are unable to philosophize clearly at their time of emotional upset, they need the pastor to hold their hands and say whatever might help them to make it through the night and retain faith in God.

There is a problem here; however, it is not a pastoral problem but a problem with the pastor and the theistic skeptics who run such a line. Their crisis of faith, although rationally explainable in terms of psychological causes, is not rationally justified because it rests upon the epistemically unwarranted belief that the evils confronting them probably are gratuitous or, at least, counterevidence to God's existence. It also follows that their emotion of horror at the evil of the Holocaust, for example, is equally irrational because based on the epistemically unwarranted belief that the apparent gratuitousness of this evil lessens the likelihood that God exists. Rationally speaking, they ought not to feel horror at the Holocaust!

Theistic skepticism appears to be an ivory tower invention of the detached epistemologist of religion that is completely out of touch with the grimy realities of everyday religious faith and experience. By neutralizing the dramatic bite of evil, it makes it too easy to have religious faith, as Kierkegaard might say.

Notes

1. See, in addition to the works referenced here, Plantinga's "Tooley and Evil: A Reply," *Australasian Journal of Philosophy*, 60, 1981, pp. 66–75; "Plantinga on the Problem of Evil," in *Alvin Plantinga*, ed. James E. Tomberlin and Peter van Inwagen, Dordrecht: Reidel, 1985, pp. 225–255; and "Reply to Robert M. Adams," in Tomberlin and van Inwagen, pp. 371–382.

2. First outlined in Plantinga's *God, Freedom, and Evil*, Grand Rapids, MI: Eardmans, 1974.

3. See Robert Adams, "Middle Knowledge and the Problem of Evil," *American Philosophical Quarterly*, 14, 1977, pp. 109–17, and "Must God Create the Best?" in *The Virtue of Faith and Other Essays in Philosophical Theology*, New York: Oxford University Press, 1987, pp. 51–64.

4. See Richard Swinburne's *Providence and the Problem of Evil*, Oxford: Oxford University Press, 1998.

5. Alvin Plantinga, "Self-Profile," in Tomberlin and van Inwagen, p. 52.

6. Alvin Plantinga, "The Probabilistic Argument from Evil," *Philosophical Studies* 35, 1979, p. 79.

7. Ibid., p. 83.

8. Gottfried Wilhelm Leibniz, *Theodicy: Essays on the Goodness of God, the Freedom of Man and the Origin of Evil*, Peru, IL: Open Court, 1985.

9. Alvin Plantinga, *God and Other Minds*, Ithaca, NY: Cornell University Press, 1967.

10. Alvin Plantinga, *Warranted Christian Belief*, New York and Oxford: Oxford University Press, 2000.

11. Alvin Plantinga, *Warrant: The Current Debate*, New York and Oxford: Oxford University Press, 1993.

12. Alvin Plantinga, *Warrant and Proper Function*, New York and Oxford: Oxford University Press, 1993.

13. Alvin Plantinga, "On Being Evidentially Challenged," in *The Evidential Argument from Evil*, ed. Daniel Howard-Snyder, Bloomington: Indiana University Press, 1996, p. 260.

14. Plantinga, *Warranted Christian Belief*, p. 257.

15. Alvin Plantinga, "Epistemic Probability and Evil," in Daniel Howard-Snyder, 1996, p. 73.

16. Ibid., pp. 75–76.

17. Robert M. Adams "Middle Knowledge and the Problem of Evil," *American Philosophical Quarterly* 14, 1979, p. 225.

18. Plantinga, "Epistemic Probability and Evil," p. 70.

3 The Modal Metaphysics of Alvin Plantinga

JOHN DIVERS

PLANTINGA'S MODAL METAPHYSICS IN (RECENT) HISTORICAL CONTEXT

Metaphysics is the part of philosophy that is concerned with the extent and content of reality: with what there is and with the nature of what there is. Matters of modality are matters of possibilities, impossibilities and necessities: what can (could, might) be, what cannot (could not, must not) be and what cannot (could not, must not) be otherwise.[1] The salient questions of the metaphysics of modality, then, are these: whether there is a modal reality – whether there is a part of reality in which modal facts consist (or which makes modal propositions true); whether such a modal consists in irreducibly modal facts or in nonmodal facts; whether modal facts consist (partly) in the existence of objects or properties of a special kind and – if so – what the nature and extent of such things is.

Perhaps these questions give a rather contemporary twist to the characterization of the metaphysics of modality; perhaps our predecessors would not have articulated their concern with the nature of modality in quite this way. But that such a concern is identifiable at many important periods in the history of Western philosophy is not seriously in doubt. It is hardly arguable that Aristotle was a practitioner of modal metaphysics[2] nor that, as a result of Aristotle's influence, such concerns figure prominently in medieval philosophy. Rather further from the specific concerns and direct influence of Aristotle, the metaphysical scrutiny of Hume[3] and Kant[4] is also trained specifically on the nature of (certain kinds of) modality at important points in their writings. If there is a moral to be drawn from consideration of the history of the metaphysics of modality prior to the twentieth century it is, perhaps, this: Enthusiasm for substantive and substantial answers to the definitive questions of the metaphysics of modality varies indirectly with the extent of influence of empiricist (and pragmatist) thought. Adopting that moral as a working hypothesis, a trajectory of the metaphysics of modality in the twentieth century can also be charted, with Alvin Plantinga emerging at its end. An explicit and substantive metaphysics of logical modality is to

71

be found in the early Wittgenstein, and a descendant of that in Carnap's intensional metaphysics of linguistic (analytic) modality.[5] However, to temper these developments, the influence of empiricist thought in the form of logical positivism brought a negative attitude to metaphysics *tout court*, and a conception of modality that was not metaphysically substantive.[6] Towards the middle of the century, then, the result of these forces was a climate of tolerance of modality – at least under the precondition that modality could be fundamentally explicated in logical and linguistic terms or, in any event, explicated without substantial metaphysical commitment. The climate of tolerance was broken by Quine, who despaired of our modal ways of speaking, finding them (variously) useless, confused and incoherent.[7] Indeed, with Quine, the prospect of a substantial metaphysics of modality reaches its lowest ebb: Insofar as we are forced into substantial metaphysical (especially, ontological) accounts of anything, it is by way of the need to interpret our best total theory, and modality – one way or another – does not merit consideration as a coherent and useful element of that theory. But then, in the late 1950s and early 1960s, the fortunes of the metaphysics of modality turned. The pivotal event of that period was the emergence of possible-worlds semantics for quantified modal logics, for this proved – rightly or wrongly – to have a massive and negative influence on the standing of Quine's antimodal agenda. The importance of possible-worlds semantic theories to our story justifies some brief and basic exposition.

If we begin with an ordinary nonmodal quantificational logic – a logic of predicates, quantifiers and variables – we can construct modal logics by adding some modal vocabulary and some axioms or rules to deal with sentences containing the modal vocabulary. The vocabulary in question is a pair of interdefinable operators ($\Box$, $\Diamond$) that, from a syntactic point of view, both function exactly as the sentential negation operator ($\sim$) does. On that basis we count as well-formed formulas such expressions as:

$$\Box\exists x[Fx] \sim \Diamond\forall x[Fx \lor Gx] \qquad \exists x[\Box Fx] \qquad \Diamond\Box\exists x[Fx] \rightarrow \Box\exists x[Fx]].$$

Intuitively, then, if we intend the box as a necessity operator and the diamond as a possibility operator, we can read these formulas (left to right) as expressing the following modal claims: It is necessary that there is something that is F; it is not possible that everything is (F or G); there is something that is necessarily F, and if it is possible that it is necessary that there is something that is F, then it is necessary that there is something that is F. So much for the intuitive meanings of the formulas. But what of the rules of inference or axioms that govern the logic of the modal operators? In fact, we get different variously strong systems of quantified modal logic by adding to nonmodal logic various combinations of axiom schemes – notably, combinations of the following:

(T*) $\square\, A \rightarrow A$

(B*) $A \rightarrow \square\,\diamond\, A$

(S4*) $\square\, A \rightarrow \square\,\square\, A$

(S5*) $\diamond\, A \rightarrow \square\,\diamond\, A$[8]

Intuitively, then, our axiom schemes would be read as expressing the principles: (T*) if it is necessary that A then A . . . (S5*) if it is possible that A then it is necessary that it is possible that A. Thus far, though, all we have is a syntactic account of modal logic allied to some intuitions about what we might like its distinctive operators to mean. But when logicians and philosophers call for a proper semantic theory of such logical systems they call for more. Principally, such a semantic theory is required to yield a) models or interpretations for the formulas, b) a definition in terms of models or interpretations of what it is for a sentence to be valid and c) results about which sentences are valid relative to certain kinds of model or interpretation. The crucial answers delivered by possible-worlds semanticists to the first two of these questions were (broadly) a) that the right models for quantified modal logics contained sets of possible worlds and sets of possible individuals that exist at those worlds and b) that what it is for a sentence of quantified modal logic to be valid is for it to be true at every possible world in every model.

Such a semantic theory can have philosophical significance for many reasons. But in the case of quantified modal logics, the most significant feature of the emergence of this semantics, in our historical and dialectical context, was that it afforded the friends of modality a direct means of replying to one potentially lethal charge of Quine. That charge was that in the face of certain paradoxes, and in the absence of an adequate semantic theory, the sentences of quantified modal logic (and their natural language analogues) stood as emblems of confusion that no philosopher could seriously use with a clear conscience.[9] The appearance of possible-worlds semantic theories did not, of course, silence Quine.[10] But possible-worlds semantics presented a framework in relation to which the defining questions of the metaphysics and ontology of modality could be posed again, and did so even as Quine would have them posed – more sharply, and by focusing, primarily, on the ontological commitments of a specific (kind of) theory, namely, a possible-worlds semantic theory. Taken at face value, a typical possible-worlds semantic theory appears to generate at least the following substantial modal metaphysical commitments: There is a modal reality, and it consists in the existence of possible worlds and the possible individuals that exist at them. The question then is whether entitlement to use such a semantic theory, and to lay claim to the benefits that it brings, really does generate these (or other) substantial modal metaphysical commitments. Thus, a certain kind of research programme in the semantics and then – crucially – in the metaphysics of modality was generated, and enthusiasm for it remains at a relatively high point now in the early years of the twenty-first century.

Many names might be mentioned in attempting an account of those whose work was seminal, crucial or most influential in this rehabilitation of the metaphysics of modality under the impetus of possible-worlds semantics. Ruth Barcan Marcus was an early champion of quantified modal logic and of essentialism, and a visible and prominent opponent of Quine in these matters both before and after the emergence of possible-worlds semantics.[11] Saul Kripke was amongst those who played a leading role in the development of possible-worlds semantics[12] and, certainly, the Kripke[13] presentation of the semantics has been the most influential on philosophers. Moreover, the development of modal themes in philosophical logic and metaphysics by Kripke[14] has been as influential as any work of late-twentieth-century philosophy. But in the specific matter of having developed systematic, comprehensive, detailed and substantive theories of the metaphysics, and ontology of modality, the two philosophers who stand out at the turn of this twenty-first century are (the late) David Lewis and Alvin Plantinga.[15] Both of these philosophers are enthusiastic practitioners of modal metaphysics, and both offer substantial answers to its defining questions about what modal reality consists in. Both might be called – indeed both call themselves – "modal realists"; however, Lewis and Plantinga differ from one another in some fundamental and important matters. In the narrative terms of this introductory section, the crucial underlying difference is in the extent of the influence of empiricist thought upon their respective modal realisms. Unqualified use of the term 'empiricist' is bound to be crass in most cases, and perhaps even bewildering if applied to Lewis. But the thought is that Lewis's metaphysics (and broader theory) of modality bears the mark of the history of empiricist (and pragmatist) thought upon it at least in those places where it clearly bears the mark of Quine – for example: in the ambition to eliminate primitive modal concepts; in the preference to limit ontology to (spatiotemporal) individuals and sets, in acceptance of the methodological precept to balance and trade ideological commitments for ontological commitments, and in the justification of ontological commitments in terms of their place in a total theory that maximizes various 'operational' virtues.[16] The contrasting, distinctive and striking characteristic of Plantingan modal metaphysics is that we find no trace within it of accommodation of any aspect of (broadly) empiricist or pragmatist thought. In particular, we find no accommodation of empiricist or pragmatist injunctions to minimize our modal metaphysical commitments.

I have introduced Plantinga as a realist, and thoroughly antiempiricist, modal metaphysician in order to create a guiding context in which to place an exposition of his views. Following that exposition, I will attempt briefly to indicate some themes of critical reaction to Plantinga's work.

PLANTINGA'S MODAL METAPHYSICS: AN EXPOSITION

The defining questions of modal metaphysics are questions about the existence and nature of a (specifically) modal part of reality. Reflection on the literature shows that we can identify under these headings a series – perhaps even a sequence – of more specific questions, to each of which there is a more substantial and more committed side. Broadly speaking, the marks of the substantial side of each question is acceptance of the existence of entities, or the acceptance of entities of kinds that are irreducible to, or metaphysically independent from, other kinds already admitted. By progressing along the line of these questions, we can measure how substantive, how committed or even how 'realistic' a position on modal metaphysics is.[17] By that measure, and by coming down on the substantial or committed side of the question for most of the way, Plantinga advocates a metaphysical theory of modality which is *almost* as committed or robust as such a theory could be. It is, at least, very probably, the most committed and robust metaphysical theory of modality that anyone actually does advocate.

(Thesis 1) The first matter is whether to endorse and practice metaphysics at all. And here we need pause only briefly to make explicit that Plantinga goes (very) boldly where certain pragmatists and positivists enjoin us not to go.

(Thesis 2) The second matter, if we entertain metaphysics at all, is whether to stop short of doing metaphysics for modality. The primary thought in this direction is that we might abstain from doing the metaphysics of modality as a result of abstaining from, or refusing to accord any serious status to, modalizing itself. Here, by way of charting some of Plantinga's fundamental departures from Quine, a brief detour through the thought of the latter may prove helpful.

We might discern in (a part of) Quine the following radical combination of views: a) that metaphysical enquiry is enforced upon us, but only in relation to those ways of speaking in which we are motivated to persist because they best serve certain identifiable (theoretical) purposes, and so b) that no metaphysical enquiry into modality is required, or merited, since there is no such purpose that stands in the way of our simply abandoning modal talk. However, once the prospect of abstaining from the metaphysics of modality is so related to the prospect of abstaining from modalizing altogether, it is natural to consider the less radical, and more immediate, prospect of partial abstention from modalizing. Quine's own three degrees of modal involvement are officially conceived in that light, but their upshot will be accommodation of a purpose associated with one kind of modal talk, and a purpose for which modal talk does not seem to be mandatory. Quine concludes that we may sanction only one role associated with talk of necessity and that is, briefly, a metalinguistic role. In that role, the use of a necessity operator on statements – the use of a necessity operator to generate a 'de dicto' modal context, as in

(1)   It is necessary that if Quine is a philosopher then Quine is a philosopher.

– is equivalent to the use of a validity predicate on names of sentences, as in

(2)   'If Quine is a philosopher then Quine is a philosopher' is valid.

But in light of that equivalence, our use of modal talk for that purpose is gratuitous. And if we do persist in using modal operators on statements for that purpose, that will encourage two further uses of modal talk of which Quine despairs. The first is that it encourages us to think that we can sensibly iterate modal operators to produce well-formed sentences such as

(3)   It is necessary that it is necessary that if Quine is a philosopher then Quine is a philosopher.

The second is that it encourages us to treat modal operators as though they may function as operators on open sentences (4) and subsequently in 'de re' modal contexts (5) – thus:

(4)   It is necessary that x is a philosopher.

(5)   ∃x(It is necessary that x is a philosopher).

But for Quine, to indulge in these sorts of modal talk – to enter into these further two grades of modal involvement – is to enter into realms where there is no good metaphysical story to be told without doing violence to the uniformity and simplicity of our best total theory – a theory which Quine interprets in a thoroughly 'extensional' manner, finding in it commitment only to spatiotemporally related individuals and sets. The upshot is a dilemma that leaves us no need to involve ourselves in modalizing nor, a fortiori, in metaphysical theorizing about the modalities: Either a) modal talk comes in a form that is useful but dispensable, with its role easily catered for within our best total theory, or b) modal talk comes in a form that is not obviously of any use and in a way that is not easily catered for within our best total theory.

Plantinga disagrees fundamentally with just about every aspect of this Quinean treatment of modal locutions. Firstly, Plantinga insists upon the good standing of a necessity operator on statements that is not apt to be 'paraphrased' as any kind of metalinguistic predicate and that, in particular, is not coextensive with the narrowly logical notion of validity (or 'logical truth'). More specifically, he champions the use of an (object-language) operator of broadly logical necessity and he illustrates his views about the extent of this necessity by giving examples.[18] Secondly, Plantinga accepts that both the iterations of such modal operators – see (3) – and their occurrences in de re modal contexts (5) are perfectly in order: The sentences (statements) in question are perfectly well formed. The relevant reasoning here will be that both kinds of use of the necessity operator are vindicated by a possible-worlds semantic theory and, further, that Quine's 'paradoxes' of de re modalizing can be resolved. Thus, Plantinga sees no good reason to avoid Quine's second and third grades of modal involvement, nor to seek a nonmodal surrogate for the first. And so, with this attempt to move us from our modalizing undermined, so is the idea that we can appeal to abstention for Quinean reasons in order to avoid an assessment of the metaphysical consequences and presuppositions of our practice.

(Thesis 3) The third matter, if we indulge in modalizing and in metaphysical theorizing about it, is whether to admit that there is a modal reality of any kind – perhaps, whether there is a part of reality in which modal facts consist (or which makes modal propositions true). One venerable philosophical tradition that advises nonadmission of modal reality is that of noncognitivism or nonfactualism about modality, and it is at this point that the empiricist or pragmatist can be expected to play his or her card against substantial modal metaphysics of modality: thus, Hume,[19] perhaps the later Wittgenstein[20] and, more recently, the modal quasi-realism of Blackburn.[21] Echoing a theme from Quine, the nonfactualists typically proceed from the question of what the function or purpose of modal judgement is. But having departed from Quine by identifying some such function, they find no need to postulate or identify any element of reality that corresponds to, or is represented by, our modal judgements in order that they serve that function. However, nonfactualism has no monopoly on metaphysical nonrealism about modality: We might still attempt to explain away the appearances of commitment to a modal reality to which our use of modal talk gives rise without accepting all (or, perhaps even any) of the nonfactualists picture. Thus, many interpretations are available that are designed to sustain the use of our modal talk without committing us to the existence of a modal reality: thus various noneists,[22] fictionalists,[23] conditionalizers[24] and agnostics.[25] So a metaphysical non-realism about modality is, one way or another, a well-populated position. However, Plantinga eschews it, and his modal metaphysics proceeds by admitting modal reality wholeheartedly and resolving to give an account of it.

(Thesis 4) The fourth issue is whether modal reality is constituted by the existence of entities of a special kind.[26] This issue is delicate, and difficult to articulate, but perhaps the best means of doing so is to consider what a negative answer might amount to. One such answer comes in the form of a *modalism* of a distinctively metaphysical stripe. The idea is that modal truths – that it is necessary that P, or that it is possible that Q – are both perfectly objective, and metaphysically perspicuous as they stand. There is nothing more metaphysically perspicuous or informative to say about what makes it true that it is possible that Q than *that it is possible that Q*. This is to take modality as real, and as metaphysically fundamental but also as nonexistential.[27] We might have to labour long and hard to make any advance on this gesture at what a nonexistential modal realism might fully amount to. But there is, I think, no need to do so in the present context since Plantinga's modal realism clearly involves many existential commitments.

The thesis that Plantinga takes to define the first degree of involvement in modal realism appears to be strictly neutral on the existence of any special, or particular, kinds of *modal* entity. The complex thesis in question is as follows:

(P1)   There are objects and there are properties and every object has some of its properties essentially and has other properties accidentally.

For what is obviously *existential* in this thesis – that there are objects and there are properties – is not that there exist any special *modal* entities. And what is obviously *modal* in the thesis – (all) objects having (some) properties *essentially* and having (some) properties *accidentally* – is not obviously *existential.* However, Plantinga goes beyond this strictly neutral position and asserts the existence of special modal entities that constitute modal reality. For Plantinga holds an auxiliary thesis that, along with (P1), entails that there exist modal properties – namely:

(P1*)   If any object x has a property P essentially (accidentally) then there is some modal property P* that x instantiates.

Thus, for example, if Socrates has the property of *being a philosopher* accidentally, then Socrates has the modal properties of *possibly being a philosopher* and of *possibly not being a philosopher* (and, no doubt, the conjunctive modal property of *possibly being a philosopher and possibly not being a philosopher*). So there exist modal properties of objects such as Socrates. But there also exist modal properties of entities such as propositions and states of affairs. The proposition *that two is even* has the property of *necessary truth*. The state of affairs of *Socrates' being a carpenter* has the property of *possibly obtaining*. This last case is of particular significance. For among Plantinga's states of affairs are those that have the modal properties of *possibly obtaining* and *being maximal*, and these are the entities that Plantinga identifies as the *possible worlds*. Thus, Plantinga takes modal reality to be constituted by the existence of both modal properties and *possible worlds*. In this latter commitment we have the ontological content of Plantinga's thesis of modal realism of the second grade (P2):

(P2)   There are such things as possible worlds and, for any temporally invariant state of affairs (or proposition) S, S is possible *iff* there is some possible world that includes (or entails) S.

Clearly, this thesis (P2) goes further than its explicitly existential first conjunct. But in the second conjunct we get an indication of some further existential information: There are at least as many possible worlds as there have to be in order that every possible state of affairs is included in at least one possible world. So, combined with some theses about how many different states of affairs are possible, we might form a view about how many possible worlds there are. Moreover, before moving beyond the second degree of modal realism, this may be the place to note that in addition to the existence of possible worlds, Plantinga admits the existence of *impossible worlds*. Crucially, impossible worlds are not states of affairs that instantiate impossible properties (e.g., *including the existence of Socrates and not including the existence of Socrates*). For Plantinga will deny the existence of *anything* that is supposed to instantiate an uninstantiable property. Rather, the impossible worlds that Plantinga admits are states of affairs that are maximal and that instantiate the property of *not possibly obtaining* – as a world will, for example, when it includes *the existence of Socrates* and *the nonexistence of Socrates*).[28]

Plantinga's thesis of the third grade of involvement in modal realism is

(P3)   All concrete objects have properties in worlds.

And this thesis is intended as expanding to

(P3*)   For every concrete object x, there is some property P and some world W such that
W includes x's having P.

But Plantinga also admits the existence of a special class of properties, *the world-indexed-properties*, and takes (P3*) to be equivalent to (P4):

(P4)   For every concrete object x, there is some property P* of the kind *having-P-in-W*
such that x has the property P*.

So, by way of illustration, given that in W, Socrates has the property of *being a carpenter*, there is a property of *being-a-carpenter-in-W*, and Socrates instantiates that property. Indeed, Socrates instantiates *that* property in every world and so for each world V, Socrates has, at a further level of iteration, a distinct and doubly indexed property of *being-(a-carpenter-in-W)-in-V*. And there is no obvious limit to the generation of properties by such 'iteration'.

Finally, in this regard, we might note that *essences* are another important element in Plantingan ontology. Plantingan essences are properties; however, despite the name, they are not invariably modal properties. An essence, E, of a thing x, is a property such that necessarily if x exists then x instantiates E and if any y instantiates E, then y is identical to x. So, for example, the property of *being identical to Socrates* is an essence (of Socrates) but it is not obvious that it is itself a modal property even though it entails modal properties, for example, *being necessarily identical to Socrates*. But essences aside, we have seen, and should emphasize, that Plantingan modal realism consists, at least in part, in commitment to the existence of many special kinds of entity – including modal properties, possible worlds, impossible worlds and world-indexed properties – in which modal reality consists.[29]

(Thesis 5) The fifth issue is whether one takes the entities of one's modal ontology (the entities that constitute modal reality) to be abstract entities. While the putative distinction between abstract and concrete entities is problematic, and there is no consensus on the criteria of demarcation of the cases, Plantinga takes his worlds, other nonmaximal states of affairs, propositions and properties to be abstract rather than concrete *relative to every salient criterion of demarcation of the abstract.* For Plantinga, a crucial consideration is that the existence of entities of these various intensional kinds is not contingent, while the existence of those concrete objects that might be identified as the worlds, propositions and so on, is contingent. He also entertains seriously the idea that properties and propositions, at least, are abstract in virtue of being entities (ideas) that exist in the mind of God. The last point aside, Plantinga's position is eminently contrastable with that of Lewis. While Lewis is sceptical of there being a unique, intended, abstract/concrete distinction, he acknowledges that his own 'genuine' possible worlds fall on the concrete side of each salient criterion of demarcation.[30] So there is justice in the slogan that Plantingan possible worlds are abstract entities, while Lewisian possible worlds are concrete.[31] But we would do better to investigate the substantial underlying metaphysical questions upon which this classification turns, and we turn to (some of) these presently.

(Thesis 6) The next issue is whether the entities in one's modal ontology are ontologically independent of (as opposed to dependent upon) concrete entities. On many, if not most, positions that make something of this question, there may be some entities – for example, some properties – that would have existed even if no concrete objects had existed. But Plantinga goes further in asserting the ontological independence of *all* states of affairs, propositions and properties from any concrete entities. For all entities of these kinds are taken to be necessary existents, and as such their existence does not depend on (the existence of) anything. The issue is, perhaps, at its sharpest when we consider (essentially) singular or *quidditative* states of affairs, propositions or properties that essentially represent (or 'make reference to') particular concrete individuals. To take the sharpest among even these cases, consider the state of affairs of *Socrates being identical to Socrates*, the proposition *that Socrates exists* and the property of *being identical to Socrates*. In each case, according to Plantinga, the entity in question could exist even though Socrates did not exist. This denial of the ontological dependence of the quidditative properties on the related individuals is the denial of the thesis that Plantinga calls *existentialism.* In denying existentialism, he takes the opposite side of the present question from many philosophers to whom he is close in his responses to earlier questions.[32] But having registered this point, we must proceed to further degrees of metaphysical commitment in order fully to explain it.

(Thesis 7) The seventh issue is whether the entities in the modal ontology are nonextensional entities. When nonextensionality is invoked as a metaphysical or ontological feature it amounts (roughly) to this: Entities of a kind or category K are nonextensional just in case two distinct entities of that kind have the same extension. Potential complications and subtleties abound in this formulation, but not in such a way that will deprive us of attributing to Plantinga a commitment to intensional entities under any reasonable precisification. For Plantinga, there are many examples of properties that are distinct even though they have the same extension, and even when they are necessarily coextensive. Thus, the property of *being identical to Socrates* and the property of *being necessarily identical to Socrates* have the same extension, both in the actual(ized) world and in every possible world: The extension is (the singleton set of) Socrates. There is an obvious, if not uncontroversial, way of considering whether Plantingan states of affairs are nonextensional entities. Indeed, by this obvious criterion, states of affairs are nonextensional, since there are cases where distinct states of affairs are even necessarily coextensive; that is, they are included in exactly the same possible worlds. Thus, for example: *Socrates' being identical to Socrates* and *Socrates' being necessarily identical to Socrates*. It is a noteworthy feature of these examples that they trade on intuitions about the identity of properties and of states of affairs – noteworthy since a) Plantinga offers no criteria of identity (specifically, no sufficient conditions) for properties or states of affairs, and b) he is hostile to the suggestion that ontological postulates should be constrained by the requirement to provide such criteria.

(Thesis 8) The eighth issue is whether the modal entities are ontologically complex. Firstly, Plantinga takes it that neither the states of affairs, nor the propositions, nor the properties are to be identified with any kind of concrete individual or set. As such, the states of affairs, properties and propositions do not have constituents in either the mereological or set-theoretic senses: They do not have parts and they do not have subsets or members. At this point a choice looms. One might hold that the entities in question are, yet, complex entities in which the mode of composition is neither mereological or set-theoretic. But the alternate view, and the view that has been, at least, associated with Plantinga, is that the entities in question are ontologically simple: They are not 'composed of' anything (save perhaps themselves).[33] Thus, for example, a possible world in which Socrates is taller than Plato is in no sense partially constituted by the state of affairs of *Socrates being taller than Plato*, nor of Socrates, nor of Plato, nor of the (relational) property of *being taller than*. The possible worlds themselves, for all the complexity they may represent, do not have complex natures, but are (abstract) simples.

(**Thesis 9**) The ninth issue is whether the categories of entity overlap – whether any entity of any one of these kinds is identical to any entity of any other kind. For Plantinga, the states of affairs, the proposi- tions and the properties are distinct and exclusive genera. Although at one time more cautious on this point, Plantinga comes to view certain 'Leibniz-Law' arguments as decisive in this regard – for example: every proposition has the property of *having a truth-value*; no set or state of affairs has the property of *having a truth-value*; so no proposition is identical to any set or to any state of affairs.[34] Certainly, Plantingan *worlds* are not *sui generis*, for they are species of the genus of states of affairs – those states of affairs that are possible and maximal. But nor (to reiterate the points of the last section) do they have any states of affairs other than themselves, nor any propositions, nor properties, nor sets nor individuals as constituents. The explanation of this subtlety requires that we bring into view at least one further, crucial metaphysical thesis.

(**Thesis 10**) **The next issue is whether there are irreducibly modal features of reality.** This question, to emphasize, is (intended as) a metaphysical question and not as a question about modal concepts; it is *not* the question whether some modal concepts have irreducibly modal content or whether some modal concepts are unanalysable solely in terms of non-modal concepts. It is also, potentially, a tricky metaphysical question. For one might think, here, of the metaphysical reducibility (in general) of the A-features of reality along the lines of their existence *supervening upon* or *being entailed by* the existence of other, B-features of reality. The problem for the application of this thought in the context of Plantingan metaphysics is the following. Since Plantinga takes *all* properties and states of affairs to be necessary existents, then on the standard accounts of supervenience and entailment, the existence of *any* properties or states of affairs will (trivially) supervene on, and be entailed by, anything. So, a fortiori, the modal features of reality will not be irreducible but, rather, trivially reducible to any others. But there is an alternative, and presently nontrivializing, take on metaphysical irreducibility that requires only that the A-features of reality are not identical to any B-features of reality. And Plantinga, I take it, will assert that the modal properties and modal states of affairs are, in this sense, irreducible to nonmodal properties or states of affairs. The properties of *being identical to Socrates* and of *being necessarily identical to Socrates* are mutually entailing. And not only in that necessarily, if one *exists* then so does the other – a matter of triviality for necessary existents – but in that necessarily, if one *is instantiated* (by any given thing) then so is the other. Yet for Plantinga this is not sufficient for them to be identical and, I believe, he would go further and assert that they are nonidentical. Similarly, mutatis mutandis, for modal states of affairs and what are (perhaps) their best nonmodal candidates for identification – for example, *Socrates being identical to Socrates* and *Socrates' being necessarily identical to Socrates*. But there is a further dimension to his question.

Take a 'merely possible' state of affairs, such as *Socrates being a carpenter*, and an 'actual' state of affairs, such as *Socrates being a philosopher*. For Plantinga this modal difference, the difference in modal status between these states of affairs, is not a difference in existence (for both states of affairs exist) but it is – it seems fair to say – a metaphysical difference, a difference in reality. The difference consists in the latter state of affairs instantiating a certain property that is not instantiated by the former state of affairs – the property of *obtaining*. This property of *obtaining*, then, is an irreducible feature of reality and the instantiation of this property is what the fundamental modal distinction between the merely possible (the possibly obtaining) and the actual (the obtaining) consists in. And on that basis, one might think, Plantinga ought to assent to the claim that *obtaining* is an irreducibly modal feature of reality.[35]

Plantinga's investment in a robust metaphysics of modality goes this far but no further. For there are at least two further claims – metaphysical, and even existential – that, arguably, represent even further degrees of involvement in modal realism but that, unarguably, Plantinga wishes to reject.

(Thesis 11) The eleventh thesis is the thesis of ontological possibilism: that there exist possible individuals that do not actually exist, that there exist mere possibilia. Plantinga rejects possibilism since he asserts the thesis of Ontological Actualism: that (absolutely) everything that exists actually exists; (absolutely) everything is actual.[36] For Plantinga, existence simpliciter is actual existence. But it bears repetition at this stage that, for him, actual existence is not actualization. Within the category of states of affairs (including possible worlds) actualization is obtaining, and Plantinga affirms that some (but only some) of those states of affairs that actually exist are not actualized. Within the category of properties, actualization is instantiation, and he affirms that some (but only some) of those properties that (actually) exist are not actualized. Within the category of individuals (of concrete particulars) there is only actual existence and there is no question of actualization. The reason why there are no actually existing but non-actualized individuals is the deep metaphysical reason that individuals are of a metaphysical category in which the distinction between the actualized and the nonactualized does not (cannot) apply.

In rejecting nonactual existents, and in so affirming ontological actualism, Plantinga finds himself diametrically opposed to Lewis. For Lewis, existence simpliciter is not actual existence: Existence simpliciter is possible existence – or in keeping with the direction of Lewis's explanatory intentions, possible existence is existence simpliciter. For Lewis, then, actual existence is some, but only some, of existence, and to call a part of existence 'actual' is not to attribute any metaphysical status to it; it is, rather, only to pick it out as 'ours' (as that which is spatiotemporally related to *us*). For Lewis, modal reality consists in a plurality of concrete possible worlds, each of which is spatiotemporally unified and spatiotemporally isolated from the others. Thus, for Lewis, many of the individuals that exist (simpliciter) exist in other possible worlds and so do not exist in that part of reality that is (from our standpoint) 'actual'. That is the explanation of Lewis's affirmation of possibilism. But our main concern is to emphasize that possibilism is one robust thesis of modal metaphysics that Plantinga robustly rejects.[37]

(Thesis 12) Our last thesis of modal metaphysics goes even further than Lewis's possibilism: It is the application to the case of possibilia (and perhaps impossibilia) of the claim that there are things that do not exist. Plantinga finds it difficult not to hear Lewis as affirming this thesis. For Plantinga, what exists simpliciter is what actually exists, and since what exists is what there is, endorsing the sentence 'there are things that do not actually exist' is apt to be interpreted as asserting that there are things that do not exist (simpliciter). But, as we have seen, Lewis seeks to resist that interpretation of his own words by distinguishing (in sense and in extension) talk of 'what exists (simpliciter)' from talk of 'what actually exists'. So if, for present purposes, we grant Lewis his semantic intentions, we go further, metaphysically, than the rejection of actualism in asserting the thesis that there are things that do not exist. Or at least with an eye trained on the *metaphysics* of modality, we must distinguish two stories about why one should assert the thesis of existential chauvinism. The first story is intended as primarily semantic and is based on distinct interpretations of a neutral particular quantifier 'there is' and an existential quantifier 'there exists' that is a restricted particular quantifier.[38] But there is a second version of the story that embraces the semantic distinction but seeks to underpin it in an overtly, and robustly, metaphysical way. On this version of the story, there are two kinds of *being*: The broadest ontological category is that of reality and reality consists in things that exist and in things that do not exist, but subsist. However, Plantinga and Lewis are at one in rejecting both versions of the story and so reject the further thesis. But the further thesis may well have had its advocates and is, at least, associated with Meinong.[39] And it is worth mentioning since it makes the metaphysical picture, in a certain sense, complete.

PLANTINGA'S MODAL METAPHYSICS: CRITICAL PERSPECTIVES

Here, I will point towards three kinds of critical thought about Plantinga's modal metaphysics.

Firstly, Plantinga's work engages deeply with some serious elements of the modal opposition but not at all with others. As I have presented Plantinga, he is the consummate realist and antiempiricist modal metaphysician. In that light, then, it is predictable that his position is apt to attract criticism for exactly the kinds of reasons that philosophers are attracted to empiricist, pragmatist and antirealist positions. From the foregoing exposition, it is clear that Plantinga has, to some extent, engaged with these positions through his engagements with Quine and with Lewis. However, there is much by way of antirealistic thought about the modal with which he has yet to engage. Plantinga takes seriously what he takes to be Lewis's reductionist conception of modal reality. But none of the various versions of the idea – both contemporary and not so contemporary, both factualist and nonfactualist – that the explanation of our modalizing does not require the postulation of modal reality, loom large among Plantinga's concerns. In this regard it is also notable that Plantinga's engagement with Quine concentrates on the defence of the semantic coherence of certain modal locutions and does not, as far as I can see, advance at all any defence of the utility, point or function of those locutions in face of Quine's suggestion that they are not only problematic but utterly dispensable. So if you are tempted towards the idea that at least some aspects of our modalizing are dispensable or subject to antirealistic construal, you will find little in Plantinga to address your concerns directly.[40]

Secondly, there is a question about the nature and the extent of explanatory advance that is earned by Plantinga's heavy metaphysical investment. Lewis claims of his own theory of modality that it offers all of the following: an account of the conceptual content of our modal and intensional talk in which no modal concept is taken as primitive; an account of the nature of various kinds of entity (propositions, properties etc.) on which each is identified with some kind of set of possible individuals; and a means of taking in the most straightforward and effective way the semantic claim that our modal expressions are various kinds of quantifier over possibilia. There is no question of Plantinga's modal metaphysics sustaining any of these claims, nor of its being intended to do so. Plantinga is explicit in his understanding that certain modal concepts are primitive, that certain kinds of intensional entity (properties, states of affairs, propositions) are *sui generis* and that the best we can do by way of accommodating canonical possible-worlds semantics is to rewrite it in such a way that our ordinary modalizing about individuals is 'modelled' as talk about associated properties.[41] Plantinga is also, of course, equally explicit in his claim that Lewis does not deliver adequate accounts of the modal concepts, the intensional entities or the meanings of our ordinary modal sayings. And clearly, we have here a certain clash of philosophical sensibilities between Lewis and Plantinga on the point of what philosophical advance consists in. But even if we take the points a) that Plantinga does not accept that Lewis has achieved his stated aims and b) that philosophical advance does not consist in the achievement of aims of this kind, that leaves unanswered the question of how Plantinga would characterize the advances that he thinks have been (or might be) achieved by his modal theorizing.

Thirdly, and finally, we can move onto ground that has less of the air of the methodological battlefield. A certain kind of paradox, familiar from set theory, generates a major worry over the consistency of Plantinga's modal metaphysics.[42] In outline the problem is this. Take as a premise that a possible world is a certain kind of maximal totality: say, a maximal consistent set of propositions. And say that set, W, is of a certain size, k. Now that means that there are $2k$ subsets of W. But then it looks as though there is at least one proposition for each of these sets (the proposition that subset-W1 is a set, the proposition that subset-W2 is a set . . .). But because W is a maximal set, then in the case of each of these propositions, either it or its negation is a member of W. But then that means that W has at least $2k$ members, and that is in contradiction to the hypothesis that W has k members (for arbitrary k). Thus, we have a kind of reductio of the hypothesis that there are possible worlds, given that the possible worlds are identified as maximal consistent sets of propositions. Now, as we know, Plantinga does not claim that possible worlds *are* maximal consistent sets of propositions. But trouble is only one step away, and in more than one direction. For in several cases we have the combination of features: a) that Plantinga is committed to the existence of a certain kind of set and b) that the foregoing argument, or a close analogue of it, serves to demonstrate that the hypothesis that there is such a set is inconsistent. Firstly, Plantinga has suggested that even though possible worlds are not identical to sets of maximal consistent propositions, there is for every possible world a corresponding book on that world that is such a set. Secondly, it is arguable that Plantinga is committed to a set of all states of affairs – or at least to a set of all of the obtaining state of affairs that is coordinate with the actualized world. Thirdly, since Plantinga does not believe in the existence of merely possible individuals, he needs a surrogate for these in his applied possible-worlds semantics, and the best candidate is the set of all instantiable essences. In all of these cases, the consistency of the hypothesis that there is such a set is dubious. And while this is by no means a decisive objection in itself, many will feel that it places upon Plantinga a substantial burden of proving either that he can rescue consistency or offer some effective alternative to believing in the existence of such a set.

I hardly need say that this brief essay has been a first rather than a last word. But I hope that it has succeeded in conveying that Alvin Plantinga's body of work on the metaphysics of modality is rich, subtle, and at the very forefront of the field.[43]

Notes

1. There are, of course many kinds of modality, but here we focus on the case of what Plantinga calls 'broadly logical' necessities and possibilities. He gives us the class by way of examples that include (narrowly) logical necessities (Socrates laughed or it is not the case that Socrates laughed), analytic truths (all vixens are foxes), mathematical truths (seven is greater than five) and certain metaphysical truths of identity (Hesperus is identical to Phosphorus, etc.). This is an alethic modality rather than epistemic (what must/might be the case *given the other things I know*) or deontic (what I must/might do *in accordance with the rules*). It is also an absolute or unrestricted modality (what must simply be the case) as opposed to a relative or restricted modality (e.g., what must be the case given that the – contingent – laws of nature are what they are).

2. Aristotle, *Metaphysics Theta*.

3. David Hume, *A Treatise of Human Nature*, ed L. A. Selby-Bigge, Oxford: Clarendon, 1739.

4. Immanuel Kant, *Critique of Pure Reason*, trans. N. Kemp-Smith, London: MacMillan, 1781 (1929 edition).

5. Ludwig Wittgenstein, *Tractaus Logico-Philosophicus*, 1921 trans. D. F. Pears and B. F. McGuinness, London: Routledge (1961 edition); Rudolph Carnap, *Meaning and Necessity*, Chicago: University of Chicago Press, 1947.

6. See A. J. Ayer, *Language, Truth and Logic*, London: Gollancz, 1936, esp. Chap. 4.

7. See, e.g., W. V. O. Quine, "On What There is," *Review of Metaphysics* 5, 1948, pp. 21–38; "Two Dogmas of Empiricism," *Philosophical Review*, 60 1951, pp. 20–43; "On What There Is," in his *From a Logical Point of View*, Cambridge MA: Harvard University Press, 1953, pp. 1–19; and "Reference and Modality," in his *From a Logical Point of View*, Cambridge MA: Harvard University Press, 1953.

8. In the cause of brevity, I am suppressing some important detail here. A standard text for philosophers that deals with modal logics and possible-worlds semantics along these lines is G. E. Hughes and M. Cresswell, *A New Introduction to Modal Logic*, London: Routledge, 1996.

9. Quine was relatively charitable about de dicto occurrences of modal operators in which they operated on closed sentences $\Box\exists x[Fx]$, reserving his harshest criticism for *de re* occurrences $\exists x[\Box Fx]$. Quine associated the latter usage with commitment to a doctrine that he called "Aristotelian essentialism" and found indefensible.

10. See, e.g., W. V. O. Quine, "Propositional Objects," in his *Ontological Relativity and Other Essays*, New York: Columbia University Press, 1969, pp. 139–160; and "Worlds Away," *Journal of Philosophy*, 73, 1976, pp. 859–863.

11. Marcus R. Barcan, "A Functional Calculus of First Order Based on Strict Implication," *Journal of Symbolic Logic* 11, 1946, pp. 1–16; "The Identity of Individuals in a Strict Functional Calculus of First Order," *Journal of Symbolic Logic* 12, 1947, pp. 12–15; *Modalities: Philosophical Essays*, Oxford: Oxford University Press, 1996.

12. Amongst others who played (at least) a prominent role in the development of possible-worlds semantics theories in that period are Hintikka, Kanger, Montague and Prior. For an (opinionated) account of the history, see J. Copeland, "Prior's Life and Legacy," in *Logic and Reality: Essays on the Legacy of Arthur Prior*, Oxford: Clarendon, 1996, pp. 1–27.

13. Saul Kripke, "Semantical Considerations on Modal Logic," *Acta Philosophica Fennica*, 16, 1963, pp. 83–94; reprinted in L. Linsky (ed.), *Reference and Modality*, Oxford: Oxford University Press, 1971, pp. 63–87.

14. Saul Kripke, "Naming and Necessity," in D. Davidson and G. Harman (eds.), *Semantics for Natural Languages*, Dordrecht: Reidel, 1972, pp. 253–355, 763–769, revised and enlarged edition *Naming and Necessity*, Oxford: Blackwell, 1980.

15. I give references to Plantinga's work later. The key works of Lewis's metaphysics of modality are his "Counterpart Theory and Quantified Modal Logic," *Journal of Philosophy*, 65, 1968, pp. 113–126; "Anselm and Actuality," *Nous*, 4, 1970, pp. 175–188, reprinted in his *Philosophical Papers Volume I*, Oxford: Oxford University Press, 1983, pp. 10–20; *Counterfactuals*, Oxford: Blackwell, 1973; and especially his *On The Plurality of Worlds*, Oxford: Blackwell, 1986. The work of Robert Stalnaker on possible-worlds semantics and related matters is also substantial and influential; however, Stalnaker is excluded from present company by his ambivalence about metaphysics and his subsequently cautious attitude to the metaphysics of modality. See Robert Stalnaker, *Ways a World Might Be: Metaphysical and Anti-Metaphysical Essays*, Oxford: Oxford University Press, 2003.

16. This is not an essay on Lewis, and so I cannot develop or defend this characterization here. But I note that Plantinga ("Two Concepts of Modality" [Abstract], *Journal of Philosophy*, 1986) is explicit in his characterization of Lewis's theory of modality as Quinean in various respects, and the theme is developed further in my "Quinean Skepticism About De Re Modality After David Lewis," *European Journal of Philosophy*, 2007.

17. This is a strategy of exposition and taxonomy that is used by both Quine, "Reference and Modality," and Plantinga, "Two Concepts of Modality." My version of the line of increasing commitment identifies more crucial points than either of those, and the account is intended to be neutral rather than partisan about how far one ought to proceed.

18. See n. 1.

19. Hume, *A Treatise of Human Nature*.

20. Ludwig Wittgenstein, *Remarks on the Foundations of Mathematics*, Oxford: Blackwell, 1956.

21. Simon Blackburn, "Morals and Modals," in *Fact, Science and Morality: Essays on A. J. Ayer's Language, Truth and Logic*, ed. G. MacDonald and C. Wright, Oxford: Blackwell, 1986, pp. 119–142.

22. R. Routley, *Exploring Meinong's Jungle and Beyond*, Canberra: Australian National University Central Printery, 1980; Graham Priest, *Towards Non-Being: The logics and Metaphysics of Intentionality*, Oxford: Clarendon, 2005.

23. G. Rosen, "Modal Fictionalism," *Mind* 99, 1990, pp. 327–354.

24. T. Sider, "The Ersatz Pluriverse," *Journal of Philosophy* 99, 2002, pp. 279–315.

25. John Divers, "Agnosticism About Other Worlds: A New Antirealist Programme in Modality," *Philosophy and Phenomenological Research*, 69, 2004, pp. 659–684. Most of these interpretations, and their metaphysical nonrealist motivation, kick in after the move has been made to conceive modality in worldly terms.

26. This is not (yet) the question of whether reality is irreducibly modal, and it is left open that a positive answer to the question of special entities should be consistent with a negative answer to the question of irreducibly modal reality (see Thesis 9, in the text).

27. See, perhaps, Prior (*Time and Modality*, Oxford: Oxford University Press, 1957) and Prior and Fine (*Worlds, Times and Selves*, London: Duckworth, 1977). I write 'perhaps' since the modalism on display in Prior is often expressed as a doctrine about modal concepts rather than a doctrine about the metaphysics of modality.

28. The point is perhaps clearer if we think of worlds in terms of the books (of propositions) that represent what is the case in the worlds. There are impossible books in the sense that there are books according to which impossible things happen. But there are not impossible books in the sense that there are books that themselves have contradictory properties such as saying that trees exist and not saying that trees exist. So, mutatis mutandis, for the states of affairs that are the worlds. It is the absence of this distinction in Lewis's ontology that prevents him from admitting the existence of impossible worlds. On Lewis's view worlds are concrete universes (see Thesis 5, in the text) and worlds represent *de dicto* by having properties. So on that view, for it to be the case that according to a world there are trees and there are no trees, there would have to exist an impossible world with contradictory properties – a universe that has the property of having tree-parts and that has the property of lacking tree-parts. And Lewis is not having that.

29. Before leaving this matter of the existential or ontological dimension of Plantinga's modal metaphysics altogether, perhaps we should note that it would not be felicitous to attribute to Plantinga a claim that is popularly associated with ontological expressions of realism: the claim that certain entities are the truthmakers for modal claims. As far as I know, Plantinga makes no such claim. And there is a familiar barrier to his, or to anyone else's, doing so to nontrivial effect. For if the truthmaking claim is that there are certain entities whose existence *entails* modal truths, then the threat is that the claim is established too quickly by the following pair of theses: a) that every necessary truth is entailed by the existence of anything and b) that modal truths are, typically, necessary truths (see my *Possible Worlds*, London: Routledge, 2002, Chap. 12).

30. Lewis, *On The Plurality of Worlds*, pp. 81–86.

31. The contrast in the case of categories of entity other than that of worlds is not so clearly marked. For Lewis's properties, propositions and states of affairs (modal and otherwise) are *sets* of concrete things, and these turn out to be abstract ontology by some, but not all, the salient criteria of demarcation.

32. E.g., Fine in the "Postscript" to Prior and Fine, *Worlds, Times and Selves*; and Adams, "Actualism and Thisness," *Synthese* 49, 1981, pp. 3–41.

33. I am not sure whether Plantinga takes an explicit stance on this point in his published work, but the commitment to abstract simples is attributed to him by Lewis (*On The Plurality of Worlds*, p. 183). It is a commitment that is embraced by Peter van Inwagen ("Two Concepts of Possible Worlds," *Midwest Studies in Philosophy*, 11, 1986, pp. 185–213).

34. The suppressed premise here is the contrapositive of (a version of) Leibniz's Law, viz.: that, for any x and y, if x and y have different properties then x is not identical to y.

35. If it helps to make the feature in question look more obviously modal, we might observe that in the Plantingan perspective, *obtaining* either is just the same property as *being actualized*, or at least the former is that species of the latter that is instantiated by the states of affairs.

36. To find another, intermediate, grade of commitment to robust modal metaphysics, we might consider the thesis that *it is possible that there exist things that do not actually exist*. To be clear, Plantinga affirms *the necessity of ontological actualism* and, so, rejects even the former possibility thesis.

37. Plantinga would likely go further in claiming that even if there are things of the kind that Lewis calls 'nonactual', that is, concrete individuals that stand in no spatiotemporal relation to us, these things are not nonactual or merely possible, but part of what there actually is – actuality thereby turning out to be spatiotemporally fragmented in a way we do not usually take it to be. This is explicitly the view of van Inwagen ("Two Concepts of Possible Worlds"), and Plantinga comes at least very close to endorsing it explicitly by declaring the irrelevance to modality of the existence of Lewis's 'nonactuals'. So Plantinga denies directly the possibilist thesis that there are things that don't actually exist, rather than the 'associated' thesis that there are concrete things that are not spatiotemporally related to us.

38. Thus, see 'noneists' Priest (*Towards Non-Being*) and Routley (*Exploring Meinong's Jungle and Beyond*).

39. Alexis Meinong, "The Theory of Objects," 1910, in R. M. Chisholm (ed.), *Realism and the Background of Phenomenology*, New York: The Free Press, 1960, pp. 76–117.

40. I believe that these comments apply also to Lewis.

41. For example, the claim that Socrates might have been a carpenter is 'associated' in the intended applied semantics with the truth-condition that at some possible world, the properties of *being identical to Socrates* and of *being a carpenter* are coinstantiated. For detailed development see Jager ("An Actualist Semantics for Quantified Modal Logic," *Notre Dame Journal of Formal Logic*, 23, 1982, pp. 335–349).

42. This line of criticism is emphasized in Charles S. Chihara, *The Worlds of Possibility*, Oxford: Oxford University Press, 1998, pp. 120–141.

43. For an alternative exposition of Plantinga's metaphysics see Matthew Davidson, "Introduction" in his edition, *Plantinga: Essays in The Metaphysics of Modality*, Oxford: Oxford University Press, 2003, pp. 3–24. For extensive discussion of Plantinga's work on modal metaphysics and related issues see James Tomberlin and Peter van Inwagen (eds.), *Alvin Plantinga*, Dordrecht: Reidel, 1985.

4 Natural Theology and Naturalist Atheology: Plantinga's Evolutionary Argument Against Naturalism

ERNEST SOSA

Natural theology has always had to contend with the argument from evil. The evil around us seemingly supports a deductive argument for the conclusion that there is no God of the sort affirmed by theology. More recently, natural theology has faced new problems, or old problems with a new urgency. Darwin, for example, showed how evolutionary design rivals Divine design, endangering the important Argument from Design. Suppose certain phenomena admit two rival, independent explanations. Any such explanation no better than its rival is insufficiently supported thereby. Theology had proposed Divine design as an explanation of the order around us. Evolutionary theory offers now a rival explanation that purports to be at least as good while independent of Divine agency.

Both of these attacks are "direct." They both confront theology directly on its own ground, by countering its theses in one of two ways. One way is by direct refutation of a theological proposition: The evil we see leaves no rational room for an omnipotent, fully benevolent God. The other way attacks, rather, the cogency of theology's rational support: by arguing, for example, that Divine agency is no longer needed to explain the order of things.

Although both of these attacks are direct, the first is *more* direct, since it clashes frontally with the theological proposition that there is a God. From the premise that there is evil, it concludes that there is no God. The second attack is not frontal. It targets not the truth of a theological thesis but the cogency of its supporting rationale.

Nietzsche, Freud, and Marx launch an even more indirect attack. They all pursue different versions of the same strategy. Their target is not so directly the truth of religious beliefs, nor even the quality of their supporting arguments. Their target is rather the *sources* of religious belief. Each deplores the factors, psychological or sociological, that originate or sustain such beliefs. For Nietzsche, religion is a way for the weak to gang up on the strong and keep them in line. For Freud, religion is wishful thinking that fills our need for a comforting view of our situation and its prospects.

For Marx, religion is opium used to distract the masses and keep them in chains.

To agree that religion can be misused in these ways is to agree with the enemies of religion only in part, for they tend to go much further. In their view, the misuse of religion is not just possible but actual: It is said to be a main use of the Christian religion in Western civilization.

If we believe these enemies of religion, religious belief has deplorable intellectual quality. No matter how practically useful it may be, religious belief will have little by way of epistemic status. Even if by chance it happens to be true, it is hardly knowledge, or even well supported. From a purely epistemic point of view, it would seem little better than irrational superstition. To avoid superstition, to attain better intellectual quality, a belief would need a more intimate connection with truth. Here we can ignore a belief's *practical* justification, its ability to fulfill human needs and desires. We focus rather on its *epistemic* justification, on its aiming at the truth in an intellectually acceptable way.

What makes a way of forming beliefs intellectually acceptable? What makes a source epistemically worthy? One minimal requirement has to be this: that it deliver truth rather than untruth reliably enough. Its deliverances must be sufficiently probable, given their origin in that source. Even the Internalist-in-Chief of the tradition agrees on this much. Recall Descartes's reasoning: Once having hit on the thought that he thinks and therefore exists, and on the thought that he is a thinking being, as his prime examples of certain knowledge, he ponders: "What could be the source of this high epistemic status, of this certainty?" Seeing no other source than its clarity and distinctness, he observes: "*But clarity and distinctness could hardly be thus a source of certainty unless it were a reliable source, indeed an infallibly reliable source.*"

If they lack intellectually reliable sources, our beliefs might be practically effective and justified, but they can hardly be epistemically justified, much less can they be knowledge, even if by luck they turn out to be true. If the enemies of religion are right about the sources of religious belief, then such belief may be comforting, or socially beneficial, but could hardly amount to knowledge.

How can the friends of religion defend against this attack? One way would be to deny what religion's enemies say about the sources of religious belief. But here the defense of religion would need empirical backing. Knowing about the actual sources of religious beliefs requires empirical inquiry. A full and credible account would need to draw on the psychology, history, and sociology of religion. Nietzsche, Freud, and Marx manage only some initial exploration of broad fields still under patient, disciplined cultivation.

However that may turn out, here I would like to consider a very different defense of natural theology, an imaginative and original turning of the tables on the enemies of religion by a contemporary philosopher/theologian. I mean the way in which Alvin Plantinga has in recent writings turned the momentum of religion's enemies against them, using their own strategy in an attempt to upend them, and indeed make them fall on their own sword. How is all this supposed to come about?

PLANTINGA'S ARGUMENT, BRUTE FORCES, AND DOUBT

Naturalism eschews or rejects appeal to the supernatural, and traces our origins back to blind and uncaring forces. Relative to forces in that sense brute, however, the probability that our cognitive faculties are reliable must be either quite low or at best inscrutable. This defeats any belief we may have in the reliability of our faculties. Absent such belief, finally, we are deprived also of epistemic warrant (authority, justification) for all beliefs deriving from such faculties. But among these beliefs is the very belief in naturalism, which therefore defeats itself.

Reply: "Surely we naturalists know more about our origins than that! We know we derive from evolutionary processes that ensure our fitness to do well in our environmental niche." Unfortunately, this ensures at most that we excel in certain respects that help enhance the fitness and survival of our species, and it is unclear just how the correctness of our beliefs can bear on such success. Even given such evolutionary considerations, accordingly, the likelihood that our faculties are cognitively reliable is only low or inscrutable. Naturalism thus remains defeated and cannot be saved by evolution.

So argues antinaturalist Plantinga, who has later defended his argument against a broad and varied set of objections gathered around it in the years since it was first sketched in his *Warrant and Proper Function*.[1]

For a defense beyond that initial sketch, Plantinga now explores in some depth the epistemology of defeat. Candidates for defeat are beliefs, and candidates for defeaters are, in the main, other beliefs and experiences. Any belief B that is part of one's noetic structure N is defeated by a newly acquired belief D if, and only if, one can preserve one's rationality while retaining belief D only by giving up belief B. It would not be fully rational to retain the noetic structure that includes both B and D. Consider, for example, this proposition:

R that one's faculties are reliable.

If one somehow believes that one is at the epistemic mercy of a demon bent on mischief, this belief is a defeater for one's trust that R is true, and is also thereby a defeater in turn for the ostensible deliverances of these faculties. Similarly, argues the antinaturalist, if one comes to believe that one is a product of brute forces, this belief also defeats one's trust in one's faculties, and in turn defeats their ostensible deliverances. (Here I have simplified Plantinga's actual argument by dispensing with the trappings of evolutionary theory and going directly to the belief that brute forces account for our existence and epistemic constitution or character.) How plausible is this? Relative to their having derived from brute forces by evolutionary processes, it is at best inscrutable how reliable one's faculties are likely to be. Let us grant, for the sake of argument, that our belief in the reliability of our faculties is indeed defeated by that fact about their derivation, that accepting this fact would preclude our rationally believing our faculties to be reliable. Even so, why should that also defeat our many ordinary beliefs derived from those faculties? Take a child at a prereflective stage wherein one takes no notice of one's faculties. Is that child irrational in forming beliefs about food, shelter, and other basic matters of its simple life? If not, why then should it be irrational to harbor such simple beliefs conjointly with a belief that we derive from brute forces relative to which the probability of our being reliable is low or inscrutable? Even if we harbor that belief about our brute derivation, and even if this requires that we not believe R, why should this lack of belief about one's faculties make it irrational to uphold our simple beliefs about food and shelter, if a similar lack does not make such beliefs irrational in a child?

It is here that Plantinga's antinaturalist argument may connect with the reflective knowledge tied to our Principle of the Criterion. What is so unfortunate in the fate of a child lacking a relevant epistemic perspective on its cognitive doings and their reliability? Perhaps he or she is unfortunate not in being irrational but in being denied the reflective knowledge that requires some such perspective. Absent belief in the reliability of one's own faculties, one is denied that higher order of knowledge. But is the naturalist necessarily denied the epistemic perspective needed for reflective knowledge? Has the supernaturalist an advantage in this respect?

Of course the belief that one's faculties are quite *unreliable* would fit ill with accepting their ostensible deliverances. Here then is an implicit assumption perhaps used by Plantinga: that if our faculties derive from brute forces, then it is quite *unlikely* that they are reliable. Absent some way of defeating this consideration, therefore, we must hold our faculties unreliable, and this would make it irrational to accept their deliverances at face value. This does require the stronger claim that our faculties are *unlikely* to be reliable if derived from brute forces (through evolution), and not just the claim that the likelihood of their reliability is inscrutable. But let us proceed on the basis of this stronger claim nevertheless, for the sake of argument.[2]

Suppose a walk down by the riverside turns up a smooth, round stone, which one picks up and admires, and about which one notes that it would reliably roll down inclines. "That stone must have derived from brute forces," thinks one, however, as a good naturalist, "and relative to that fact there is only a low or inscrutable probability that it be either round or a reliable roller." Have we now in this consideration a defeater of the belief (call it S) that the stone is indeed both round and a reliable roller?

We can plainly see and feel the stone's smooth roundness, and we know through much experience that such an object would roll reliably. The improbability of its having been rounded so smoothly, given its origin in brute forces, is then, surely, no bar to our still knowing it to be smoothly round, and even a reliable roller, nor does our justification for so believing seem defeated, even if we retain the belief that here the improbable has occurred.

If that is a plausible response in the case of the round stone, why are we deprived of it when it comes to our own nature as reliable perceivers endowed with eyes and ears, and so on, by means of which we have reliable access to the colors, shapes, and sounds around us? Start first with someone else, a friend whom we believe to be a reliable perceiver of the colors and shapes of things seen in good light, and so on. Can't we forestall the alleged defeat by appeal to our perceptual and other means of knowing that our friend is as described?

Perhaps it's when one turns to one's own case that we run into real trouble? Not if the belief concerns only some introspectible feature of one's present state of consciousness or some perceptible feature of one's body. I can know that I now ache or that I have hands, no matter how improbable it may be that brute forces should produce someone aching or with hands, and despite my believing us to derive from such forces.

So it must be something concerning the specific belief about oneself involved in R that might make one's belief in R susceptible to defeat in the ways noted by Plantinga. And what exactly could that be? What might be the basis for the conclusion or for the assumption that R specifically is thus susceptible? Here is a possibility.

One might suppose that a deliverance of a faculty when accepted is based on an implicit reliance on the reliability of the faculty, and that this reliance takes the form of an assumption that plays the role of an implicit premise in reasoning whose conclusion is the acceptance of the deliverance. Call this the *implicit premise thesis.* On ordinary assumptions, then, as soon as the implicit belief in the reliability of the faculty is put in question, one can hardly find support for that belief by appeal to the ostensible deliverances of that faculty. Such appeal would, after all, require a prior trust in the reliability of the faculty, and we would be in a vicious circle.

Is it perhaps on the basis of such reasoning that belief in one's own cognitive reliability is held importantly distinct from belief in the reliability as a roller of a smooth stone, and even from belief in the cognitive reliability of someone else? In these other cases, one can rationally base one's belief on one's perceptions, memories, and reasonings, overcoming thus any doubts based on the fact that the entity derives from brute forces. In one's own case, it would be viciously circular to argue in parallel fashion from the deliverances of one's perception, memory, and reason to the reliability of these faculties seated in oneself.

How defensible is the implicit premise thesis? Compare the following three theses:

R   That one's faculties are reliable.
S   That the stone by the riverside is smoothly rounded and would roll.
F   That one's friend is a reliable perceiver of colors and shapes.

If not on the basis of that thesis, how then might we support the required distinction between R, on the one hand, and the likes of S and F, on the other? How to support the claim that R is subject to defeat by brute origins, whereas S and F are exempt from such defeat? What accounts for this distinction if not the implicit premise thesis?

Something like the implicit premise thesis may be found in Thomas Reid, where it raises subtle and difficult issues. While unable to discuss these issues here, I elsewhere conclude that no vicious circularity need be involved.[3] As a consequence, I can see no way to support the required distinction between R, on the one hand, and S and F, on the other. So I do not believe that the foregoing line of argument can be successful.

REFLECTIVE KNOWLEDGE

That brings us to the more promising reasoning in terms of the requirements of perspectival or reflective knowledge, reasoning that we now explore briefly: Does it offer better support for the case against naturalism? Reflective knowledge requires an epistemic perspective underwriting the knower's belief from his or her own epistemic perspective. It might perhaps be argued that the naturalist, unlike the theist, is denied such a perspective, and is hence at an epistemic disadvantage. This I have argued to be the leading idea of Descartes's epistemological project. Descartes crafts for himself, and invites us to share, a theological perspective meant to underwrite his faculties and beliefs. If the faculties valued are those of a priori reflection, moreover, such as intuition and deduction, and if one wants to cast these in a good light, and if the best light is that attainable only by use of these very faculties – if these are "the most sure routes to knowledge, such that the mind should admit no others" – what might one invoke other than rational theology? In fact, it is easy to see why Descartes, with his background and in his milieu, would feel strongly drawn to that recourse.

Is the naturalist at an epistemic disadvantage? Is the naturalist indeed in a position that is rationally self-defeating? This seems implausible in light of the following. As a supernaturalist, one might use certain faculties (as does Descartes his faculties of a priori reflection) in devising an epistemically comforting view of one's universe, according to which one is so constituted, and so related to one's environment, that one's faculties would be truth-conducive, not misleading. I take that to be Descartes's strategy.

What denies such a strategy to the naturalist? Why can't you as a naturalist develop a view of yourself and your surroundings that shows your situation to be epistemically propitious? You would need to be able to self-attribute ways of acquiring and retaining beliefs that put you so in touch with your surroundings, relative to the fields of interest relevant to you, that you would tend to believe correctly in virtue of using those ways. What precludes your doing so, by means of science, as a naturalist, if the supernaturalist can do so by means of theology?

And now comes a key question in assessing Plantinga's strategy: Is there any proposition O in a relevant sense just about our origins, whose inclusion in a view V would preclude V's enrichment by an epistemic perspective of the sort required for reflective knowledge? In other words, would any O-containing view V repel any possibility of being enriched coherently (while still including O) in a way enabling the holders of the enriched V to become thereby reflective knowers?

I myself can see no bright prospect for showing that the following would be such a proposition O: that we humans derive from brute forces. That proposition seems to me tenable compatibly with the view that, in fact, we are quite good cognizers of our surroundings through our use of vision, hearing, and so on; that these faculties put us reliably enough in touch with the truth about empirical and contingent goings-on around us, and that we are thereby enabled to know about these goings-on. Issues of circularity do arise as to how we can rationally and knowledgeably adopt such a view about our own epistemic prowess. But these problems of circularity are not exclusive to naturalism, as Descartes was soon to find out from his critics.[4]

EVOLUTIONARY THEORY AND COGNITIVE SCIENCE

Perhaps Plantinga's argument is unfairly gutted of crucial content if we omit the part of his reasoning that draws on naturalist evolutionary theory and cognitive science. Naturalism, we are told, leads to acceptance of evolutionary theory. Given evolutionary theory, however, it is at best inscrutable how reliably truth-conducive our cognitive mechanisms may be. Thus, we have little reason to suppose that the beliefs delivered by our mechanisms will be reliably enough true. So, once again, we are led to the conclusion that our beliefs have little by way of epistemic justification, and this includes the belief in naturalism itself.

After all, evolution cares fundamentally about adaptation and fitness. If it cares at all about the truth of our beliefs, this will have to be because of how our true beliefs contribute to our adaptation and fitness. But the probability that our true beliefs make any such contribution is low or at best inscrutable. According to naturalist cognitive science, beliefs are brain states with cognitive content. Their place in the causal order is thus at the juncture between afferent and efferent nerves. But how then can the content or truth of a belief gain any purchase in the causal order? It is presumably the physical, electrochemical properties of the brain and nervous system that link up with our sensory receptors on one side and with our muscles on the other, serving thus as causal intermediaries between perceptual stimulus and behavioral response. It is those electrochemical properties that matter causally. The propositional content of a belief thus seems epiphenomenal, its causal efficacy preempted by the physical properties of the constitutive brain state.

The advocate of naturalism now appears more vulnerable than the friend of religion. For it is naturalism *itself* that yields the bad result about our belief formation, that its reliability is low or inscrutable. No such result about religious sources is supposed to follow from religious beliefs themselves; not even religion's enemies suppose otherwise. Accordingly, the enemies of religion are *not* able to convict religious belief of any sort of self-defeat. Their attack on religion is based on claims about the sources of religious beliefs, but they are not able to draw these claims from religion itself. Plantinga, by contrast, does take his reasoning to convict naturalism of self-defeat, since he does draw his premises from naturalism itself.

The naturalist contends that we, and our faculties, derive from *brute forces*, from forces that are blind and uncaring about human welfare, including our cognitive welfare. Plantinga responds that once we accept such a brutish etiology for our faculties, we cannot rationally hold on to our implicit trust in their reliability as sources of truth. But if we cannot trust our faculties, then we cannot rationally accept anything we regard as a deliverance of those faculties. If you are a naturalist, however, then your naturalism is itself something you regard as a deliverance of your faculties, in which case you cannot rationally hold on to that belief. This is how, according to Plantinga, naturalism defeats itself.

Consider now any subjects who face the question whether their faculties are reliable, and realize that if they do have reliable faculties, this is a contingent matter, and that they cannot just assume so and let it go at that. Given the contingency of the reliability of their faculties, what assurance is there that though they *might* be unreliable, in fact they are reliable? Wouldn't the inability to give a rational, nonarbitrary answer to this question itself constitute a problem?

Compare your situation as a naturalist facing the fact that your faculties derive from brute forces. If you agree that your faculties are brutely derived, does this not defeat your belief in their reliability? Suppose you try through your faculties to attain a picture of yourself and the world around you offering assurance that your faculties are reliable despite their brute derivation. Is this to proceed circularly? Well, it is to proceed in a kind of circle. Will it be said that the circle is vicious? Yes, but *such* a circle cannot possibly be avoided once we face so fundamental a question.

What, in sum, should we say to Plantinga's antinaturalist argument? If our faculties are brutely derived, their reliability is then perhaps low or

inscrutable, relative to that fact. This can be debated, but let us grant it
for the sake of argument. Even granting this, it will defeat our belief in
the reliability of our faculties only if we have no other basis for believing
them reliable. We do have another basis, however, beyond anything we
may believe about the etiology of our faculties. For the deliverances of these
faculties themselves give us an additional basis. And what, more specifically,
is this basis? Is it the mere fact that our faculties are self-supportive and
yield belief in their own reliability? No, that cannot suffice on its own; for
superstitious "faculties" might easily have that property with little epistemic
effect. At a minimum, our faculties must satisfy two conditions: first, that
they be thus self-supportive, that is, productive of a picture of the believer
and his or her world according to which those very faculties are reliable;
second, that they be *in fact* reliable.

Can that be a sufficient response? Can the naturalist rest with a naturalist
picture according to which we are animals with sensory receptors that enable
causal commerce with our surrounding world to the effect of perceptual and
eventually other knowledge of that world? How well can this stand up once
we reflect that, given the brutish etiology of our faculties, it would be a
near-miracle for us to be reliably attuned through our sensory receptors?
Suppose I think that, much more easily than not, my brain could have been
placed in a vat, rather than being left to develop in its cranial housing.
May I hold that view while still assuming that my brain is cranially housed
and receives input through the connected sensory receptors? Suppose it is
incoherent to combine these beliefs. Suppose instead that believing I could
so easily have been envatted would require me to suspend judgment on
what has actually happened to my brain. I could then hardly continue to
accept the deliverances of my faculties, of the very faculties whose epistemic
standing is now in doubt.

What seems bad for the naturalist is not just that, given our brutish etiology, it is monumental luck that we exist at all. That would seem acceptable
and not to preclude that, *given* our existence, however lucky, our faculties
are indeed reliable, and not just accidentally so. What seems bad for the
naturalist is that however accidental our existence, it is a *further* accident
that our faculties are reliable, if indeed they are. Suppose we have no basis
for supposing that things have turned out well enough for our faculties,
despite how little reason we have to suppose they would turn out that way,
given their evolutionary origins. This would be bad. It would put us in an
epistemic situation about as bad as if we knew that we had taken a pill that
nearly always disables one's faculties terminally, except for those in some
minuscule subset. If one believes that one did take such a pill, it seems

incoherent to think that one is still cognitively reliable. This would require believing that one falls in the favored minuscule subset. But how could one rationally believe that one is so lucky, unless one had some special reason for so believing? And how could one gain such a reason, given how likely it is that one's cognition is disabled?

STRATEGIES FOR NATURALISTS

Naturalists face Plantinga's argument that the success of our cognitive faculties *would* indeed be a huge accident, *if* we go by evolution and by the naturalist conception of our minds as our contentful brains. As I suggested, the tables have been turned on the naturalist opposition, and a fully adequate response remains to be formulated. In conclusion, I would like to point in two directions where such a response might be found.

In the first place, perhaps we could not possibly have been in existence, all of us, deprived of our successful cognitive faculties. Perhaps the human species could not have come about while entirely deprived of such faculties. If so, it would not be just an accident that humans qua human come outfitted with reason, memory, and perception, and with the social framework that forms the basis for credible testimony. This might be a strategy for the naturalist to use, one inspired by recent externalist accounts of how our minds acquire conceptual and propositional contents. A line of reasoning championed most prominently by Hilary Putnam and Donald Davidson opposes skepticism through a kind of transcendental argument, according to which we could not possibly have contentful beliefs without a substantial amount of built-in truth. The conditions required for our acquisition of empirical concepts, for example, will entail that our application of such concepts could not be too far off the mark. For it is only through adequate sensitivity to the presence or absence of perceptible properties that we acquire corresponding concepts of those properties.

Finally, I will sketch an alternative strategy that the naturalist might employ, one that goes beyond the externalism just indicated, though the two are complementary. Again, Plantinga's critique requires naturalists to show how they can reasonably trust their cognitive faculties. For a start, while our evolutionary derivation may not *entail* our reliability, neither does it *preclude* our reliability; we may be reliable *anyhow*. We would of course need some basis for believing that we are, and this basis will unavoidably involve the circularity already noted, that of issuing from the very faculties whose reliability is to be affirmed. But no conceivable defense of our reliability could possibly avoid *that* sort of circularity, and so this cannot be a disabling objection in the end.

This line of defense appears to crash, however, on the example of a cognitively disabling pill – call it DISABLEX. This is a pill that terminally disables one's cognitive faculties, so that none is any longer reliable. How can you right now be sure that you have never taken any such pill? Appealing to the present deliverances of your faculties would seem vicious, since these are of course deliverances that would be made misleading by your having taken the pill.

Does DISABLEX pose a problem for us? Well, consider right now the possibility that we did once take such a pill. How *do* we properly get to assume that we did not? How so, if not just by relying on our faculties in the sort of default way in which we normally do? But by so relying, we manifest our commitment to the claim that our faculties are indeed reliable, our commitment to this shown at least in our intellectual practice. If we are justified in that commitment, moreover, what could then prohibit our reflectively making our practice explicit? Certainly we would be within our rights in giving voice to what we were already rightfully committed to in practice. And once we do give voice to this, what prevents our deducing further that we must not have taken any such pill? Surely we would then be entitled to deduce that we cannot have done so. For if we had done so, then we could not have what we are committed to believing we do have, namely, the reliability of our faculties.

 We are supposing ourselves entitled to rely on our commitment in intellectual practice to the reliability of our faculties, and to be within our intellectual rights in making that commitment explicit upon reflection. But on a closer look that might seem viciously circular: The step here appears rather too close for comfort. Even so, the step to our having taken no DISABLEX would not be quite so close; it would require some further information and argument. We would need the information that such pills terminally disable you. Only by adducing such further information, and reasoning from it, do we reach the conclusion that this is a pill we cannot have taken. And indeed, how else can you attain justification for your explicit denial right now that you have never taken any such pill?

Of course, there are conceivable scenarios where you acquire considerable evidence that you have taken a disabling pill. But these scenarios cannot render you justified in believing what they initially suggest, that you have in fact taken such a pill. Nor can they even justify you in suspending judgment on the question. For the claim that you have taken any such pill is a self-defeating claim. Both believing that you have taken the pill and even suspending judgment on that question are epistemically self-defeating. The contrary claim, that you have taken no such pill, follows logically from what is epistemically obligatory and self-sustaining, namely, the commitment to the reliability of your faculties. Therefore, it is hard to see how you could possibly go wrong epistemically not only in affirming the reliability of your faculties but also in affirming anything you can see to follow logically from that, including the consequence that you have never taken any such pill.

And the same goes for Plantinga's evolutionary argument. Again, believing that our faculties are unreliable is self-defeating, as is even suspending judgment on that question. On the question whether your faculties are reliable, you have no rational choice but to assent, therefore, and so you would be within your rights to draw the further conclusion that if your origins are evolutionary, then such origins cannot make your faculties unreliable. Would that necessarily preclude a naturalist from believing in evolution? Only if evolutionary origins entailed the unreliability of our faculties. But nothing like this is shown by any of the considerations adduced in Plantinga's evolutionary argument. At most, what those considerations show is that the probability that our faculties are reliable is low or inscrutable. And this is compatible with our faculties being reliable. Indeed, from those considerations it cannot even be inferred that it is *unlikely* that our origins are evolutionary, for inscrutability would permit no such inference.

What exactly is the question that we have no rational choice but to answer in the affirmative? What is the question to which we can respond neither with a no nor even with a suspending maybe? It is the question *whether one's faculties are cognitively reliable.* By this I mean whether they are faculties that reliably guide us to the cognitively proper doxastic stances. Sometimes the proper stance is to believe, sometimes it is to disbelieve, and sometimes it is to suspend judgment. According to externalists, the propriety of these stances will be determined by what would properly enable us to attain truth and avoid error in the circumstances. Why might it be thought that we have no rational choice but to answer in the affirmative the question as to our reliability? Well, consider the alternatives. Suppose we say no. How then can we still coherently trust our faculties in sustaining that negative answer? Indeed, suppose that we so much as suspend judgment on the question, saying "maybe so, maybe not." Even here, how can we coherently commit to *this* attitude while saying that we have no idea whether, in so proceeding, we are proceeding cognitively aright? This still seems less than fully coherent. Again, on that question the only coherent stance would seem to be the confident affirmative. Once we see this stance

to be rationally required, that surely entitles us to draw its deductive consequences, including a) that we have never taken any disabling pill, and b) that
our faculties do not have *disabling* evolutionary origins. Moreover, we have
not been shown that evolutionary origins would necessarily be disabling.
Compatibly with one's inevitable rational trust in the reliability of our faculties, therefore, one is free also to retain belief in a naturalistic, evolutionary
account of our origins. And this for the naturalist would seem properly to
counter the allegedly defeating belief that our evolutionary origins render
our faculties unreliable.

Notes

It is an honor and a pleasure to join in this tribute to a most admired philosopher
and friend.

1. Alvin Plantinga, *Warrant and Proper Function*, New York and Oxford: Oxford
   University Press, 1993.
2. Note how well the stronger claim comports with acceptance of the Argument
   from Design. But here we shall focus on *reflective knowledge* specifically. It is then
   plausible to require belief in the reliability of one's faculties as a condition for
   enjoying (reflective) knowledge through their ostensible deliverances. Of course,
   this distinguishes that higher sort of knowledge from the "animal" knowledge
   that requires no such reflection (like the *cognitio* that Descartes allows to an atheist
   mathematician).
3. I take up these issues in my discussion of Reid's epistemology, "Reidian First Principles," which is my part of a contribution, jointly with James Van Cleve, on Reid,
   to *The Modern Philosophers: From Descartes to Nietzsche*, ed. Steven Emmanuel,
   Oxford: Blackwell, 1999.
4. I myself think that Descartes was actually right on the issue of circularity, and
   the critics wrong. My forthcoming *Virtuous Circles* contains a fuller defense.

5 | Two Approaches to Epistemic Defeat
JONATHAN KVANVIG

The concept of epistemic defeat, or some surrogate for it, is essential for any fallibilistic epistemology. If knowledge requires infallibility, then the epistemic grounds of belief have to be strong enough that no further information could be made available to the cognizer to undermine these grounds of belief. When knowledge requires no such infallibility, however, grounds of belief can be undermined by further information, information that defeats the power of the original information to put one in a position to know that the claim in question is true. Even if some combinations of conditions for knowledge are sufficient for truth, if there is a nonpsychological condition for knowledge that is not sufficient for truth, that condition will need to appeal to some concept of defeat (or a surrogate of it).

I mention here the notion of a surrogate for the concept of defeat only to ignore it in what follows, for the following reason. Reliabilists, such as Alvin Goldman, recognize that a belief can be produced by a reliable mechanism, without putting one in a position to know.[1] For example, one may form a perceptual belief in circumstances that one has good reason to believe are deceptive. This further information defeats the confirming power of the perceptual experience. Since reliabilists wish to construe talk of reasons and confirmation in terms of reliable processes and methods, they cannot be satisfied simply to note that these reasons defeat the confirming power of one's perceptual experience. Instead, they must construct a surrogate for this language of defeat. Goldman, for example, talks in terms of alternative reliable processes available to the individual, which, if displayed, would not have resulted in the formation of the belief in question.[2] Such a proposal is not adequate as it stands, and those familiar with the sorry credibility of counterfactual proposals in the history of philosophy can anticipate what the problems will be.[3] For example, suppose there is a competent cognizer who disagrees with you about something you know to be true (and heaven help the epistemological theory that claims this can't happen). There is a reliable process that if you had used it, would have resulted in a different belief: namely, ask this cognizer and believe what is reported.

It is not important to claim that such examples show decisively that no surrogate for the concept of defeat can be successful. What is important is to note that the concept of defeat is necessary in any fallibilistic epistemology, and if a theory prefers to avoid talk of the disconfirming power of defeaters by introducing a surrogate for this notion, their theory will be subject to the constraint that the ways in which defeat can occur have to be explained by the surrogate in question. Explaining defeat is inescapable, even if explained only indirectly via some surrogate of it. In what follows, then, I will speak freely about defeat, leaving it to those who need to find a surrogate for this concept asea amid the demands of their own theory. If they can find such a surrogate, nothing in what follows will be affected by the substitution of the surrogate for my language of defeat; if they cannot find such a surrogate, so much the worse for their theory.

Here, I want to explore two fundamentally different approaches to the concept of defeat, and argue that only one of them has any hope of success. One theory begins with propositional relationships, only by implication describing what happens in the context of a noetic system. Such a theory places information about defeat up front, not informing us of how the defeat relationships play out in the context of actual belief, at least not initially. The other theory takes a back door to the concept of defeat, assuming a context of actual belief and an entire noetic system, and describing defeat in terms of what sort of doxastic and noetic responses would be appropriate to the addition of particular pieces of information. Where the house is the noetic structure itself, the front-door approach characterizes the concept of defeat in terms of the propositional contents a belief might have, thus characterizing defeat at the front door. It presumes that once let into the house, some changes will be required, but the characterization of defeat is logically prior to any account of such changes. The backdoor approach characterizes defeat in terms of what leaves the house, in terms of beliefs that exit the noetic system in response to intrusions into the system, in terms of what the staff of a well-run household kicks out the back door for making a mess of things. The best-developed example of a backdoor theory is Alvin Plantinga's, and here I will argue that his theory and approaches like it will be unable to explicate accurately the concept of epistemic defeat. I will argue that a front-door approach is needed, rather than a backdoor approach.

I will also argue that the differences between these two approaches mirror fundamental differences in approaches to the theory of justification or warrant. The approaches I have in mind I have characterized elsewhere as the difference between propositional and doxastic, or Aristotelian,

approaches in epistemology.[4] The doxasticist wishes to characterize justification in terms of appropriate doxastic responses to input, without having to
characterize some intrinsic justificatory relationship between the contents
of input and output. The doxasticist can describe the machine of justification solely in terms of the quality of the box that takes input and generates
doxastic output: Perhaps the box is a reliable one, or a properly functioning
one, or one that displays the right sorts of intellectual virtues or excel-
lences. The propositionalist, however, tells a different story. According to
the propositionalist, there are confirmation relationships between contents,
independent of whether or not those contents are believed.

The recent history of epistemology can be seen as a conflict between
these two fundamentally different approaches to epistemology. Reliabilism,
proper functionalism, and virtue epistemologies can be seen as a reaction
to the immense difficulty of finding necessary, and perhaps a priori, principles of evidence on which to construct a theory of justification. Their
opponents react negatively to the idea that the operations of cognition can
generate justification without involving the notions of rational intelligibility
and insight that we should expect from the application of suitable principles
of evidence. Traditional approaches to epistemology such as foundationalism and coherentism are typically propositionalist in character, and more
recent accounts such as reliabilism and proper functionalism are doxasticist
in character.

Each approach has an explanatory burden, since justification is correctly
attributable both to beliefs and propositions that are not believed. Propositionalism takes the propositional notion of justification or warrant to be the
basic notion, and understands the doxastic notion in terms of propositional
appraisal plus proper basing. Doxasticism attempts the reverse, trying to
understand propositional appraisal in terms of what would be doxastically
justified were it believed.

As already noted, given the truth of fallibilism, an account of justification
will have to include an account of the nature of epistemic defeat, since that
which makes for justification in one circumstance might be undermined in
another circumstance. In the process of characterizing the concept of defeat,
either theoretical perspective might sell its soul to find a good theory. That
is, an explicit doxasticist might characterize defeat in propositionalist terms,
and a propositionalist might adopt a doxasticist account; in the language
of the aforementioned metaphor, a doxasticist might resort to a front-door
theory and a propositionalist to a backdoor theory. This point in itself is
no objection to such a mixed theory, but it is an objection to a theory that
pretends to purity, whether doxasticist or propositionalist purity. Moreover,

such a mixed theory faces an additional explanatory burden. If, for example, a theorist explicitly adopts a doxasticist approach on the basis of expressed dissatisfaction with the usual versions of propositionalism, such a theorist will need to explain why, after returning to feed at the propositionalist table when trying to understand the concept of defeat, there is some special reason not to always and everywhere dine at the propositionalist table when constructing an epistemological theory. It is worth noting, in this context, that the usual versions of doxasticism express skepticism about the existence of the confirmation relationships between propositions needed to sustain the propositionalist program, and so if doxasticists end up having to appeal to these very same relationships to clarify the concept of defeat, they have undermined their reason for looking elsewhere for a good epistemology in the first place.[5]

It is not surprising, then, that paradigm doxasticists offer backdoor approaches to the concept of defeat, since they need to do so in order to preserve their doxasticism. I will argue here that such purity cannot be maintained, that a proper theory of the concept of defeat needs to be a front-door theory, and thus that the only pure approach available is a propositional one. As a result, doxasticists will be in the position of needing to explain their aversion to propositionalism without undercutting their appeal to that view when it comes time to explain the concept of epistemic defeat.

PLANTINGA'S BACKDOOR THEORY

As I pointed out earlier, the best-developed doxaticist account is Plantinga's, and so I will begin with the details of his account and some emendations of it. Plantinga's official account is the following:

D is a purely epistemic defeater of B for S at *t* iff

1. S's noetic structure N at *t* includes B and S comes to believe D at *t*,
2. any person S*

   a. whose cognitive faculties are functioning properly in the relevant respects,
   b. who is such that the bit of the design plan governing the sustaining of B in his or her noetic structure is successfully aimed at truth . . . and nothing more,
   c. whose noetic structure is N and includes B, and
   d. who comes to believe D but nothing else independent of or stronger than D, would withhold B (or believe it less strongly).[6]

This official account, however, does not represent Plantinga's full thinking on the matter, for he says:

> Still, argument is one way to give me a defeater. Is there another way? Yes;
> you can put me in a position where I have *experiences* such that, given those
> experiences (and given my noetic structure), the rational thing to do is to
> give up the purported defeatee.[7]

This quotation calls for a revision of the official account, since we
shouldn't want to require that the person form a reflective belief to the
effect that one is having experience D in order for that experience to function as a defeater. Clause d requires such a reflective belief, however, and
so some change is necessary. The required change is obvious, though. Just
change the beginning of d to read "one who comes to experience D or
believe D . . ." and change clause 1 in a similar fashion.

Notice the backdoor character of this account. The account characterizes a defeater in terms of epistemically appropriate responses to the
presence of a defeater in a noetic system: We insert the defeater into the
noetic house, and see which belief gets expelled out the back door.

THE PROBLEM OF DEFEATER DEFEATERS

Because of this backdoor approach, this account has some difficulty with
Plantinga's acknowledgment that defeaters can themselves be defeated
(he calls them "defeater defeaters," and some defeaters are supposed to
be immune from any sort of defeater defeater, called Humean defeaters,
in Plantinga's argument against evolutionary naturalism).[8] No adequate
account of defeat can ignore this issue, since the possibility of such follows
straightforwardly from an appropriate understanding of the fallible character of reasons for belief: Defeaters are no more infallible reasons to abandon
belief than is evidence an infallible reason to hold a belief. On the afore-
mentioned account, however, there is no talk or possibility of higher-level
defeaters at all. If something that should count as a defeater is inserted into
a noetic system containing a defeater defeater, the conclusion that follows
on this account is that the purported defeater is not in fact a defeater at all
(since no belief exits the system if the system is properly functioning). This
point leaves one wondering what to make of Plantinga's talk of defeater
defeaters.

One way to deal with this issue is to treat talk of defeater defeaters on
the model of talk of former senators and decoy ducks. A former senator is

not a senator, and a decoy duck is certainly not a duck. So maybe a defeater defeater need not defeat something that is really a defeater; it need only block some item of information from being a defeater in the first place.

Let us say, then, that when a defeater defeater is present, the original defeater is merely a potential defeater, rather than an actual one. One way to understand this concept of potential defeat is suggested by the previous discussion:

D is a potential defeater of B for S at t iff

1. S's noetic system N includes the belief B and the belief or experience D, and
2. There is some aspect DD of N which is such that, if it were not present, D would be a defeater of B for S at t.

Those familiar with the sad track record of counterfactual theories will know that this account is not going to work; those who believe that counterfactual theories hardly ever work may despair or salivate, depending on their attraction to the backdoor approach exemplified here. Whatever the attitude, however, this approach cannot succeed as it stands, since DD might be entailed by other aspects of a noetic structure, or the noetic structure might contain other compelling grounds for DD. In such cases, dropping DD won't turn D into a defeater of B, since there is other information in the system that would still block this result. We can address these concerns by replacing the above account with the following:

D is a potential defeater of B for S at t iff

1. S's noetic system N includes the belief B and the belief or experience D, and
2. There is some aspect DD of N which is such that, if it and any aspect of N giving adequate grounds for DD were not present, D would be a defeater of B for S at t.

We've now removed DD from the system, as well as anything that confirms it, in order to see if D is a defeater of B for S at t. Here's a possibility we need to be able to rule out, however. Consider the implications of this account if the grounds for DD are also part of the grounds for B itself, so that in removing these grounds, we've made the grounds for B less than adequate. In that case, this definition counts everything in N distinct from B as a potential defeater of B for S at t.

It is important to note that such a possibility cannot be ruled out. Suppose Joe believes that the leaves on a certain tree are red on the basis of being told this by Jeff and Jimmy, a pair of complementary color-blind individuals who are known by Joe to be honest and sincere with him on, but only on, color reports: They are so self-conscious about being colorblind, they overcome their deceptive natures, hoping to hide their color blindness from others by a special display of sincerity and honesty. The ground of this belief for Joe is not their testimony alone, since Joe is like us in being suspicious of color reports by color-blind people. In this case, however, they both report that the leaves are red. Joe knows that the leaves have to be brown, red, or green, and since Jeff confuses brown and red but not red and green and Jimmy confuses red and green but not red and brown, Joe comes to believe that the leaves are red.

The ground of Joe's belief is thus a complex combination of testimony and reasoning. If Joe just had the testimony of Jeff and Jimmy, he wouldn't believe them. If you add the information that it's a color report, Joe still wouldn't believe them, since they are color-blind. What grounds his trust includes his belief about their color blindness, their self-consciousness about it, and the specific details about their color blindness that confirms that the leaves are red. In order to explain how their color blindness is a potential defeater in this case, we must leave the defeater defeater out of the noetic system. That is, we must leave out the information about how their color blindness combines to show that the leaves are red. But if we take this information away, Joe wouldn't believe that what they say is true. Not only is their color blindness a potential defeater of Joe's belief, but so is everything else that Joe believes (by this account of potential defeat).

Perhaps our difficulty here is the result of trying to characterize the notion of a potential defeater in terms of being an actual defeater. Perhaps what we should try to do is to characterize the grounds or reasons why the belief in question would be absent if the actual defeater were removed. Here is a suggestion along these lines:[9]

D is a potential defeater of B for S at t iff

1. S's noetic system N includes the belief B and the belief or experience D, and
2. There is some aspect DD of N which is such that, if it and any aspect of N giving adequate grounds for DD were not present (and nothing else were added to the system, and the system in question remained a properly functioning one with the operative aspect of the design plan successfully aimed at truth), S would withhold believing B on the basis of D.

That is, what would ground, or explain, the absence of the belief in question would be the presence of D in S's noetic system. This suggestion avoids the previous case of Joe, since not everything in Joe's noetic system will explain or ground Joe's withholding of belief in the conditions in question.

The concept of withholding here is ambiguous between mere absence of belief and the mental attitude of suspension between believing B and believing ~B. Only one of these readings is helpful here, since requiring the attitude of suspension of belief is too strong. One need not take any attitude at all toward a claim one doesn't believe in order for believing that claim to be defeated for one, and so we should interpret the notion of withholding in the consequent of the second condition in terms of mere absence of belief.

If we interpret the claim in this way, if we suppose that the withholding is not itself a propositional attitude taken by the person toward the proposition in question, this account requires the truth of the claim that the ground or explanation of a nonevent involves the defeater in question.

Both concepts yield problems. First, if we are thinking about explanations, then much of the noetic system will explain the lack of a mental attitude toward B by S, and so much in the noetic system beyond D will also count as potential defeaters of B for S. Yet, not everything in a noetic system that helps explain the absence of a particular belief is a defeater of that belief – to continue the previous example of Joe, Joe's noetic system contains the information that his only sources of information about the color of the leaves is from Jeff and Jimmy, and were their testimony removed, the loss of the belief in question would be partially explained by Joe's knowledge of his sources. But this knowledge about who reported the color of the leaves is not itself a defeater or potential defeater of the belief in question.

The other option relies on the concept of a ground of failure to believe. The appeal to grounds of failure to believe appears to be subject to the same problem as the earlier appeal to explanation, but there is a way to avoid that problem. It is natural to understand an appeal to grounds in terms of reasons, so that D itself gives S a reason not to believe B. Such an approach abandons the backdoor character of Plantinga's theory, since D will constitute such a reason in virtue of confirming that the content of B is not true (or not supported by adequate evidence). By hypothesis, D is present in the noetic system but does not require a properly functioning system to abandon B, and so if we characterize the rationalizing power of D with respect to B in a negative fashion, we will have to say that D disconfirms, or counts against the truth of, B. In short, the definition faces the dilemma of either being inadequate or abandoning the doxasticist purity of a backdoor approach to the concept of defeat.

So Plantinga's language of defeater defeaters is going to cause problems for his theory of defeat. These problems are a direct result of the backdoor strategy Plantinga employs. The front-door strategy yields a straightforward solution: a defeater of the support generated for *p* by *e* is a claim *d* such that *d*&*e* does not epistemically support *p*; and a defeater of *d* is a further proposition *dd* where the combination *dd*&*d*&*e* does epistemically support *p*.[10] So one cost of the backdoor strategy is that it threatens to undermine Plantinga's reliance on the language of defeater defeaters.

THE QUINE/DUHEM ISSUE

The problem that provided the focus of the last section is a foreshadowing of the problems faced by Plantinga's definition of defeat itself. In general terms, the problem is one that has been highlighted by Quine and Duhem regarding confirmation and disconfirmation for scientific theories and hypothesis. Their point is that when we test a hypothesis and get results in conflict with the hypothesis, the existence of auxiliary hypotheses involved in the testing prevents the test from forcing the conclusion that the tested hypothesis is false. Instead, there is a variety of rational responses to an anomalous experimental result. As a consequence, one may expect properly functioning noetic structures to display no single response to the introduction of a defeater. Instead, there can be a variety of changes displayed by systems that are both reliable and properly functioning.

In this way, introducing a defeater into a noetic system is the epistemic equivalent of a *reductio* argument. The reductio itself doesn't tell you which assumption is at fault, and so information beyond the reductio itself is needed to determine what assumption to reject. Just so with defeaters. The defeater doesn't tell you how to fix the cognitive dissonance it introduces; it only tells you that something needs to be fixed. Any epistemological theory suitably sensitive to the difference between a permissible change to a noetic structure in light of further learning and an obligatory change will have to allow that when faced with a defeater, there will be cases in which there is more than one permissible option open for addressing the defeater.

It is tempting to say here that what is defeated is not a particular claim but a conjunction of all the claims that together conflict with the defeater. This temptation should be avoided, for two reasons. The first reason is that it forces our understanding of defeat to be modeled too strongly by the deductive analogue of reductios. It is true that the only thing that follows logically from a reductio is that a conjunction of claims is false, but we shouldn't conclude from this fact that a defeater is only evidence against an entire collection of things with which it is incompatible. This point leads to a second one. In the case of a reductio, paralysis ensues at the end of the proof, if one's hope was to discharge one of the assumptions. The only conclusion that follows logically from a reductio is that the conjunction of all the assumptions is false. If we extend this analogy into the epistemic domain, a similar paralysis will ensue. We will tell cognizers that the only change they are entitled to make when confronted with a defeater is to abandon a conjunction representing all the different assumptions that might be abandoned in order to remedy the cognitive difficulty faced. This description, though, borders on incoherence: If there are multiple possible ways of accommodating a defeater, the notion of possibility here, one would think, would be normative, implying that each of the ways is permissible. The view in question, however, denies that any of them are permissible; only the disjunction of all possible accommodations is allowed as a response to a defeater.

Can we solve the Quine/Duhem problem by changing the last clause of the definition from a "would" counterfactual to a "might" counterfactual? That is, instead of saying that any person in similar circumstances *would* abandon the belief, can we say that any person in similar circumstances *might* abandon the belief?[11]

This change makes the account too weak, however, for on it, too many elements of the system of beliefs will count as defeaters. If we take the Quine/Duhem issue seriously, rational responses by properly functioning systems can vary quite considerably, but we don't want to disqualify your belief from counting as knowledge merely because someone might give up that belief in the process of making quite dramatic changes to his or her noetic structure in response to a given experience.

The proper response is not, then, to move to a weaker last clause in light of the Quine/Duhem point, but rather look at the problem more carefully to see how to qualify the present account. To see how to do so, let's return to the scientific example that motivates the Quine/Duhem point. In that example, a contrary experiment prompts the need for making some changes regarding one's commitment to the combination of the hypothesis being tested together with the auxiliary hypotheses that play a role in the setup of the experiment. In response to the experiment, there are a number of rational responses that can be taken. The revealing question, however, is this: When we consider two different scientists who embody different rational responses to the experiment, what explains the difference in their responses? If we can answer this question, we are on the way to finding an adequate way to qualify Plantinga's account, since we can include this explanatory difference when describing how a properly functioning system of that sort would respond to the presence of a defeater. The point of the Quine/Duhem thesis is that the difference need not always appeal to background assumptions, beliefs, experiences, and so on, of the two scientists. The differences would have to be able to be explained in other terms, at least in some cases.

If the difference can be explained, we should be able to refine Plantinga's approach to accommodate it. My concern here is not the precise nature of the explanation, but it is clear that the explanation will have something to do with the overall intellectual character of the different scientists. Some are disposed to seek originality more than others, some tolerate greater risk of error in their pursuit of the holy grail of truth, and others value precision and meticulous detail over grand visions. In each such case, differences in overall intellectual character are compatible with identical noetic structures prior to the anomalous experimental result, and so we can accommodate the Quine/Duhem point by supplementing the account under consideration with a further condition requiring sameness of overall intellectual character.

There is a further restriction that is needed as well, and it will be more efficient to incorporate the changes together. Notice that the time frame for the second clause can't be synchronic through all the clauses: clause d, where B is abandoned, must be later than the other clauses, since those clauses include the presence of B. Consider, then, a "road to Damascus" experience, an experience to which a response will occur, but where the response will not in any way be explicable in terms of rational strictures on belief change. In such a situation, nearly any change whatsoever might occur in a system that, up to the moment of change, was properly functioning. In such situations, however, the change to the system is explained other than in terms of the proper functioning of the system with respect to a design plan aimed at truth. Because of this difference, we can accommodate this problem by including the restriction that the response itself is a display of a properly functioning system involving a part of the design plan aimed at truth. Putting these two changes together gives us the following revision of the official account:

D is a purely epistemic defeater of B for S at t iff

1. S's total intellectual character C and noetic structure N at t includes B and S comes to believe or experience D at t,
2. Any person S*

   a. whose cognitive faculties are functioning properly in the relevant respects,
   b. who is such that the bit of the design plan governing the sustaining of B in his or her noetic structure is successfully aimed at truth... and nothing more,
   c. whose intellectual character is C and noetic structure is N, including B, and
   d. who comes to believe or experience D but nothing else independent of or stronger than D and whose response to D is a display of a part of the design plan successfully aimed at truth of a properly functioning cognitive system, would withhold B (or believe it less strongly).

DEEPER PROBLEMS AND LEARNING ONE'S LESSONS

The previous account is a proper response to the Quine/Duhem point about the openness of possible rational responses to anomalous experiential results. The developments that led to this formulation, however, include a number of possibilities relevant to our assessment of the backdoor strategy, but not pursued in the last section. We saw that defeat needs to be compatible with a certain optionality of response; that sometimes a response is simply nonrational rather than rational or irrational; and that this latter possibility of things being in good rational order prior to a response raises the question of what to say when things are not in good rational order prior to a response. As we have seen, it is essential to the backdoor approach to imagine the prospective defeater as being "in the house," to see what emerges from the back door. The problem just noted is analogous to noting that houses come in various stages of disrepair, just as noetic systems do. Sometimes the very belief regarding which a prospective defeater is being evaluated is part of what's in disrepair. Less metaphorically, one can acquire a defeater for a belief that is already unwarranted, already a display of improper function or of a part of the design plan not aimed at truth.

Just as convicted felons can be guilty of further crimes, so can an unwarranted belief be guilty of further epistemic improprieties. In such cases, clause 2 of the previous account will be vacuously true, since it is not possible to be characterized by the noetic system in question and also have the belief be the product of a properly functioning system whose design plan is aimed at truth. Furthermore, no account of defeat is complete without an account of this phenomenon; no account of defeat is complete when it limits the concept of defeat so that it is applicable only to systems of belief in good repair.

This problem is not one that calls for a bit more Chisholming away at a better definition of defeat. We can't consider the responses of systems in such disrepair, for the same reason that we don't follow the advice of the insane. The only option is to allow the noetic system of the properly functioning individuals in clause 2 to be different from the noetic system of the individual in question. This path is a dead end, however. There are too many possible remodeling designs for a house in disrepair to be able to determine what aspects of the house will, or would, be preserved. All we could hope for is some idea of what might remain, and we've already seen why such a weak modality isn't adequate. So even though our exploration of the Quine/Duhem issue found a path to a suitable response by backdoor theorists to the particular difficulties raised there, that issue points us to a deeper problem for the backdoor theory. That deeper problem is one that full reflection reveals to be insoluble.

There is a better approach to characterizing the nature of defeat. Instead of putting prospective defeaters in the house and seeing what comes out the back door, a better approach is to identify defeaters before they enter the front door. Instead of beginning with noetic structures and beliefs within them, we can begin instead with propositions and what is evidence for them. In a word, the better approach is a propositional rather than a doxastic theory of defeat. On such an approach, the fundamental notion will be the notion of evidence, and the fundamental form of defeat is where the conjunction of e and the defeater is not evidence for p.[12]

Such an approach handles the major problems we've seen here for Plantinga's theory. First, it allows a straightforward account of defeater defeaters. Where dd is a defeater defeater of d, the conjunction of any evidence e conjoined to d does not justify p, but the conjunction of e plus d plus dd yields at least as much justification for p as provided by e itself. Moreover, the Quine/Duhem problem ceases to worry as well, for even if d is a defeater of the $p|e$ relation (where e is the evidence for p), it need not be a defeater of the $p\&r|e$ relation. That allows rational adjustments to a system of beliefs in response to learning d that don't require abandoning p. All learning d requires (on the assumption that there are no restorers present) is that some evidentially suitable adjustment is made, one of which is abandoning p, but not the only one. This way of proceeding is very much like that of John Pollock's,[13] though there are two important differences. First, he doesn't mention the Quine/Duhem issue and doesn't give a way to accommodate it. Second, his theory takes the relations of evidence and defeat to be relations between mental states, rather than relations between the contents of mental states.[14] It is worth noting on the latter point, however, that he cannot sustain consistency on this point. It turns out that to represent the concept of provisional defeat in his system, he has to represent provisionally defeated conclusions in the system that can play a role in future changes of belief, even though they are not believed; as Pollock and his coauthor Anthony Gillies say, "Thus more than beliefs (undefeated conclusions) must be included in a representation of an agent's epistemological state."[15] As a result of the need to represent provisionally defeated conclusions, a representation of a person's epistemological state will require representation of contents that play a role in determining the epistemic status of other beliefs. In such a case, there may be no mental state whatsoever with that particular propositional content, and hence no way for Pollock to represent all epistemic relations as relations between mental states.

This difficulty can be avoided by adopting propositionalism. Pollock and Gillies note a problem for this view, however; they say:

> Note that this makes the *reason-for* relation a relation between mental states, not the contents of the mental states. This is important because we reason quite differently from different kinds of mental states with the same content, e.g., the percept of there being something red before me, the desire that there be something red before me, and the belief that there is something red before me.[16]

The worry here is that a thoroughgoing propositionalism will not be able to explain why a desire that p is not a reason for belief, whereas a belief or experience that p is. This objection is important but not decisive, though I do not have space here to discuss the matter thoroughly. Instead, I will only point in the direction I think an adequate reply can be found. A point to note is that we can distinguish between affective and cognitive states, and note that for the purely cognitive purposes in epistemology, the only kind of reasons that are relevant as a basis for a belief are going to be cognitive reasons. That still leaves a distinction between belief and experience, and it is a harder matter to say what the difference between these is, even though such a difference there must be (since no belief is a reason for itself and yet an experience of something red is a reason to believe that something is red). Recent work in the theory of consciousness and phenomenal content suggests a possible response, however, in terms of the self-representational character of phenomenal content.[17] On this view, intrinsic to the character of experience is an awareness that one is having the very experience in question, and if that is correct, allowing an experience as if p to confirm a belief that p via the content of the awareness that is intrinsic to the experience itself. In this way, the confirming power of an experience as if p will differ from the confirming power of a belief that p without having to abandon the propositionalist view that confirmation is a matter of a relationship between possible contents of mental states, rather than the mental states themselves.

Finally, this approach allows an explanation of the defeat of an already unwarranted belief. Such beliefs fall into two categories. The first is where there is some evidence for the belief, but enough counterevidence that the belief is not warranted. In such a case, one can possess a defeater in addition to the counterevidence, a further piece of information that, together with the evidence for the belief, fails to provide a justification or warrant for it. The second case is where there is no evidence at all for the belief. A further piece of information can be a defeater for such an unwarranted belief in several different ways. The primary way would be for the defeater to be evidence against the belief, but it could also be evidence that there are no reliable methods of learning that the belief is true. In either case, the front-door approach has resources that the backdoor approach lacks.

The last possibility considered made reference to reliable methods and procedures, and it is worth noting that adopting a backdoor reliabilist approach in place of Plantinga's backdoor proper functionalist approach is not going to help with these problems. Such a reliabilist alternative will identify defeaters with reliable processes or methods whose use would have led to the abandoning of belief. Such an approach will face precisely the difficulties faced by Plantinga's proper functionalist approach: It will have to address the problem of defeater defeaters, and it will have the same difficulties with the Quine/Duhem problem.

It won't help here to talk of reliable indicators rather than reliable processes, either.[18] Such a theory works best when it is a front-door rather than a backdoor theory, as can be seen when we ask about the nature of the indicators in question. A front-door approach will take these to be a relationship between some piece of information and a proposition that may or may not be believed. The reliabilist component of the view, then, is simply a requirement that the indicator relationship be a reliable one, that is, objectively a likelihood of truth. The theory could be given a backdoor rendering as well: It could be claimed that the notion of a reliable indicator is to be clarified with reference to the proportion or percentage of true beliefs generated by a mechanism or process that takes awareness or belief in the indicator as input. Taken in this way, the reliable indicator theory has all the difficulties of the reliabilist approach cited in the last paragraph.

The lesson to learn is that if one is attracted to a reliabilist approach here, the best option is the front-door, propositionalist option. The alternative, backdoor version shares with Plantinga's account the fundamental problem of beginning with talk of B as a belief, trying the characterize defeat in terms of conditions under which a belief would be abandoned. Backdoor approaches to the concept of defeat are bound to fail, precisely because of this core.

One final point by way of comparison of the two approaches, a point especially instructive in the context of Plantinga's epistemological agenda. Some defeaters engender mental apoplexy, since they tell you that something has to be changed, but you can't tell what to change. Call these "paralyzing defeaters." Such was Russell's paradox for Frege regarding his set theory: He knew that something must be changed but had no idea what to change. Plantinga thinks that something similar plagues the evolutionary naturalist.[19] He holds that such naturalists have an undefeated defeater for their view, but in order to sustain this conclusion, Plantinga must hold as well that those who understand his argument but do not abandon their view are somehow malfunctioning.

It's easy to see how a propositionalist account of defeat could reach this conclusion: Argue that there is a propositional defeater of which evolutionary naturalists are aware, show that there couldn't be a propositional defeater defeater for this defeater; point out that the evolutionary naturalists have been shown the evidence against their view but remain unpersuaded; and conclude that they must be malfunctioning in some way. It is interesting to note that this strategy is strikingly like the one Plantinga follows. Instead of addressing the question of proper functioning directly, his discussion focuses on the issue of whether the content of his argument gives a reason not to believe evolutionary naturalism. Once we see the distinction between front-door and backdoor approaches to defeat, and the underlying distinction between propositionalism and doxasticism, we can see that Plantinga's actual practices fit well with a propositionalist approach in spite of his official doxasticist dogma. His practice shows all the signs of illicitly partaking of propositional fruit here, "illicit" given his backdoor doxasticism of his official account of defeat.

In any case, the right approach is propositional, whether or not Plantinga is implicitly relying on one. This result is more bad news for doxasticists, since now they cannot remain doxasticists and include the concept of defeat in their epistemological theory. The theory of defeat provides just one more reason to be a propositionalist and to abandon doxasticism.

Notes

1. See, for example, "What Is Justified Belief?" in George Pappas, ed., *Knowledge and Justification*, Dordrecht: Reidel, 1979, pp. 1–25.
2. "What Is Justified Belief?" p. 13.
3. The locus classicus for an account of the implausibility of counterfactual accounts in philosophy is Robert Shope's "The Conditional Fallacy in Contemporary Philosophy," *Journal of Philosophy* 75, 1979, pp. 397–413.
4. See, e.g., "Plantinga's Proper Function Theory of Warrant," *Warrant and Contemporary Epistemology*, J. L. Kvanvig, ed., Lanham, MD: Rowman & Littlefield, 1996; "The Basic Notion of Justification," Christopher Menzel, coauthor, *Philosophical Studies* 59, 1990, pp. 235–261; and "Propositionalism and the Perspectival Character of Justification," *American Philosophical Quarterly* 40(1), 2003, pp. 3–18.
5. One of the most forthright epistemologists in expressing this motivation is Ernest Sosa. See, in particular, his explanation for preferring a version of virtue epistemology to some Chisholmian collection of epistemic principles in *Virtue in Perspective*, Cambridge: Cambridge University Press, 1991.
6. Alvin Plantinga, *Warranted Christian Belief*, New York and Oxford: Oxford University Press, 2000, p. 363.
7. Ibid., p. 367.
8. See "An Evolutionary Argument Against Naturalism." *Logos* 12, 1991, pp. 27–48; and the collection of essays on the argument, *Naturalism Defeated?: Essays on Plantinga's Evolutionary Argument Against Naturalism*, James Beilby, ed., Ithaca, NY: Cornell University Press, 2002.
9. Thanks to Chad Mohler in his comments on the epistemology weblog, *Certain Doubts*, for this suggestion.
10. This account of defeaters in terms of a heirarchy of overriders is the one articulated by John Pollock in *Contemporary Theories of Knowledge*, Totowa, NJ: Rowman & Littlefield, 1986, and which, in a developed form, plays a central role in his Oscar project.
11. The interpretation of this modal notion is in terms of the denial of a stronger, opposite counterfactual: To say that A might occur were B to occur is to say that it's false that $\sim$A would occur were B to occur. More formally, using the standard notation for such conditionals, $A \diamond \rightarrow B = df. \sim (A \square \rightarrow \sim B)$. For the source of this view, and more on the logic of counterfactuals, see David Lewis, *Counterfactuals*, Oxford: Blackwell, 1973.

12. In the text, I ignore the issue of partial defeat, where a defeater lowers the credibility of a claim, but not so much as would require the loss of belief. Ignoring this issue means that what I say would require elaboration and adjustment, but such changes would lead us too far afield for present purposes.

13. See *Contemporary Theories of Knowledge*, pp. 38–39.

14. See "Belief Revision and Epistemology," coauthored with Anthony Gillies, *Synthese* 122, 2000, pp. 69–92. See, especially, p. 74, where they say, ". . . it must be borne in mind that it is really the beliefs, and not their contents, that are reasons for each other."

15. Ibid., p. 82.

16. Ibid., p. 74.

17. See Uriah Kriegel, "The Same-Order Monitoring Theory of Consciousness," in U. Kriegel and K. Williford, eds., *Self-Representational Approaches to Consciousness*, Cambridge, MA: MIT Press, forthcoming.

18. For an example of such, see John Greco's "Holding Defeat to the Fire," manuscript.

19. See "An Evolutionary Argument Against Naturalism," pp. 27–48, and the collection of essays in *Naturalism Defeated?*

6 Plantinga's Model of Warranted Christian Belief

JAMES BEILBY

INTRODUCTION

Warranted Christian Belief [1] is undoubtedly Plantinga's magnum opus, not only because of its size – 508 pages with routine interludes of fine print – but also because it constitutes the culmination of a research project in which Plantinga has been actively engaged for nearly forty years. Even those diametrically opposed to his assertions will find much with which to be impressed. For instance, Paul Moser – someone who shares Plantinga's theistic beliefs, but whose epistemological convictions differ markedly – has commented that some of Plantinga's insights on sin and its cognitive consequences "are alone worth the price of admission." [2] And Richard Gale, who shares neither Plantinga's theism nor his epistemology, praises the "depth, rigor and brilliance" of *Warranted Christian Belief* [3] (hereafter, WCB).

WCB is unique in a number of respects. While Plantinga is undoubtedly a philosopher through and through, his book is clearly not written *primarily* for specialists in philosophy. [4] While philosophers will find plenty of sophisticated philosophical arguments with which to satiate their appetite, many may be surprised at the overtly theological nature of much of this volume. Moreover, those who are unfamiliar with his thought may be taken aback by the unabashedly conservative disposition of his theology; he unapologetically accepts the inspiration of Scripture, the divine instigation of faith, the noetic effects of sin, and other theological concepts that many in academia have relegated to a bygone era. Finally, while philosophical monographs are typically something less than scintillating, his winsome, lucid writing style offers unexpected treasures of humor.

Given the breadth of Plantinga's project, one of the real challenges facing a would-be commentator is deciding what to consider and how to do so. Consequently, before attempting to evaluate the fruits of his labors, it is worthwhile to take a step back and survey his project from afar.

PLANTINGA'S APOLOGETIC PROGRAM

The perennial target of Plantinga's philosophical animadversions has been the evidentialist objection to belief in God, the idea that Christian belief is epistemically substandard because it lacks an appropriate kind and amount of evidential support. Plantinga first challenged this notion in 1967 with the publication of *God and Other Minds*[5] (hereafter, GOM). In this seminal volume, he argued that there are beliefs for which compelling evidence or arguments are lacking that we are nevertheless strongly inclined to accept as true, the paradigm example being belief in the existence of other minds. He concludes that since some of what we rationally believe, and even know, is held in the absence of propositional evidence or arguments, then the evidentialist objection to belief in God is called into question. In 1983 with the publication of "Reason and Belief in God"[6] (hereafter, RBG), Plantinga radicalized this suggestion by arguing that Christian belief could be perfectly rational in the absence of propositional evidence or supporting argumentation – belief in God could be 'properly basic'.

The profundity, distinctiveness, and iconoclastic nature of Plantinga's early religious epistemology is matched only by its unfinished state. Not long after the publication of RBG, Plantinga came to realize that his work left many important questions unanswered, the most fundamental of which was: What epistemic quality is denoted by the 'properly' in 'properly basic'? In GOM he identified this epistemic quality as rationality, and in RBG he alternates between referring to it as rationality and justification. In both works, however, he seems to construe these epistemic qualities deontologically – a rational or justified belief is a belief that can be held without flouting any epistemic duties. But what is it to be 'rational' and 'justified', and what sorts of things are 'epistemic duties'? More importantly, what is the connection between these epistemic constructs and knowledge? Plantinga's own evaluation of his early work speaks volumes:

> In *God and Other Minds*...I was trying to address [the evidentialist objection] – *trying* to address it, because I didn't then understand it very well. From my present vantage point, *God and Other Minds* looks like a promising attempt by someone a little long on chutzpah but a little short on epistemology.[7]

Plantinga's first steps toward repairing that deficiency came in 1993 with the publication of the first two volumes of his *Warrant* trilogy,[8] and the journey was completed in 2000 with the publication of WCB. In *Warrant:*

The Current Debate (hereafter, WCD), he argues that none of the major contemporary epistemologies provides a satisfactory theory of knowledge, and in *Warrant and Proper Function* (hereafter, WPF), he develops a comprehensive account of the epistemic virtue that when added to true belief yields knowledge – namely, warrant. In so doing, Plantinga parted from the long and distinguished tradition that defined knowledge either explicitly or implicitly in terms of justification. This is important because justification and warrant are not merely different sides of the same epistemic coin; they are fundamentally different epistemic properties. This difference is most clearly expressed by pointing out that justification is a property of *persons*, whereas warrant is a property of *beliefs*. In other words, for any person *S* and belief *p*, to say that a belief is justified is to say that 'person *S* is justified in holding belief *p*'. On the other hand, to say that a belief is warranted is to say that 'belief *p* is warranted for person *S*'.

For Plantinga, a warranted belief *p* for person *S* is one that meets the following four conditions:

1. *p* is produced in *S* by properly functioning cognitive faculties.

2. *p* is formed in an appropriate epistemic environment.

3. *S*'s cognitive faculties are operating according to a design plan reliably aimed at truth.

4. *S* has no defeaters for *p*.

Applying this account of warrant to knowledge requires one additional stipulation:

5. *S* holds *p* with sufficient firmness to yield a degree of warrant sufficient for knowledge.

While the epistemological spadework in WCD and WPF is tremendously valuable in its own right, for Plantinga it was a means to an end; it provided the epistemological canvas on which to paint his account of religious knowledge. But WCB is more than just a simple application of the epistemology he developed in WCD and WPF to the topic of belief in God. Before even attempting to consider the epistemic status of Christian belief, he first addresses a logically prior question: Is it even sensible to talk about 'Christian belief' in a realist, nonconstructionist fashion? He considers the work of Immanuel Kant, John Hick, and Gordon Kaufman as representative of this sort of objection and concludes that the attempt to dismiss a robust Christian epistemology on the grounds that human beings cannot refer to or predicate properties of God is not successful. Second, Plantinga considers the nature of the de jure objection to belief in God. What, exactly, is the epistemic property the evidentialist objector is claiming that belief in God lacks? After considering various permutations of classical foundationalism, deontological justification, and assorted forms of rationality, Plantinga concludes that the most sensible version of the de jure objection is found in the machinations of Freud and Marx – belief in God, according to 'the F&M complaint' (as Plantinga calls it), is epistemically invalid because it lacks warrant.[9] Third, he formulates a pair of models – the A/C and Extended A/C Models – that jointly describe how Christian belief, if true, can have warrant. Finally, he addresses the possibility that there could be defeaters for warranted Christian beliefs that would require the believer to reject them (or hold them less strongly, with insufficient strength to be counted as knowledge).

Plantinga has not one but two purposes for WCB. First, "it is an exercise in apologetics and philosophy of religion, an attempt to demonstrate the failure of a range of objections to Christian belief."[10] He claims that beliefs about the Christian God, if true, can possess epistemic warrant sufficient for knowledge, and consequently, de jure objections – objections to the epistemic acceptability of Christian belief – depend for their success on de facto objections, objections to the truth of Christianity.[11] This is because

> what you properly take to be rational, at least in the sense of warranted, depends on what sort of metaphysical or religious stance you adopt. It depends on what kind of beings you think humans are, what sorts of beliefs you think their noetic faculties will produce when they are functioning properly, and which of their faculties or cognitive mechanisms are aimed at the truth. Your view as to what sort of creature a human being is will determine or at any rate heavily influence your views as to whether theistic belief is warranted . . . for human beings.[12]

If successful, this aspect of Plantinga's argument would invalidate many atheistic arguments, and the skeptic would have to shoulder the formidable task of demonstrating the falsity of Christian belief.

Plantinga's audience with regard to this first purpose, therefore, is readers in general, Christians and non-Christians alike.[13] But his second purpose is less obvious, and so will be more readily misunderstood. In addition to apologetics, in WCB Plantinga engages in what he calls 'Christian philosophy' – the project of considering and answering the sorts of questions philosophers ask and answer from a Christian point of view.[14] His attempt to articulate "a plausible account of the way in which Christian belief is, in fact, justified, rational, and warranted" is aimed not at a general audience but specifically at Christians.[15] In other words, in developing his 'models' of warranted Christian belief, he is attempting to answer the question: 'How should Christians think about their beliefs *from their perspective?*' It is not an answer to the question: 'How should Christian belief be thought of from the standpoint of a neutral observer?' (as if there was such a thing), and it is certainly not the attempt to think through these issues from the perspective of the skeptic or the naturalist.

In order to focus attention on his *religious* epistemology, I will grant Plantinga his underlying epistemology.[16] After summarizing the essential features of Plantinga's project, I will offer a critique – albeit a sympathetic critique – of his approach to religious epistemology and his understanding of the formation of the cognitive aspect of faith. While the conceptual fecundity of his religious epistemology provides many avenues for discussion, given that the design plan of this essay is to discuss the essential features of Plantinga's work, I am warranted in considering only those topics that are directly relevant to the proper function of his account of religious knowledge.

PLANTINGA'S RELIGIOUS EPISTEMOLOGY

1. Faith and Warranted Beliefs about God

Plantinga's religious epistemology is expressed in terms of two models: The A/C Model, which provides a general description of how Christian beliefs might be warranted, and the Extended A/C Model, which applies specifically to our postlapsarian epistemic environment. While the A/C Model draws on a shared insight of Thomas Aquinas and John Calvin, much of the flavor of the model is Reformed, reflecting dependence on Calvin, Jonathan Edwards, and Abraham Kuyper. Crucial to the A/C Model is a description of the innate tendency for humans to see the hand of God in creation, a tendency that Calvin called the *sensus divinitatis*. This innate tendency is occasioned by a wide variety of circumstances. I may see God's majesty while observing the night sky, while you receive a sense of God's presence while listening to a Mozart symphony.[17]

The defining characteristic of Plantinga's religious epistemology – a feature that is decidedly more Calvinistic than Thomistic – is his insistence that the deliverances of the *sensus divinitatis* are not inferential beliefs. One does not see a beautiful sunset and *infer* from that beauty that 'only God could have created all of this'. Rather, the belief arises immediately and spontaneously.[18] As such, there is epistemic parity between the deliverances of the *sensus divinitatis* and perceptual beliefs. Both can be 'properly basic' – fully appropriate from an epistemic point of view. In fact, they can be properly basic with respect to warrant; that is, despite not being based on arguments or evidence, they can meet the conditions necessary for warrant.[19]

The notion that there is epistemic parity between Christian beliefs and the mundane beliefs of perception and memory is one of the defining characteristics of Plantinga's religious epistemology, originating in GOM. It is also commonly misunderstood. When Plantinga claims that there is epistemic parity between belief in God and, say, memory beliefs, he is not claiming that belief in God is *phenomenologically* identical to perceptual or memorial beliefs. Perceptual and memorial beliefs are accompanied by a "detailed phenomenological basis" and "rich and highly articulated sensuous imagery."[20] Moreover, there are the obvious differences in the universality of these experiences. Most everybody forms perceptual and memorial beliefs, but the same is not the case with regard to belief in God. However, while belief in God, memorial beliefs, and perceptual beliefs differ with respect to the circumstances of formation, they share at least one thing in common. From the point of the believer, they all seem exactly right, a proper result of their epistemic situation. What creates epistemic parity between beliefs about God and mundane perceptual beliefs is two features: 1) *the cause of the beliefs* – they are both formed by properly functioning cognitive faculties, and 2) *the psychological response associated with the formation of those beliefs*. In both cases the beliefs seem appropriate, right, approved.

To account for our postlapsarian context, Plantinga develops the Extended A/C Model. The Extended A/C Model acknowledges that human beings have fallen into sin and, as a result, the *sensus divinitatis* is both damaged and narrowed in the scope of its operation. In circumstances where we would have naturally formed beliefs about God, no theological beliefs are formed. Further, sin introduces in us not only a resistance but also a hostility to the deliverances of the *sensus divinitatis*; we not only are unable to see what we ought to see, we do not desire to see those things.[21]

As a response to sin, the Extended A/C Model includes God's plan of salvation. Since humans are unable to extricate themselves from the ruinous cognitive and moral effects of sin, God provided his Son, Jesus Christ, to be born, suffer, die, and be resurrected. Through belief in the person and work of Jesus Christ, the believer can experience spiritual rebirth and regeneration, "a process (beginning in this life and reaching fruition in the next)."[22] Most importantly for our current topic, the Extended A/C Model includes an explicitly cognitive element – a three-tiered process whereby humans become aware of the plan of salvation God has graciously made available. God's revelation of his plan of salvation typically proceeds first through Scripture, humanly authored but divinely inspired.[23] The second tier is the presence and action of the Holy Spirit, something promised by Jesus Christ. Through the "internal instigation of the Holy Spirit" we come to see that the Bible is true and contains divine "testimony."[24] Finally, the principal work of the Holy Spirit is the production of the third element of the process, faith. Faith is a divine gift and includes both cognitive and affective dimensions. In the words of John Calvin, faith is "a firm and certain knowledge of God's benevolence towards us, founded upon the truth of the freely given promise in Christ, both revealed to our minds and sealed upon our hearts through the Holy Spirit."[25] While the cognitive content of faith is what Jonathan Edwards called *the great things of the gospel* – "the central teachings of the gospel; it is contained in the intersection of the great Christian creeds"[26] – to have faith is not only to know God; it is also to have a proper affectional disposition toward God. Consequently, through the work of the Holy Spirit, the person with faith not only knows about God ('belief that' God exists); he or she also comes to trust, love, and serve God ('belief in' God).

There is an important difference between the *sensus divinitatis* and the internal instigation of the Holy Spirit. Where the *sensus divinitatis* is a part of humanity's original cognitive equipment, the internal instigation of the Holy Spirit, whereby we come to realize the central truths of the gospel, is a special gift given by God that comes with salvation and is part of the process designed to produce faith. Hence, the internal instigation of the Holy Spirit is not a cognitive faculty in the same way that perception, memory, or even the *sensus divinitatis* are; it is a cognitive process or "a means by which belief, and belief on a certain set of topics, is regularly produced in regular ways."[27] Consequently, according to Plantinga, the immediate cause of the beliefs associated with faith are "not to be found just in [the believer's] natural epistemic equipment."[28]

Just as with regard to the *sensus divinitatis*, Plantinga claims that the deliverances of the internal instigation of the Holy Spirit can be fully rational and justified for the believer – he or she will be flouting no epistemic duties with regard to acquiring and maintaining beliefs. In fact, given the work of the Holy Spirit, Plantinga asserts that "it would be dysfunctional *not* to form [those beliefs]."[29] Further, he claims that the deliverances of the internal instigation of the Holy Spirit can "satisfy the conditions that are jointly sufficient and severally necessary for warrant."[30] First, the belief will be produced by a properly functioning cognitive process. This cognitive process is specially designed by God to produce this very effect, just as vision is designed to produce certain kinds of perceptual beliefs.[31] Second, Plantinga's environmental condition is met. Since the Extended A/C Model was designed for a postlapsarian context, the "maxi-environment" in which the beliefs are produced is appropriate. Further, the typical context in which the individual forms beliefs, the "mini-environment" "is also favorable."[32] Finally, this cognitive process is designed to produce true beliefs, and does so reliably – it is *successfully* aimed at the production of true beliefs.

Crucial to understanding Plantinga's project is an understanding of the function of a 'model' in this context. According to Plantinga, a 'model' is a set of propositions (or a state of affairs) that jointly describe how beliefs about God *could be* warranted.[33] His claim is that the Extended A/C Model is *epistemically possible*. Epistemic possibility is stronger than strict logical possibility or broadly logical possibility. An epistemically possible proposition, according to Plantinga, is "consistent with what we know, where 'what we know' is what all or most of the participants in the discussion can agree on."[34] For example, while the propositions *My computer has a mass greater than the solar system* and *China has a population of four* are broadly logically possible, they are not epistemically possible.

Consequently, since the Extended A/C Model explains how belief in God could have warrant, if the state of affairs described by the model obtains or is actual, then belief in God does in fact possess warrant.[35] Plantinga's claims regarding the Extended A/C Model can therefore be summarized in the following conditional: *If the Extended A/C Model is true, then beliefs formed as described by the model are warranted.* Given this conditional claim, the truth of the antecedent – whether the Extended A/C Model is actually true – is obviously of crucial importance. Plantinga closes the book by addressing this question:

> But is [the Extended A/C Model] true? This is the really important question. And here we pass beyond the competence of philosophy, whose main competence, in this area, is to clear away certain objections, impedances, and obstacles to Christian belief. Speaking for myself, and of course not in the name of philosophy, I can say only that [the Extended A/C Model] does, indeed, seem to me to be true, and to be the maximally important truth.[36]

So while he believes the Extended A/C Model to be true (or versimilitudinous, close to the truth) he *does not* argue that it is true.[37] He says: "The only way I can see to argue that Christian belief [is warranted] is to argue that Christian belief is, indeed, *true*. I don't propose to offer such an argument. That is because I don't know of an argument for Christian belief that seems very likely to convince one who doesn't already accept its conclusion."[38]

Plantinga's rejection of the task of arguing for the truth of Christian theism is one of the most distinctive aspects of his methodology. It is also the aspect that has received the most criticism. Unfortunately, space restrictions and the existence of another chapter in this book dedicated to Plantinga's objection to natural theology prevent me from going into much detail on this subject here.

2. Plantinga and the Reformed Objection to Natural Theology

Taken generally, natural theology refers to what can be justifiably believed or known about God apart from the guidance of Scripture or mystical revelation; it relies solely on human reasoning capacities. The project of natural theology has been most commonly identified with the task of providing arguments for God's existence that appeal to evidence that is in principle public. Most who have considered the question of the epistemic status of religious belief have accepted that something like natural theology is required to give warrant to religious beliefs. Skeptics and natural theologians unite in accepting this requirement but differ with respect to the success of theistic arguments. Fideists reject both the requirement and the notion of religious knowledge. Some, however, maintain the value and possibility of religious knowledge despite rejecting the necessity of natural theology.

Many in the Reformed theological tradition fall into this final category. While Reformed scholars often mention philosophical objections, most object to natural theology for a variety of theological reasons. One of the most common of these is the noetic effects of sin – the notion that sin mars not only the function of the human will and emotions but also the intellect. A second common Reformed objection to natural theology is that it is presumptive; it involves humans trying to come to knowledge of God on their own terms, rather than submitting to God's means of making his nature and plans known: Scripture. A third Reformed objection to natural theology emphasizes the irrelevance of logical arguments to faith – a robust, dynamic, sincere faith does not require philosophical argumentation. Some push this line of thinking even futher; natural theology is not only irrelevant to faith, it is injurious to it. The speculative, theoretical dimension emphasized by natural theology actually undercuts a vital, experiential relationship with God, and the arguments of natural theology, if they suggest the existence of a god of any sort, point not to the Christian God but to a vague, semideistic 'God of the philosophers' who is relationally remote and unaffected by genuine religious concerns.[39]

Plantinga's objection to natural theology clearly includes philosophical considerations. As he sees it, an argument that makes Christian belief probable with respect to public evidence, even if it makes it highly probable, is insufficient for its being warrantedly believed with the requisite degree of firmness. He says that "the most such an argument can accomplish is to show that Christian belief isn't particularly improbable."[40] The best such arguments, by Plantinga's lights, are those of Richard Swinburne, but his arguments do not have as their goal (what Plantinga deems to be) full-fledged, warranted Christian belief, but only to be "sufficient to make sensible a commitment to achieving a certain goal."[41]

In fact, Plantinga believes that natural theology is insufficient for full-fledged Christian belief being warrantedly believed with *any* degree of firmness.[42] Suppose a theistic argument was produced that made the probability of Christian belief with respect to the public evidence as high as 0.9. Plantinga claims that this argument would place the believer in a situation analogous to hearing the weatherman announce that the probability of rain this afternoon is 0.9. He says, in such a case, "if I am thinking straight, I won't believe that it will rain this afternoon; I will *believe* only that it is very *likely* that it will. And if I do rashly believe that it will rain, this belief will have little by way of warrant. Even if, as it turns out, it does rain, I didn't know that it would."[43]

Consequently, Plantinga contends: "If it's to be the case that at least some people actually *know* some of the claims of Christianity, or even are rational in actually *believing* them, there will have to be a separate source of warrant for such belief, something like, following Calvin and Aquinas, the internal testimony (Calvin) or instigation (Aquinas) of the Holy Spirit."[44] Therefore, by Plantinga's lights, "if Christian beliefs are true, then the standard and most satisfactory way to hold them will not be as the conclusions of an argument."[45]

But Plantinga's dim appraisal of the efficacy of natural theology extends beyond his philosophical objections. Like many of his Reformed compatriots, Plantinga finds the project of natural theology wanting for a variety of theological or religious reasons, including the noetic effects of sin. He says: "We human beings, apart from God's special and gracious activity, are sunk in sin; we are prone to hate God and our neighbor."[46] Consequently, "given our fallen nature and our natural antipathy to the message of the gospel, faith will have to be a gift... one that wouldn't come to us in the ordinary run of things, one that requires supernatural and extraordinary activity on the part of God."[47] The basic idea is clear: Even if there was sufficient evidence to produce religious knowledge in humans in the absence of sin, the presence of sin makes that evidence moot.

As much as Plantinga emphasizes the noetic effects of sin, the irrelevance of natural theology objection seems to be equally important in his fustigations against natural theology. According to Plantinga, natural theology is irrelevant with respect to the production of faith and warranted beliefs about God because natural theology addresses only a part of what is involved in robust Christian belief – the cognitive, intellectual dimension – but ignores completely the affective aspect of faith. In addition to having the truths of Christianity "revealed to our minds," we must have them "sealed on our hearts"; what is required is not just a change of doxastic attitudes vis-à-vis God but a change of affection.[48]

Plantinga does not, however, follow many of his Reformed compatriots in holding that natural theology is not only irrelevant but injurious. He repeatedly acknowledges that there are other acceptable models of Christian belief, many of which acknowledge a larger role for theistic argumentation.[49] In fact, he points to Stephen Wykstra[50] and Michael Sudduth[51] as philosophers who have developed models of this very sort. (Of course, he thinks his model is closest to the sober truth.) But there is a different sense in which Plantinga *does* deem natural theology to be injurious. Specifically, he holds it to be profoundly deleterious to accept that natural theology (or something like it) is *necessary* for faith and knowledge of God. In such a case, he says: "only a few people would acquire the knowledge in question, and only after a great deal of effort and much time; furthermore, their belief would be both uncertain and shot though with falsehood."[52] Moreover, according to Plantinga, acceptance of the necessity of natural theology would encourage a dangerous overemphasis on the cognitive aspects of faith to the detriment of the experiential and affective dimensions.

So Plantinga believes that natural theology is neither necessary nor sufficient to ground the cognitive aspects of faith, the 'firm and certain knowledge' of which Calvin speaks. Warranted Christian beliefs, if they are to be had, must therefore come as a gift from the Holy Spirit. Plantinga's reticence to base belief in God on argumentative or evidential grounds has led Michael Martin and others to charge him with fideism.[53] I'm not convinced, however, that the charge is valid. While he argues that faith should not be *based on* arguments, he acknowledges that faith can be *affected by* arguments. Atheological arguments can negatively affect the epistemic status of Christian belief, and theistic arguments can increase the warrant of a Christian's beliefs.[54] In fact, Plantinga acknowledges that logical arguments *can be* sufficient to eliminate the warrant a believer has for aspects of the faith. The Christian, he says, "is not to hold [Christian] beliefs in such a way as to be invulnerable to criticism.... If I find good reason to modify my understanding of the Christian faith, then (so far forth) I should do so. 'Good reason' could come from many sources: logic, obvious ethical principles, common sense beliefs of various kinds, science and the like."[55] Understanding this matter requires a closer look at the relationship between defeaters and warranted Christian beliefs.

3. The Extended A/C Model and Defeaters

Many of the misconceptions of Plantinga's religious epistemology stem from a failure to understand his specific goals and claims. Plantinga's claim is that his model is epistemically possible. He does not claim that all beliefs about God are formed exactly as described by the Extended A/C Model, nor does he claim that beliefs about God are warranted only if they are so formed. In fact, he readily affirms that there are "a whole range of models for the warrant of Christian belief, all different but similar to [the A/C and Extended A/C Model]."[56] Consequently, for any given belief *p* about the Christian God, there are a range of possibilities:

1. *p is* formed as specified by the Extended A/C Model and *is* warranted.

2. *p is not* formed as specified by the Extended A/C Model and *is* warranted.

3. *p is not* formed as specified by the Extended A/C Model and *is not* warranted.

4. *p is* formed as specified by the Extended A/C Model and *is not* warranted.

The first of these options represents Plantinga's paradigm of Christian belief; the second is an example of an alternate model of warranted Christian belief; the third occurs when the cognitive faculties producing the relevant belief either fail to function properly (as in the case of hallucinations) or are not aimed at truth (as in the case of Freudian wish fulfillment); and the fourth represents initially warranted Christian beliefs that get defeated either fully or partially by an atheological argument or an experience deemed by the person in question to be incompatible with the belief in God.

The last of these options raises the host of interesting issues that surround the matter of defeaters. Plantinga claims that the recipient of the internal instigation of the Holy Spirit need not be ignorant of the objections to Christian belief. He says: "I shall argue further that Christian belief can be justified, rational, and warranted not just for ignorant fundamentalists or benighted medievals but for informed and educated twenty-first century Christians who are entirely aware of all the artillery that has been rolled up against Christian belief since the Enlightenment."[57] Objections like projective theories of religious belief, the findings of historical biblical criticism, and the fact of religious diversity and the problem of evil can be defeated in two ways: either by a counterargument (an extrinsic defeater-defeater) or by the fact that the warrant for the relevant Christian beliefs exceeds the warrant for the defeater (an intrinsic defeater-defeater). Consequently, epistemic defeat is relative to the content of a person's noetic structure.[58] You and I might have identical beliefs, but mine might be defeated and yours not because you have significantly more warrant for your belief than I have for mine.

What determines whether and when an objection to Christian belief – the problem of evil, for example – will actually function as a defeater for Christian beliefs? For Plantinga, the answer is the design plan. When one's cognitive faculties (including the *sensus divinitatis*) are functioning as designed, because humans were designed to believe in God, beliefs about God will possess far more warrant than the premises of any atheological argument from evil. Evil and suffering may be troubling and even shocking, and the believer might be perplexed at God's permitting it, but he or she will feel no inclination toward agnosticism when confronted with cases of horrifying evil.[59] In such a case, the fact of evil and the existence of God are separate issues from an epistemological point of view.

To fully appreciate Plantinga's point, we need a distinction between *a belief* D *being a defeater for another belief* B and *circumstances being such that person* S *will reject* B. Even if the circumstances of evil are such that some Christians do in fact give up belief in God, that does not entail that the existence of horrendous evil constitutes a defeater for Christian belief. To illustrate this, consider the design plan of an air-raid siren: to produce a constant, very loud noise:

When the electric current is fluctuating because of a problem in the wiring, the air-raid siren emits a weak and pathetic squeak; it doesn't follow that the vibrating disc that produces the sound was designed to produce that squeak under those circumstances. True, it is designed in such a way that in fact it *will* produce that squeak then; but its doing so is not part of the design plan.... [It is] instead, an unintended by-product rather than part of the design plan itself.[60]

Similarly, if, for example, the presence of horrendous evil in the world constitutes a defeater for belief in God, it is the result of cognitive dysfunction – bad wiring – somewhere in the system. When no dysfunction is present, there is no defeater.

But what if, as is the case in our postlapsarian world, the *sensus divinitatis* is profoundly damaged; then does evil constitute a defeater for belief in God? For the unbeliever, very likely; but for the recipient of the internal instigation of the Holy Spirit, no. This is because one of the functions of the internal instigation of the Holy Spirit is to repair the *sensus divinitatis*. Therefore, because

> what a rational person will do when confronted with suffering and evil depends on what the cognitive design plan for humans is; but from a filled-out Christian perspective, that design plan will be such that someone who (like Mother Teresa, e.g.) continues to accept Christian belief in the face of the world's suffering and evil displays no irrationality whatever. Indeed, it is the person who gives up belief in God under these circumstances who displays cognitive dysfunction.[61]

Suppose something like this is the case. Nevertheless, this explanation cannot be the entire picture, for there must be some provisions in the design plan for an atheological objection to cause the Christian to give up on beliefs.[62] If there are no such provisions, that would entail that Christian belief is insulated from defeat, something that Plantinga explicitly denies. So what circumstances are such that there be a defeater for Christian belief? There would be defeaters for Christian belief if Christianity was, in fact, not true. Remember that for Plantinga de jure considerations ultimately boil down to de facto considerations. If the Christian God did not exist, the design plan covering the production of beliefs about God, *if aimed at truth*, would require that personal experiences of evil *be* a defeater for Christian belief.[63] But suppose theism is true, and suppose that a Christian's belief was maintained by cognitive processes *aimed at truth*;[64] could there be a defeater in such a case? Yes, if the *sensus divinitatis* was only partially repaired, something that Plantinga acknowledges is likely.[65] In such a case, due to the disordering of the *sensus divinitatis*, the warrant for beliefs about God would be significantly lower than the design plan requires, and consequently, an atheological argument could function as a defeater for Christian beliefs.

4. Uncovering Plantinga's Motivations

Why is Plantinga's religious epistemology shaped like it is? Although important, this is a difficult and mildly ostentatious question. Nevertheless, I will offer two *tentative* explanations as to why his project is structured as it is. The first of these is theological in nature. Plantinga's understanding of what a successful piece of religious epistemology would look like is heavily informed by his Reformed theological heritage. His view of the nature and implications of the noetic effects of sin and his definition of faith as 'firm and certain knowledge' conspire to require that knowledge of God cannot (and should not) be based on argument but on a source of warrant that does not deal in probabilities. One cannot base 'firm and unwavering' belief in Christianity on an argument the conclusion of which is that the probability of theism on the public evidence is 0.9.

The second reason why Plantinga argues as he does is less obvious, but I believe also important. Consider the environment in which he began his career as a philosopher. In 1958 (the year he defended his dissertation), logical positivism still had a firm grip on American academia, and as a consequence, the traditional conception of God was under attack from many different quarters. As he was a Christian studying in this environment, the necessity of engaging in negative apologetics reinforced Plantinga's pre-existing allergic reaction to natural theology. Consequently, even if he had wanted to engage in natural theology, the environment would have steered him away from doing so. Plantinga acknowledges that his first teaching post at Wayne State had a profound affect on his philosophical methodology with respect to religious questions. He says:

> [While at Wayne State] I was never able to get beyond a sort of defensive posture. I concentrated on arguing (contrary to my colleague's claims) that theism was not *wholly irrational*. . . . I often felt beleaguered and, with respect to my Christianity, alone, isolated, nonstandard, a bit peculiar or weird, a somewhat strange specimen in which my colleagues displayed an interest that was friendly, and for the most part uncensorious, but also incredulous and uncomprehending. It wasn't that this atmosphere induced doubt about the central elements of Christianity; it was more that my philosophical horizons were heavily formed by my colleagues and friends at Wayne.[66]

He is, I submit, still focused on minimalist, defensive arguments. While there are theological and philosophical reasons for this, I think that he does so at least partially out of habit. His way of approaching apologetic questions has been informed consciously or unconsciously by the antagonistic state of academia at the start of his academic career.

While there is much more that might be said about Plantinga's seminal contribution to religious epistemology, I turn now to critique. I will discuss a number of possible objections to his approach to religious epistemology and his account of faith formation.

AN EVALUATION OF PLANTINGA'S METHODOLOGY

Evaluating Plantinga's approach to religious epistemology is like standing at the foot of a very long and technically difficult climb – there are many different routes that can be taken, but none of them is taken without some degree of fear and trepidation. Methodological questions are invariably and notoriously difficult, and especially in Plantinga's case, thoroughly intertwined with theological commitments.

In my evaluation of Plantinga's approach to religious epistemology, I will touch on three different but conceptually related topics. First, I will briefly address the role of the Christian community in his model; second, I will evaluate his conception of the task of natural theology; and third, I will consider the success of the now-famous 'Great Pumpkin Objection'. While the first two are troublesome, the third unveils considerations that suggest the failure of one of Plantinga's goals for his project: to provide a good way for Christians to think about the warrant of Christian beliefs.

1. The Extended A/C Model and the Christian Community

An immediate red flag for many theologians regarding Plantinga's religious epistemology is the fact that he seemingly completely ignores the role of the religious community in his description of the formation of faith. This omission is particularly striking (and worrisome) given that the scriptural model of faith development is invariably communal. While Plantinga is aware of this omission, his comment on it is relegated to a footnote:

> Presented in this brief and undeveloped way, this model can seem unduly individualistic. But of course it doesn't at all preclude the importance of the Christian community and the church to the belief of the individual

Christian. It is the church or community that proclaims the gospel, guides the neophyte into it, and supports, instructs, encourages, and edifies believers of all sorts and conditions.[67]

Fair enough. But one is still tempted to wonder whether the Christian community is *epistemically* important in Plantinga's model. If the interesting and efficacious work is being done by the *sensus divinitatis* and the internal testimony of the Holy Spirit, what of importance is left for the Christian community to do?

The simple fact of the matter is that Plantinga does not say, and so we will have to hypothesize. While he does not develop the ecclesiological component of his model, there is nothing in his model that is logically or practically incompatible with an epistemic role being played by the Christian community in faith formation. For example, there is no reason to assume that the internal instigation of the Holy Spirit cannot assume or even elaborate on the teaching a person receives in church. The Holy Spirit might provide a divine imprimatur on the teaching of the Christian community or build on the value a person ascribes to his or her religious community in the rebuilding of a person's religious affections. Most importantly, the value Plantinga ascribes to his own ecclesial community is reason to believe that his religious epistemology *could* have a robust ecclesiological emphasis. So while it is worrisome that this rather significant lacuna exists, there are many different ways to flesh out the communitarian aspect of his model, and even if he does not do so himself, his silence should not necessarily be taken as an implicit devaluation of the topic.

2. Plantinga's Objection to Natural Theology

In a previous section, I considered Plantinga's assessment of natural theology. I now turn to a deeper question: Does the practice described by Plantinga as 'natural theology' adequately describe what Christians have actually practiced throughout the centuries?[68] What is striking about his definition of natural theology is how high he sets the bar; the 'success conditions' for natural theology, as envisioned by Plantinga, are enormously stringent. According to Plantinga, a successful piece of natural theology must start with self-evident premises, utilize a self-evidently valid argument form, and produce conclusions with maximal epistemic status.[69]

There are, I believe, two problems with Plantinga's stance on this matter. First, the rationale behind his lofty expectations of natural theology are less than clear. He says: "I don't know of an argument for Christian belief that seems very likely to convince one who doesn't already accept its conclusion."[70] As Paul Moser points out, however, it is difficult to see what his claim amounts to.[71] What kind of 'likelihood' is relevant here? In any event, it seems ill-advised to base the propriety of an argument for the truth of Christian belief on the likelihood that some people will not be convinced. No argument, not even an argument with the pedigree of Plantinga's own Free Will Defense, will convince *everyone*, and it is lamentable that nearly any argument will convince *someone*.[72] The second problem with Plantinga's stance on natural theology concerns his understanding of the 'success conditions' for natural theology. Why does he demand that theistic arguments yield maximal epistemic warrant when it seems that warrant *sufficient for knowledge* will suffice? Three possible answers come to mind, one philosophical and two theological. The philosophical answer can be dismissed immediately; it could be that Plantinga believes maximal warrant is necessary for knowledge. But this isn't the case. In WPF he says: "Clearly the faculties relevant with respect to a given belief need not be functioning perfectly for me to have warrant for my belief; many of my visual beliefs may constitute knowledge even if my vision is not 20/20."[73] For Plantinga warrant comes in degrees, and the degree of warrant is a function of the belief of belief; when the degree of belief is sufficient, knowledge is the result.

So the answer is theological. First, for Plantinga, the arguments associated with natural theology address only part of what is involved in faith. Faith involves the heart, affections, and will every bit as much as the intellect.[74] While this is true, it is only an argument against the *sufficiency* of natural theology for faith. Natural theology might be wholly worthless with respect to the affective component of faith but might still play a role with respect to the epistemic component. The second reason Plantinga sets the bar so high for natural theology is that here, as in other areas, he is following Calvin. For Calvin, faith is a "firm and certain knowledge."[75] Even the best probabilistic argument is just not sufficient to provide the degree of certainty required by Calvin's understanding of faith. But this merely explains Plantinga's standard; it does not justify it. The problem is that it's not obvious that the brand of certainty invoked by Calvin is *epistemic* certainty – in fact, I think that it is likely that it is *not*.[76] Because epistemic certainty requires both maximal warrant and the highest possible degree of belief, it is beyond the grasp of humans on this side of Eden. So if natural theology requires epistemic certainty, it is doomed to failure. But what if the brand of certainty necessary for faith were not epistemic but psychological?[77] Psychological certainty occurs when a person has a very high degree of confidence that a given proposition is true. On this view, since for Plantinga the amount of warrant associated with a given proposition is a function of the degree of belief, there is an important role for natural theology – even within the confines of his own religious epistemology – namely, increasing the warrant of Christian beliefs. As a consequence, his construal of natural theology is unnecessarily stringent in that he doesn't seem to have a place for good arguments that are unlikely to convince the skeptic.

3. The Return of the Great Pumpkin

A fairly standard objection to Plantinga's approach to religious epistemology has been labeled the Great Pumpkin Objection. The essence of this objection is that in granting that Christian beliefs can be warranted in the absence of propositional evidence, Plantinga must grant that absurd beliefs like 'the Great Pumpkin will return to the pumpkin patch tonight' can also be warranted. If successful, this objection would function as a reductio ad absurdum for his model. Plantinga himself first called attention to this objection in "The Reformed Objection to Natural Theology"[78] and again in RBG,[79] but despite his low opinion of its success, numerous commentators have identified this argument as the Achilles heel of his religious epistemology.[80]

At first glance, the Great Pumpkin Objection is a nonstarter. There is nothing in Plantinga's acknowledgment that some beliefs are properly basic with respect to warrant that requires him to hold that all beliefs (or even other phenomenologically similar beliefs) are properly basic with respect to warrant. But there is, I think, the kernel of a more troubling objection here. The objection is not merely that in claiming that belief in God is properly basic, Plantinga *himself* must accept all sorts of irrational beliefs. Rather, the objection is that other systems of belief could use his exact strategy to argue for the warrant basicality of their beliefs. For example, couldn't members of other world religions develop a model by which their beliefs could have warrant if they were true, just as Plantinga has? He acknowledges just as much:

> For any such set of beliefs, couldn't we find a model under which the beliefs in question have warrant, and such that given the truth of those beliefs, there are no philosophical objections to the truth of the model? Well, probably something like that *is* true for the other theistic religions: Judaism, Islam, some forms of Hinduism, some forms of Buddhism, some forms of

American Indian religion. Perhaps these religions are like Christianity in that they are subject to no *de jure* objections that are independent of *de facto* objections.[81]

Plantinga's suggestion seems to be that the methodological parity among theistic religions is a function of their shared theistic perspective. But why restrict this possibility to theistic religions? Rose Ann Christian, for example, has argued persuasively that a follower of the Advaita Vedanta religion could develop a model similar to Plantinga's:[82]

> For both Plantinga and exponents of Advaita Vedanta, reality and human knowers are metaphysically constituted in such a way that the latter are possessed of a capacity to grasp a deep truth about the former. In certain conditions, this capacity is activated. On these occasions, belief that reality is what it is (created by God, essentially Brahman) is not the result of inference or evidence, but is immediate (basic). And such a belief is warranted (properly basic).[83]

The problem for Plantinga is that Advaita Vedanta beliefs are not as easily dismissed as those of the Great Pumpkinite. It will not do, for example, for Plantinga to assume that (as he did regarding the Great Pumpkin) "reality is not Brahman, and therefore there is no capacity or tendency for apprehending it as such."[84] Consequently, Plantinga's methodology seems applicable to nontheistic religions as well.[85]

Maybe if suitably nuanced models of nontheistic religious belief were advanced, Plantinga would grant this point. Yet he maintains that this still doesn't open the door to all worldviews. Even if many of the world religions could benefit from Plantinga's line of argumentation, he claims "that isn't true for just *any* such set of beliefs. It isn't true, for example, for voodooism, or the belief that the earth is flat, or Humean skepticism, or philosophical naturalism."[86] Whether something like his model will work for philosophical naturalism is open for debate.[87] But why couldn't the followers of voodooism employ a similar model? What if voodooism represented the work of an extremely powerful supernatural being, a being that desired to cause people to believe in the efficacy of a particular set of religious practices? What if this being could take advantage of a particular epistemic situation and through the manipulation of cultural norms create 'belief-forming' processes that functioned properly in an appropriate environment, and was guided by a design plan reliably aimed at truth? Of course, these 'truths' would not be 'the great things of the gospel'; they would involve the reality and power of the spiritual world, the existence of the supernatural being behind the practices of voodooism, and the like. Given this background, it seems difficult to claim that 'voodoo epistemologists' could not take advantage of a model similar to Plantinga's. But Plantinga is still probably right. His argumentative methodology is not open to every belief system. Belief systems that have no place for the notion of a 'design plan' or 'proper function' will be unable to utilize his approach. But it is open to many different belief systems, and maybe even to some belief systems widely deemed to be both false and irrational. But all of this might not trouble Plantinga at all. He might aver that this sort of pluralism is an expected by-product of human finitude and sinfulness, and he would undoubtedly reiterate that his project is not designed to demonstrate the rationality of the Christian faith, to show that competing belief systems are irrational, or to adjudicate religious truth claims. It is 'religious epistemology for the Christian'. It is "a recommendation as to how Christians can profitably understand and conceive of the warrant they take Christian belief to have."[88]

Nevertheless, my supposition is that most Christians would be unimpressed if they were told that the explanation of how Christian beliefs could have warrant could also be used by Advaita Vedanta Hindus, 'Voodoo Epistemologists,' and maybe even atheists. They would, I think, reject Plantinga's Extended A/C Model as a good explanation of the epistemic status of their religious beliefs and maybe conclude that this state of affairs was supportive of some version of religious pluralism. Of course, Plantinga would be pleased by neither of these conclusions. In the final analysis, therefore, a consideration of the Great Pumpkin Objection focuses attention on what may be the most disturbing problem with his approach to religious epistemology – its applicability to Christian belief.

Admittedly, this claim may seem both impertinent and preposterous. No one in contemporary philosophy has done more to bring Christian belief into meaningful conversation with philosophy, and no work in religious epistemology is as theologically focused as WCB. The problem is not that Plantinga does not address theological matters or write from a specifically Christian perspective – he certainly does. The problem lies in his minimalist approach to religious epistemology.[89] While his minimalism has served him well throughout his career, giving him the reputation as an extremely careful philosopher, fully discussing certain topics requires a more fine-grained, less-minimalist approach. Because of the diversity of epistemic practices in the Christian tradition and the diversity of situations in which faith is formed, not to mention the diversity of understandings of the nature, antecedents, and consequents of faith, I submit that religious epistemology is one of those topics.

Plantinga's minimalism creates two problems, one epistemological and one theological. The Great Pumpkin Objection highlights his epistemological minimalism. His unwillingness to argue for the truth of the Extended A/C Model saddles him with an argumentative methodology that applies too widely, to too many religious traditions. The result is that what he sells as 'religious epistemology for the Christian' is in fact 'religious epistemology for any worldview that has a suitably strong notion of design and proper function'.

Plantinga's theological minimalism can be seen in the lack of applicability of his Extended A/C Model to the faith of typical Christians. While he speaks a great deal about the recipients of faith, those who have had their religious affections cured and who have been given the divine gift of firm and certain belief in the great things of the gospel, it is far from clear whether there are _any_ people whose faith looks like that described in Plantinga's model.[90] Plantinga acknowledges that the description of faith in WCB is 'paradigmatic' in the sense that it describes ideal or "fully formed and well-developed faith."[91] He says that "for the person with faith (at least in the paradigmatic instances) the great things of the gospel seem clearly true, obvious, compelling."[92] Elsewhere he states: "It is only in the pure and paradigmatic instances of faith that there is "utter certainty."[93] And he acknowledges that "the model represents things the way they go when they go really well; only paradigmatic cases of faith are like the model. But for most of us, the model isn't a wholly accurate description."[94]

While it is undoubtedly easier to describe and defend the warrant of "epistemological saints,"[95] because the Extended A/C Model describes the ideal, fully formed faith of paradigmatic believers rather than the usual, in-process faith of typical believers, Plantinga's attempt to use the Extended A/C Model to provide a good way for Christians (including, I assume, typical Christians) to think about the epistemology of Christian belief is in jeopardy. Since the faith of typical believers looks very different from that described in Plantinga's model, they have a choice between questioning the warrant of their belief about God or rejecting Plantinga's model as a good explanation of the warrant of their religious beliefs. Since Plantinga himself argues that the beliefs of "most Christians" are "both externally rational and warranted,"[96] the most reasonable option for the typical Christian is the latter. To repair this deficiency, he needs to generalize his model to the typical believer or give some guidance as to what such a generalization might look like. Just as, according to Plantinga (and Calvin), faith requires not only believing in God and realizing that there is a scheme of salvation "but also and most important, that this scheme applies to and is available to me,"[97] Plantinga's model, to be successful with respect to his second goal, must give the typical believers some reason to believe that the model applies to them.[98]

In summary, to be successful with respect to his second goal, to offer his models as a way for Christians to think about the epistemic status of their religious beliefs, he must restrict the application of his religious epistemology so that it applies less widely and expand the application of his account of faith development so that it applies more broadly, to typical as well as paradigmatic Christians.

AN EVALUATION OF PLANTINGA'S EXTENDED A/C MODEL

An evaluation of a model such as Plantinga's is complicated by the fact that he does not argue that the theological details of his model are true. Because Plantinga takes this approach, arguments against the truth (or actuality) of the theological details of the model are of dubious merit. Consequently, an effective critique of his Extended A/C Model will have to demonstrate either that an aspect of the model is not epistemically possible – it is not consistent with widely accepted facts – or that it does not accomplish his stated goals – it does not demonstrate that Christian belief can be warranted if true and provide a good way for Christians to think about the epistemology of religious belief.

1. Is Belief in God Properly Basic?

One of the most distinctive aspects of Plantinga's Extended A/C Model is that the deliverances of the internal instigation of the Holy Spirit are properly basic with respect to warrant. He says: "In the typical case, Christian belief is immediate; it is formed in the basic way. It doesn't proceed by way of an argument from, for example, the reliability of Scripture or the church."[99] For Plantinga, beliefs formed by the sensus divinitatis and the internal instigation of the Holy Spirit are both *psychologically* direct – they are not inferred or accepted on the evidential basis of other beliefs – and *epistemically* direct – they do not receive their warrant from another belief.

It is probably true that the vast majority of mature Christians do not believe *solely* on the basis of arguments or propositional evidence. Instead, their beliefs are based (at least partially) on their experience of God, on a sense of his communication, disapproval, or forgiveness. And for some (Plantinga's 'paradigmatic believers'), their core religious beliefs are properly basic. But Plantinga's claim is that the beliefs of the *typical* believer, not merely the paradigmatic believer, are properly basic. It is this claim that I propose to question. Contrary to Plantinga's models, I suggest that the religious beliefs of the typical Christian are more likely based on a complex mixture of personal, social, and evidential factors in addition to pneumato-logical factors such as the internal instigation of the Holy Spirit. In doing so, I call into question not the logical or theological validity of Plantinga's model but its applicability. I will discuss two reasons to think that belief in God may not be properly basic for many Christians, one philosophical and the other theological. The former concerns the relationship between basic and derived beliefs, and the latter concerns the diachronic or developmental aspect of beliefs about God.

Plantinga's contention that belief in God is properly basic assumes some form of foundationalism. While his critique of *classical* foundationalism is well known, he nonetheless remains a foundationalist of a 'modest' or 'broad' variety. Like all versions of foundationalism, in Plantingian foundationalism properly basic beliefs receive their warrant from an immediate source, an experience or something similar; it is not transferred from other propositions or beliefs.[100] In other words, the basis-relation for Plantinga is unidirectional; basic beliefs can provide warrant for derived beliefs, but not the reverse.

Lurking behind Plantinga's brand of foundationalism seems to be an assumption that belief in God should be *based on* a single source of warrant. Other sources, he allows, can *contribute* to the warrant of Christian belief, but they cannot ground or stand in a basing relationship to it.[101] I demur. While it could be (and perhaps occasionally is) the case that Christian beliefs enjoy a single source of warrant, it is difficult to see how Plantinga might support the claim that multiple sources of warrant are logically or theologically impossible. Consider the following counterexample developed by Keith DeRose.[102] Imagine a very simple noetic structure of subject S, composed of two beliefs, A and B. A and B possess a good deal of immediate warrant for S, but not enough to be considered knowledge. S, however, notices that A and B are mutually supporting and on that basis gains significant additional confidence in A and B individually. Because A and B are mutually supporting, they each transfer some of their immediate warrant to the other and in so doing increase the warrant of the other enough to be considered knowledge. In this case, not only is the basis-relation *not* unidirectional, but there are *multiple* sources of warrant – belief A is based partially on immediate grounds, and partially on inferential grounds (the warrant transferred from *B*).

If the scenario described by DeRose is possible, then it could be that Christian beliefs receive warrant from both immediate and inferential sources. How would this alternate understanding of faith formation cash out in practical terms? Perhaps like this. Suppose that after confessing a sin, a neophyte Christian is in a situation in which he or she has a strong sense of being forgiven by God. This experience is distinct, but a lack of theological perspective leaves the neophyte mildly incredulous of his or her experience. Consequently, the neophyte's belief in such forgiveness, while possessing significant immediate warrant, falls short of the warrant necessary for knowledge because it is not accompanied by a sufficient degree of belief or psychological certainty. It is not until he or she has a conversation with a spiritual mentor who recounts a similar experience of feeling forgiven that the neophyte's degree of belief is sufficient to yield the degree of warrant necessary for knowledge. In such a case, the warrant for the belief that the neophyte has been forgiven is based partially on the doxastic evidence associated with his or her original experience and partially on trust in the friend's testimony.

Because the context of faith formation in Plantinga's Extended A/C Model is individualistic rather than communitarian, the plausibility of the proper basicality of beliefs about God is increased. However, because the Christian model of faith formation always occurs in a communal context, the beliefs of the typical Christian will often be based on testimonial as well as pneumatological grounds.

The second reason to question Plantinga's contention that belief in God is properly basic for the typical Christian is related to the first. For the typical Christian, belief in God may cycle back and forth between basicality and nonbasicality because of 'developmental' issues associated with faith – issues grouped under the heading 'sanctification'. Despite the fact that Plantinga often gives the impression that warranted beliefs about God are produced in the believer immediately and simultaneous to conversion, he does acknowledge that faith may have a processive quality:

> Perhaps the conviction arises slowly, and only after long and hard study, thought, discussion, prayer. Or perhaps it is a matter of the belief's having been there all along (from childhood, perhaps), but now being transformed, renewed, intensified, made vivid and alive. This process can go a thousand ways; in each there is a presentation or proposal of central Christian teaching and, by way of response, the phenomenon of being convinced, coming to see, forming of a conviction.[103]

Plantinga is correct in seeing the diversity of avenues by which faith is appropriated; the problem is that in many of these cases, the proper basicality of core beliefs about God is much more difficult to maintain than on Plantinga's model. To illustrate this, consider the faith development of the noted Christian writer and apologist C. S. Lewis.

Born in 1898, Lewis was raised a Christian but fell into agnosticism in his teens and twenties. By 1929, however, through extensive research, Lewis came to accept the Christian worldview, although he continued to reject Christianity. For the next couple of years he studied the claims of Christianity closely, and specifically the life of Jesus and the historicity of the Gospels. His famously reluctant conclusion was that he was "nearly certain that it really happened."[104] Then in a conversation on September 19, 1931, with J. R. R. Tolkien and Hugo Dyson, the truth of Christianity struck Lewis in a powerful way. Whether the internal instigation of the Holy Spirit made its first appearance to Lewis during this conversation or was present in Lewis from childhood, but only partially effective, what seems difficult to deny is that Lewis's beliefs about God *before* the conversation with Tolkien and Dyson possessed significant warrant for him. It is cases like this, however, together with the fact that they are not at all atypical, that create problems for Plantinga's claim that the beliefs of the *typical* Christian are properly basic. Even if there is a final moment in which faith is created in the individual, the *sensus divinitatis* is finally (or sufficiently) repaired, and as a result the great things of the gospel seem utterly compelling, how can this new conviction be completely divorced (epistemically speaking) from one's previous reflection on the matter? Consequently, even if Lewis *could have* held his beliefs in the basic way (assuming a sufficient repair of the *sensus divinitatis*), it seems difficult to claim that his religious beliefs were not based at least partially on the arguments and evidences uncovered in his previous study. If this is correct – and I believe it is – it seems that in the many cases like Lewis's, Christian beliefs are not properly basic but are based on a complicated web of arguments, experiences, testimony, and pneumatological intervention.

But if belief in God is based, at least partially, on propositional grounds and arguments, what explains the fact that the typical believers stubbornly and steadfastly believe in God, even in the face of arguments to the contrary? This phenomenon, I believe, is due to the fact that the beliefs associated with faith have a very high, perhaps maximal, depth of ingression. 'Depth of ingression' is Plantinga's term; a belief with a high depth of ingression is a belief the abandonment of which would require massive changes in one's noetic structure.[105] My point is that a belief can be based at least partially on propositional evidence and arguments, and thereby fail to be properly basic but still have a maximal depth of ingression. And I think that belief in God, for many committed believers, is exactly that kind of belief.

2. The Internal Instigation of the Holy Spirit and the Contribution of the Believer

My second objection to Plantinga's Extended A/C Model concerns the specific mechanism by which faith is created in the believer, and specifically the fact that it is produced by a cognitive process, not by means of the believer's native cognitive faculties. The fact that the internal instigation of the Holy Spirit is a cognitive process is not as benign as Plantinga suggests. In fact, the very fact that Plantinga defends the warrant of a cognitive process is a bit surprising. In WCD he argued extensively, and I think correctly, that process reliabilism is too permissive – beliefs produced by a reliable cognitive process can fail to be warranted.[106] But even if some properly attenuated version of process reliabilism were vindicated, it would still not answer all the questions associated with Plantinga's adoption of the internal instigation of the Holy Spirit as a properly functioning cognitive process. As Andrew Dole has perspicuously argued:

> It cannot simply be assumed that a criterion which determines whether beliefs produced by cognitive faculties are warranted can perform the same function with regard to cognitive processes. Cognitive faculties are a subset of the set of cognitive processes, a subset whose members we are to a certain extent familiar and comfortable with. But the larger set of imaginable cognitive processes contains members which bear little if any resemblance to our own cognitive processes. A belief produced by a non-faculty cognitive process which meets the criterion for warrant may well suffer from defects sufficient to suggest that the belief should not be considered warranted.[107]

In other words, even if a part of humanity's native noetic equipment, say the *sensus divinitatis*, produced a belief that met Plantinga's criterion for warrant, it isn't obvious that beliefs produced by the internal testimony of the Holy Spirit, a cognitive process *not* a part of humanity's original equipment, would also be warranted.

The essence of the problem with non-native cognitive processes lies in the potential for the deliverances of these processes to be unfamiliar, to seem to come from 'out of the blue' and, by virtue of that fact, be discounted by the recipient of the beliefs in question. To avoid this problem, Plantinga must treat the internal instigation of the Holy Spirit in such a way that it does not fall prey to counterexamples like "Mr. Truetemp."[108] Mr. Truetemp is an unlucky soul who undergoes brain surgery and unknowingly is implanted with a device that measures his body temperature (properly and reliably according to a design plan aimed at truth) and then hourly produces a belief regarding his current body temperature. Upon awaking from his surgery, Mr. Truetemp says: 'You know, I am suddenly convinced that my temperature is 98.6 degrees.' While Mr. Truetemp has no defeaters for his belief, because the doctors do not inform him of their surgical shenanigans, he also has no explanation for why he believes as he does. Of course, Mr. Truetemp has no reason to believe that his temperature is *not* 98.6 degrees, but because his belief about his body temperature will lack any prior context or coherence with other beliefs of his, rationality would seem to require that he withhold belief as to his temperature. This sort of defeater has been called a 'no-reason' defeater (so called because 'person *S* realizes that he or she has *no reason* to believe belief *p*').[109] While commenting on the Mr. Truetemp example in a response to Keith Lehrer, Plantinga acknowledges that Mr. Truetemp's beliefs should not be considered knowledge because even if Mr. Truetemp doesn't have a rationality defeater for his belief, he should.[110] For a belief to be rational, Plantinga holds that one must have "considered how it fits with your other beliefs, engaged in the requisite seeking for defeaters, considered the objections that you have encountered, compared notes with the right people, and so on."[111]

The problem for Plantinga is that since there are potentially significant phenomenological similarities between Mr. Truetemp's belief and the deliverances of Plantinga's internal instigation of the Holy Spirit, it seems possible that a recipient of the internal instigation of the Holy Spirit might treat her religious beliefs just as Mr. Truetemp treats his beliefs about his temperature. Even though the beliefs in question are formed in a reliable manner, an appropriately reflective cognizer may question those beliefs either because she has no expectation of having access to the information concerned or because she realizes her degree of belief exceeds what seems reasonable given her experiences. To avoid this unwanted conclusion, Plantinga's Extended A/C Model must be fleshed out with respect to the cognitive context in which the internal instigation of the Holy Spirit can be expected to provide reliable beliefs for which there will be no defeaters of this sort. In other words, Plantinga must make the deliverances of the internal testimony of the Holy Spirit similar *in the relevant respects* to the deliverances of the native cognitive faculties that might produce the same beliefs in similar situations.

Of course, specifying these 'relevant respects' is a complex matter. I do not intend to claim that whatever produces beliefs about God must be a 'natural process', whatever that amounts to.[112] What is necessary is that beliefs produced by the internal instigation of the Holy Spirit must be phenomenologically similar *from the perspective of the cognizer* – they must seem to flow from native cognitive faculties rather than seem to be produced apart from them (or, if the belief seems divorced from usual cognitive channels, the cognizer must not see this as problematic). The following revision of the Mr. Truetemp example provides a sketch of this sort of thing. Suppose that the mischievous doctors implant in Mr. Truetemp a device that produces 'current temperature beliefs' but does so *indirectly*. The device produces an inclination to determine one's temperature, and at the behest of that inclination, Mr. Truetemp places his hand on his forehead and the implanted device registers the belief: *My temperature is X*. While Mr. Truetemp might be initially surprised at the specificity of his belief ('exactly 98.6, huh?'), before long he accepts the deliverances of his implanted device as arising from an unusual skill he has developed – much like one who develops the skill of determining the time of day by looking at the sun. With respect to the production of religious beliefs, John Greco notes that Thomas Aquinas seems to provide a template for a parallel move. He says: "The act of believing is an act of the intellect assenting to the Divine truth at the command of the will moved by the grace of God."[113] The Holy Spirit might be the cause of the belief in question, but the means to the belief is found in the believer's native cognitive faculties.

3. The Noetic Effects of Sin and 'Firm and Unwavering' Belief in God

My final objection to Plantinga's Extended A/C Model concerns what seem to be failures of the internal instigation of the Holy Spirit, cases in which beliefs about God have decidedly less warrant than the model seems to imply they should have. My claim here is not that the Extended A/C Model always fails, but that there are instances of belief in God that are not explained by the model, or are explained only awkwardly.

Let's start with what seems obvious: Different Christians hold their beliefs about God with different degrees of firmness. I don't mean to say merely that there are people whose religious beliefs are held for nonalethic reasons, such as the desire to belong to an ecclesial community or to avoid eternal punishment in hell; such beliefs are not even candidates for warrant because they are not produced by cognitive faculties aimed at truth. My point is that even among Christians whose beliefs are 'alethically aimed', the beliefs of some Christians approach 'firm and certain' while other Christians' beliefs are tentative, shot through with doubt, and fail to exhibit a degree of belief sufficient for knowledge.

While Plantinga speaks of faith as a 'firm and certain knowledge', he acknowledges that "*in typical cases*, as opposed to paradigmatic cases, degree of belief will be less than maximal. Furthermore, the degree of belief typically varies from person to person, from time to time, and from circumstance to circumstance."[114] Let's call this 'the variability of belief problem' (abbreviated 'VB problem'). I will suggest that the variability of belief among seemingly sincere, alethically motivated Christians raises an interesting question for Plantinga's religious epistemology. Given Plantinga's stance on the formation of beliefs about God – associated as it is with a divinely instigated cognitive process – how should VB be understood?

There are, so far as I can see, four possible explanations of the VB phenomenon. The first explanation is that those who demonstrate VB have not received the internal instigation of the Holy Spirit. Their beliefs about God vary in intensity and clarity because they are the products of cognitive faculties that are still wholly mired in sin. While this explanation is logically coherent and theologically possible, it cannot be the explanation of VB for Plantinga because he explicitly says in a number of places that doubt is not eliminated by the inward instigation of the Holy Spirit.[115]

Second, VB could be accounted for by citing the 'epistemic distance' between God and the believer; God's utterly transcendent nature is beyond the ken of human beings. While there is undoubtedly epistemic distance between God and the believer, Plantinga argues extensively in Part I of WCB that it is not a barrier to human knowledge of God. Moreover, his desire to make his Extended A/C Model compatible with Calvinist soteriology undercuts his capacity to use epistemic distance as an explanation of VB. After all, the sine qua non of Calvinist soteriologies is that God is necessarily the cause of the beliefs associated with faith. Consequently, given a Calvinist soteriology, whatever epistemic distance that undoubtedly exists between God and the believer is irrelevant, for the belief in question is not ultimately produced by the believer; it has a divine cause that transcends mundane or 'this worldly' explanations. In other words, even if there was epistemic distance between God and humanity, it would not compromise God's ability to produce religious knowledge in an epistemic agent.

A third explanation for VB is that those whose religious beliefs are not 'firm and certain' have received a weakened version of the internal instigation of the Holy Spirit. While this is compatible with Plantinga's affirmation that "for whatever reason, the deliverances of the internal instigation of the

Holy Spirit seem to come in all different degrees of strength,"[116] this explanation is unsatisfactory for two reasons: First, it is difficult to explain why God would deliberately mute the effectiveness of his preferred means to produce faith in humans; second, Plantinga explicitly says that the gift of faith – including, I assume, the cognitive benefits thereof – "is given to anyone who is willing to accept it."[117]

A final explanation for VB is the noetic effects of sin *on the believer*. On this view, the reason believers experience doubt is because the effects of sin on the mind are not *wholly* cured by the regenerating effects of the Holy Spirit. While the noetic effects of sin have always played a significant role in Reformed theology, there has been some debate over the extent of those effects and particularly the extent to which the noetic effects of sin continue to affect the believer. The majority of Plantinga's discussion of the noetic effects of sin concern their effect on the unbeliever. This is understandable since his discussion of this topic is designed to set the table for his introduction of the Extended A/C Model, the model designed for our postlapsarian epistemic environment. Still, Plantinga does acknowledge that the noetic effects of sin continue to affect the believer. He says: "Regeneration heals the ravages of sin – *embryonically in this life*, and with ever greater fullness in the next."[118] Since the cognitive benefits of regeneration are 1) the repair of the *sensus divinitatis*, 2) a clearer picture of the reality and nature of God, and 3) a greater recognition of the truth of the gospel message,[119] a partial or 'embryonic' regeneration would obviously involve, inter alia, a less clear picture of God's existence and nature and a greater degree of doubt about the truth of the great things of the gospel. In short, it seems clear that for Plantinga, VB is best explained by the noetic effects of sin on the believer.

There is, I submit, a tension between Plantinga's claim that the cognitive aspects of faith can constitute a 'firm and certain knowledge' and his affirmation that the noetic effects of sin continue to rage in the believer.[120] Specifically, the presence of VB in those who putatively are the recipients of the internal instigation of the Holy Spirit seems to undercut one of Plantinga's conditions for warrant, his environmental condition. For Plantinga, a warranted belief must meet the proper function, environmental, alethic, and no-defeater conditions. Whatever causes a particular belief to fail to meet one or more of these conditions is considered a warrant defeater. If the presence of VB is accounted for by a feature of our epistemic environment – the noetic effects of sin – then there is reason to question whether Plantinga's environmental condition for warrant is met. And if his environmental condition is not met, then we have reason to believe that the beliefs formed as described by the Extended A/C Model, even if they are true and even if they are held with a high degree of confidence, will not be warranted. In other words, VB is a warrant defeater for beliefs about God.

A little reading between the lines leads me to believe that Plantinga would respond to this objection in the following way: If God designed the Extended A/C Model for a world in which sin exists, of course the design would be a good one – it would 'fit' the situation for which it was designed, and therefore the environment would be favorable. I'm not sure this follows, because there are many things an omnipotent being cannot do, and guaranteeing that 'firm and unwavering' beliefs will be created in a postlapsarian epistemic environment is perhaps one of those things. But suppose Plantinga is right: The design plan for the cognitive maxi-environment is congenial to the formation of warranted beliefs about God. Even so, there is no guarantee that the cognitive *mini-environments* in which many believers find themselves will be similarly congenial.[121]

4. Plantinga's Theological Minimalism

The problem underlying many of the previous objections to Plantinga's Extended A/C Model is theological in nature. For the most part, the problem is not that the theology contained in the his models is flawed, but that it is not sufficiently fine-grained to explain the phenomenological diversity of faith formation. It is precisely this lack that constitutes a barrier to Plantinga's suggestion that his models represent a good way for Christians to think about the epistemic status of their religious belief. My three objections detail three respects in which the theological content of his models requires augmentation. First, because he relies on paradigmatic instances of faith formation, Plantinga's models explain only awkwardly, if at all, the theologically complex nature of most Christians' apprehension of faith. Second, even if the cognitive process involved in faith formation meets Plantinga criteria for warrant, since he does not provide a theological context in which its deliverances will seem appropriate and familiar, there is a very real possibility that the beliefs of the internal instigation of the Holy Spirit will be subject to no-reason defeaters. Finally, the paucity of theological detail in Plantinga's models makes it difficult to explain the diversity of degrees of belief without violating one of his own criteria for warrant.

One of the crucial steps toward remedying these lacunae is discussing the role played by human freedom in the process of faith formation.[122] Plantinga affirms that "it is a part of much traditional Christian teaching to hold that a necessary condition of my receiving the gift of faith is my acquiescing, being willing to accept the gift, being prepared to receive it. There is a contribution to this process that I myself must make, a contribution that I can withhold."[123] Curiously, immediately after making this important qualification, he states that the Extended A/C Model "need take no stand on this issue."[124] The reason for this is that Plantinga wants to keep the Extended A/C Model as simple as possible because the more theological details that are added, the more the probability of the whole model is diminished and the more the model describes the warrant of a proper subset of Christian belief, rather than Christian belief generally considered.[125]

While this approach is understandable, I think that ultimately it is problematic. Even if the addition of theological details diminishes the probability of the model as a whole, they are necessary to avoid what I see as several substantial objections to the model. Moreover, since Plantinga's religious epistemology is already articulated from a particular theological perspective (in methodology if not in soteriology), I fail to understand why he is reticent to flesh out the theological details of his model. The result is that his model is neither inclusive enough to be truly ecumenical nor theologically detailed enough to handle some of the pressing theological questions asked of it.

In fact, Plantinga's *own* theological commitments involve an affirmation of the role of human freedom in the production of faith. He says:

> I'm thinking of the Holy Spirit as giving us a chance to see something of the beauty and truth of the great things of the gospel: but it is still possible to freely accept and freely reject. The work of creating faith in us is subsequent to such an acceptance. But that's not part of the model – that's just the way I do in fact think it works. The Holy Spirit does not, on my way of thinking, cause me to accept the invitation.[126]

The image of the Holy Spirit's 'enabling us to see' the truth of the great things of the gospel is a fruitful explanation of how the internal instigation of the Holy Spirit might function with respect to the role of the believer in the formation of faith. On this understanding, the Holy Spirit repairs and utilizes human cognitive equipment, 'removing the scales from our eyes', so to speak. This correlation with our native cognitive equipment goes a long way toward resolving questions regarding the warrant of beliefs produced by a cognitive process rather than a cognitive faculty. In the absence of such a revision, Plantinga's Extended A/C Model remains vulnerable to counterexamples like Mr. Truetemp.

Moreover, including an account of the role of the human will in the formation of faith will allow Plantinga to explain the VB phenomenon by acknowledging that willingness on the part of the epistemic agent is a necessary condition for the creation of faith via the internal instigation of the Holy Spirit. Without reference to human freedom, or even if the issue is bracketed (as Plantinga does), the warrant of Christian beliefs is called into question because the cause of the VB phenomenon must be located in the cognitive environment. The Extended A/C Model, it seems, is best served by following Plantinga's own theological intuitions and including human freedom in the equation.

CONCLUSION

My critique of Plantinga's religious epistemology has repeatedly called attention to problems associated with his minimalism. His unwillingness to argue for the truth of his model, his reference to the faith of 'paradigmatic' believers rather than that of typical believers, and his unwillingness to flesh out the controversial theological details of the context of faith formation all conspire to undercut the applicability of his model.

The conclusion to be drawn, however, is not that belief in God cannot be warranted – I believe it can. Neither should one conclude that Plantinga's model is irredeemably flawed. Rather, my objection is that his mature religious epistemology, like its more inchoate predecessor, is unfinished. Despite the depth and breadth of Plantinga's project, there are lacunae that need to be addressed, lacunae that are primarily theological in nature. I am aware that this objection might seem a bit unfair. After all, WCB is more than 500 pages and is part of a trilogy that covers just shy of 1,000 pages. (Plantinga's exasperation shows in his response to one critical reviewer: "It [WCB] was already a 500 page tome; should I have made it longer yet?")[127] This objection, therefore, is less an indictment of Plantinga's work and more a testimony to the mind-numbing complexity of religious epistemology.

Despite its foibles, Plantinga's magisterial project will be the standard by which future religious epistemologies will be judged for many years. (One reviewer favorably compares WCB to *Summa Theologica* and *Church Dogmatics*.)[128] While its virtues are many, I will close this essay by mentioning just two. First, Plantinga's proposal represents the most complete and comprehensive attempt to think through important philosophical issues from a distinctively Christian point of view. He does not restrict his philosophical work to addressing those questions deemed 'sensible' or 'interesting' (whatever that means) by the majority of academics. Consequently, his religious epistemology applies not only to 'mere Christianity' but to a full-fledged version of Christian theism, complete with many of the trimmings. Those who castigate Plantinga's approach as isolationistic, fideistic, or a "distortion of the spirit of philosophical inquiry"[129] have failed to grapple with the extent to which *all* academic work – not just that of conservative Christians – builds on presuppositions the truth of which cannot be conclusively demonstrated to those who do not share them. Consequently, while Plantinga's approach *could become* isolationistic or fideistic, it is not necessarily so. For these reasons, Plantinga's religious epistemology is an important step in what I think is the right direction.

Second, Plantinga's work has shown the interconnectedness of theological and philosophical issues in religious epistemology, especially in two respects. Plantinga brings the topic of the role of the religious affections to the fore. This is important because many contemporary religious epistemologies have – I believe, to their detriment – been articulated in purely cognitive terms. The affective, volitional aspect of faith has been ignored, or to the degree it has entered into the conversation, it has been relegated to the status of an ancillary issue. In addition, Plantinga's argument that de jure objections are not independent of de facto objections also serves to draw attention to the interconnectedness of theological and philosophical matters in religious epistemology. Even if my critique in this essay is successful, Plantinga's claim that what one takes to be true affects what one deems to be reasonable is still absolutely correct. For instance, if someone became convinced (say, on the basis of an independent argument) that God existed only as 'the ground of being' or as 'being as such', that would greatly affect what sorts of features one would take as 'evidence' of God's existence and what sorts of beliefs would be reasonably formed about God in various situations. Consequently, Plantinga's work exposes the attempt to articulate a 'purely agnostic' or 'methodologically naturalistic' religious epistemology as either impossible or hopelessly tendentious. In the final analysis, this might be the most important attribute of Plantinga's magisterial contribution to religious epistemology.

Notes

In this chapter I draw on material found in my *Epistemology as Theology: An Evaluation of Alvin Plantinga's Religious Epistemology*, Aldershot: Ashgate, 2006.

1. Alvin Plantinga, *Warranted Christian Belief*, New York and Oxford: Oxford University Press, 2000.
2. Paul Moser, "Man to Man with *Warranted Christian Belief* and Alvin Plantinga," *Philosophia Christi* 3.2, 2001, p. 369.
3. Richard M. Gale, "Alvin Plantinga's *Warranted Christian Belief*," *Philo* 4.2, 2001, p. 139.
4. Something Plantinga acknowledges in WCB, p. xiv.

5. Alvin Plantinga, *God and Other Minds*, Ithaca, NY: Cornell University Press, 1967.

6. In *Faith and Rationality: Reason and Belief in God*, ed. Alvin Plantinga and Nicholas Wolterstorff, Notre Dame, IN: University of Notre Dame Press, 1983, pp. 16–93.

7. "Afterword," in *The Analytic Theist: An Alvin Plantinga Reader*, ed. James Sennett, Grand Rapids, MI: Eerdmans, 1998, p. 353.

8. Alvin Plantinga, *Warrant: The Current Debate* and *Warrant and Proper Function*, New York and Oxford: Oxford University Press, 1993.

9. WCB, pp. 152–153.

10. Ibid., p. xiii.

11. Ibid.

12. Ibid., p. 190.

13. Alvin Plantinga, "Rationality and Public Evidence: A Reply to Swinburne," *Religious Studies* 37.2, 2001, p. 215; WCB, p. xiii.

14. WCB, p. xiii.

15. Plantinga, "Rationality and Public Evidence," p. 215.

16. For two reasons: first, the topic is addressed elsewhere in this volume; second, my own epistemological views are similar to Plantinga's. See my *Epistemology as Theology*, Chapter 5.

17. WCB, p. 174.

18. Ibid., p. 175.

19. Ibid., p. 179.

20. Ibid., p. 264.

21. Ibid., p. 205.

22. Ibid.

23. Ibid., p. 243. Plantinga refers to this process as 'typical' because he acknowledges that God could have made us aware of his plan of salvation in many ways and that some Christians have come to know about God in a different way.

24. WCB, p. 251.

25. *Institutes of the Christian Religion* (1536) III, ii, 7, p. 551; ed. John T. McNeill; trans. Ford Lewis Battles, Philadelphia: Westminster, 1960; cited in WCB, p. 244. Subsequent page numbers will refer to the McNeill edition.

26. WCB, p. 248; notes omitted.

27. Ibid., p. 256.

28. Ibid.

29. Ibid, p. 255.

30. Ibid., p. 258.

31. Ibid., p. 257. In fact, Plantinga goes so far as to claim that this cognitive process "cannot fail to function properly" (WCB, p. 246, n. 10).

32. Ibid., p. 257.

33. Ibid., p. 168.

34. Ibid., pp. 168–169.
35. Ibid., p. 168.
36. Ibid., p. 499.
37. See WCB, pp. 169–170, 201, 271, and 351–352.
38. WCB, pp. 200–201; see also pp. 169–170.
39. C. Stephen Evans, "Apologetics in a New Key: Relieving Protestant Anxieties Over Natural Theology," in *The Logic of Rational Theism*, ed. William Lane Craig and Mark McLeod. Problems in Contemporary Philosophy Series, vol. 24, Lewiston, NY: Edward Mellen, 1990, p. 66.
40. "Internalism, Externalism, Defeaters, and Arguments for Christian Belief," *Philosophia Christi* n.s. 3.2, 2001, p. 398.
41. Ibid.
42. "Rationality and Public Evidence," p. 220; italics mine.
43. Ibid., pp. 220–221; italics original. See also WCB, p. 271 n. 56.
44. Ibid., pp. 220–221.
45. WCB, pp. 200–201.
46. Ibid., pp. 268–269.
47. Ibid., p. 269.
48. Ibid., pp. 269–270.
49. Plantinga says: "Of course [the beliefs constituting faith] could be accepted on the basis of other propositions, and perhaps in some cases are. A believer could reason as follows: I have strong historical and archeological evidence for the reliability of the Bible (or the church, or may parents, or some other authority); the Bible teaches the great things of the gospel; so probably these things are true. A believer could reason this way. But in the [Extended A/C] model it goes differently" (WCB, p. 250). See also Plantinga's comments in WCB, pp. 170, 176 n. 12; and "Reply [Ad Wykstra]," *Philosophical Books* 43.2, April 2002, p. 124.
50. Stephen Wykstra, "Not Done in a Corner: How to be a 'Sensible Evidentialist' About Jesus," *Philosophical Books* 43.2, April 2002, pp. 92–116.
51. Michael Sudduth, "The Prospects for 'Mediate' Natural Theology in John Calvin," *Religious Studies* 31.1, March 1995, pp. 53–68.
52. WCB, p. 270.
53. Michael Martin, *Atheism: A Philosophical Justification*, Philadelphia: Temple University Press, 1990, p. 276. See also Patrick J. Roche, "Knowledge of God and Alvin Plantinga's Religious Epistemology," *Quodlibet* 4.4, November 2002, and Charles Gutenson, "Can Belief in God Be Properly Basic? A Pannenbergian Perspective on Plantinga and Basic Beliefs," *Christian Scholar's Review* 29, Fall 1999, pp. 49–72.
54. WCB, p. 368; "Rationality and Public Evidence," p. 217.
55. "Response to Keller," *Faith and Philosophy* 5.2, 1988, p. 162.
56. WCB, p. 170. See also "Reply [Ad Wykstra]," p. 124.
57. WCB, p. 242.

58. Ibid., p. 360.

59. Ibid., p. 490.

60. Ibid., p. 486.

61. Ibid., p. 492.

62. A point made by Michael Sudduth, "Reformed Epistemology and the Role of Natural Theology," Chapter 4, sections III and IV in *The Reformed Objection to Natural Theology*, unpublished; cited with permission. See also his "Can Religious Unbelief Be Proper Function Rational?" *Faith and Philosophy* 16.3, 1999, pp. 297–314.

63. See WCB, pp. 186–188.

64. The alethic goal is essential because Plantinga acknowledges the existence of what he calls *purely epistemic defeaters*. Even if a belief *B* is central to a person's noetic structure and is therefore functionally immune from defeat, that person still has a pure epistemic defeater since maintaining *B* is caused by nonalethic features of his or her epistemic environment. See WCB, p. 363. He refers to the same concept in "Reply to Beilby's Cohorts" (in *Naturalism Defeated? Essays on Plantinga's Evolutionary Argument Against Naturalism*, ed. James Beilby, Ithaca, NY, and London: Cornell University Press, 2002, under the term *purely alethic defeater*), p. 209.

65. "The repair of the *sensus divinitatis* is a gradual thing, part of the process of sanctification" (personal correspondence; e-mail dated December 20, 2005; cited with permission).

66. "A Christian Life Partly Lived," in *Philosophers Who Believe*, ed. Kelly James Clark, Downers Grove, IL: InterVarsity, p. 65; italics mine.

67. WCB, p. 244 n. 8.

68. This question is raised by Hunter Brown, "Alvin Plantinga and Natural Theology," *International Journal for Philosophy of Religion* 30, August 1991, pp. 1–19.

69. "The Prospects for Natural Theology," *Philosophical Perspectives*, Vol. 5, *Philosophy of Religion*, ed. James Tomberlin, Atascadero, CA: Ridgeview, 1991, pp. 288–289.

70. WCB, pp. 200–201.

71. Moser, p. 371.

72. Ibid., pp. 371–372.

73. WPF, p. 10.

74. WCB, pp. 244, 290–294.

75. *Institutes* III, ii, 7, p. 551.

76. Plantinga's discussion of what is meant by his many references to 'certainty' in WCB is uncharacteristically sparse.

77. For a discussion of epistemic and psychological certainty, see Walter Cerf, "Certainty and Certitude," *Philosophy and Phenomenological Research* 13.4, June 1953, pp. 515–524.

78. *Christian Scholar's Review* 11.3, 1982, pp. 195–196; originally published in *Proceedings of the American Catholic Philosophical Association*, Vol. 54, *Philosophical*

Knowledge, ed. John Brough et al., Washington, DC: Catholic University of America Press, 1980, pp. 49–62.

79. RBG, pp. 74–75.

80. See, for example, Michael Martin, "A Critique of Plantinga's Religious Epistemology," in *Philosophy of Religion: An Anthology*, 2d ed., ed. Louis P. Pojman, Belmont, CA: Wadsworth, 1994; and Jay Van Hook, "Knowledge, Belief, and Reformed Epistemology," *Reformed Journal* 31, 1981, pp. 12–17.

81. WCB, p. 350; italics original.

82. See "Plantinga, Epistemic Permissiveness, and Metaphysical Pluralism," *Religious Studies* 28.4, 1992, pp. 568–569. Christian makes this point about Plantinga's religious epistemology generally considered, not about the Extended A/C Model in particular, because her article precedes the publication of WCB.

83. Christian, p. 569.

84. Ibid. Note Plantinga's declaration regarding the Great Pumpkinite: "there being no Great Pumpkin and no natural tendency to accept beliefs about the Great Pumpkin," RBG, p. 78.

85. In addition, in a recent article, David W. Tien argues that a Confucian could utilize a model parallel in all the relevant aspects to Plantinga's A/C Model to demonstrate the warrant of Confucian beliefs. See his "Warranted Neo-Confucian Belief: Religious Pluralism and the Affections in the Epistemologies of Wang Yangming [1472–1529] and Alvin Plantinga," *International Journal for Philosophy of Religion* 55.1, 2004, pp. 31–55.

86. WCB, p. 350.

87. Plantinga believes that his argumentative methodology is not open to philosophical naturalists because his evolutionary argument against naturalism shows that the conjunction of naturalism and contemporary evolutionary theology cannot rationally be held. See WCB, pp. 350–351, as well as Plantinga's essays in *Naturalism Defeated?* pp. 1–12, 204–275. This argument raises a huge number of highly vexed issues, and even if it is ultimately successful, it is far from obvious that it is. Obviously, however, I cannot try to adjudicate this matter here.

88. WCB, p. xiv.

89. Of course, there are aspects of Plantinga's proposal that are not minimalist. For example, while William Alston in *Perceiving God* limits his discussion to God's perceivable qualities – his love, sustenance, forgiveness – Plantinga's project discusses the whole Christian system of belief: what Plantinga calls the 'great things of the gospel'. So it might be said that Plantinga's methodology is minimalist while his theological content is maximalist. (One might argue that the former is a necessary result of the latter.)

90. A point also raised by Andrew Chignell ("Epistemology for Saints: Alvin Plantinga's Magnum Opus," *Books & Culture*, March/April 2002, p. 21), and Julian Willard, "Plantinga's Epistemology of Religious Belief and the Problem of Religious Diversity," *Heythrop Journal* 44.3, 2003, pp. 275–293, especially pp. 280–282.

91. WCB, p. 248 n.14.

92. Ibid., p. 264.

93. Ibid., p. 260 n. 35.

94. "Reply [to Wykstra]," p. 127.

95. A term borrowed from Andrew Chignell. See his "Epistemology for Saints," p. 20.

96. WCB, p. 201; see also p. 242.

97. Ibid., p. 248.

98. See Plantinga's comments in WCB, p. 291 n. 1.

99. WCB, p. 259.

100. Plantinga makes this explicit in WCD, p. 74, and WCB, p. 10.

101. It's not clear to me whether this assumption is driven by theological or philosophical concerns, or both.

102. DeRose, "Are Christian Beliefs Properly Basic?" unpublished, p. 2; cited with permission.

103. WCB, p. 251.

104. Humphrey Carpenter, *The Inklings: C. S. Lewis, J. R. R. Tolkien, Charles Williams, and Their Friends*, London: George Allen & Unwin, 1978, p. 44.

105. RBG, p. 50.

106. WCD, pp. 195–197.

107. Andrew Dole, "Cognitive Faculties, Cognitive Processes, and the Holy Spirit in Plantinga's Warrant Series," *Faith and Philosophy* 19.1, 2002, pp. 32–33.

108. Keith Lehrer, "Proper Function vs. Systematic Coherence," in *Warrant in Contemporary Epistemology: Essays in Honor of Plantinga's Theory of Knowledge*, ed. Jonathan Kvanvig, Lanham, MD: Rowman & Littlefield, 1996, pp. 31–33.

109. See Michael Bergmann, *Internalism, Externalism, and Epistemic Defeat*, Ph.D. diss., University of Notre Dame, 1997, pp. 102–103.

110. "Respondeo," in *Warrant in Contemporary Epistemology*, ed. Kvanvig, p. 333; italics original.

111. WCB, p. 255.

112. See Plantinga's comments in WCB, p. 258.

113. *Summa Theologiae* II.II, q. 2; cited in Greco, "Review of *Warranted Christian Belief*," p. 465.

114. WCB, 264 n. 43; italics mine. John Calvin himself clearly rejected the notion that believers never waver in their faith (*Institutes*, III, ii, 17; p. 562).

115. WCB, p. 260 n. 35, p. 343.

116. Personal correspondence. E-mail dated December 20, 2005; see also WCB, p. 264 n. 43, p. 280.

117. WCB, p. 244.

118. Ibid., p. 280; italics mine.

119. Ibid., p. 281.

120. This tension does not concern the soteric dimension of faith. Whatever the divine aspect of the act of salvation consists in, it seems to be compatible with the continued presence of the noetic effects of sin, and therefore, the divine act of soteric regeneration is compatible with VB. The tension concerns the cognitive aspects of faith.

121. Plantinga defines a favorable mini-environment for the exercise of one's cognitive faculties as one where those faculties "can be counted on to produce a true belief" (WCB, p. 159; italics removed). This seems odd. Of course, the mini-environment must be favorable with respect to truth, but shouldn't it also be favorable with respect to warrant?

122. The nature of human freedom is a vexed issue, one that I cannot consider here. In referring to 'human freedom', however, I am assuming something like what is often labeled 'libertarian' or 'incompatibilist' freedom.

123. WCB, p. 257.

124. Ibid.

125. See Plantinga's comments in "Internalism, Externalism, Defeaters, and Arguments for Christian Belief," p. 383.

126. Personal correspondence. E-mail dated January 12, 2002; cited with permission.

127. "Internalism, Externalism, Defeaters, and Arguments for Christian Belief," p. 398.

128. Andrew Chignell, "Epistemology for Saints," p. 20.

129. See D. Z. Phillips, "Advice to Philosophers Who Are Christians," *New Blackfriars* 69.820, 1988, pp. 416–430.

7 | Pluralism and Proper Function

KELLY JAMES CLARK

INTRODUCTION

Religious diversity,[1] the fact of a wide variety of religious beliefs and traditions, raises the problem that apparently sincere and equally cognitively capable truth seekers reach widely divergent conclusions about the nature of ultimate, perhaps divine, reality. Religious exclusivists hold that their own religious beliefs are true and, therefore, that all competitor beliefs are false. Critics of exclusivism allege that it smacks of arrogance and intolerance and also seems to make moral and spiritual transformation a matter of luck. If you happen to have been born to a conservative, Christian family in the heart of America, you would have likely been a Christian; but, if you had been born in India, say, more than likely you would have been a Hindu (or in China, an atheist; or in Jordan, a Muslim; or in California, Mickey Mouse).

Just how religious diversity is offered as a defeater for one's warrant for exclusive religious beliefs can be seen in John Hick's defense of religious pluralism, which holds that the multifarious religious beliefs are equally efficacious at moral and spiritual transformation. Hick claims that there is a variety of religious traditions each of which, so far as we can tell, is equally successful in the transformation of human lives. Although they differ in their characterizations both of the goal of human life and of the processes necessary for the attainment of such goals, each of the disparate processes seems nonetheless equally well suited for the goal of the transformation of human lives from self-centeredness to what he terms 'Reality-centeredness'. Salvation/liberation/fulfillment/enlightenment are among the many and most prominent names of this goal. Hick claims that the epistemic grounds for diverse religious beliefs, typically religious experience, are virtually identical: Neither Christianity nor its competitors has any epistemological advantage. Because of the pragmatics of transformation (all religions seem equally successful at transformation) and the alleged identical epistemic grounds of their competing beliefs, Hick contends that no religious belief can stake any claim to moral, spiritual, or epistemic superiority or exclusivity.[2] To claim otherwise is arrogant, intolerant, arbitrary, and unjustified.

Alvin Plantinga, in his defense of Christian exclusivism, responds to these sorts of criticisms.[3] He notes that the Christian belief consists in, roughly,

1. The world was created by an almighty, perfectly good and personal God

and

2. God has provided a unique way of salvation through the incarnation, life, sacrificial death, and resurrection of his divine son.

To accept (1) and (2) and to deny the truth of any beliefs that are incompatible with (1) and (2) is Christian exclusivism.[4] Let us take exclusive Christian belief to be (1), (2) and the rejection of beliefs incompatible with (1) and (2).[5] Plantinga rejects the allegation that Christian belief is unwarranted because awareness of religious diversity provides a defeater for traditional Christian beliefs: Exclusivist Christian belief is not unjustified and may even be warranted even if one is keenly aware of the challenges of religious diversity. In this chapter I will discuss Plantinga's contention that Christian belief can be warranted in such circumstances.

Critics of either Plantinga's views specifically or exclusive Christian belief generally contend that awareness of religious diversity either eliminates warrant or requires the Christian to offer non-question-begging evidence for his or her Christian beliefs. Gary Gutting alleges that Christian belief is unjustified and immoral because a) there is no evidence to support specifically Christian doctrines, and b) there is widespread disagreement about Christian belief. He contends that "believing *p* because its truth is supported by *my* intuition is thus an *epistemological egoism* just as arbitrary and unjustifiable as ethical egoism."[6] The Christian, then, thusly afflicted with (a) and (b) is both epistemologically unjustified and morally pernicious in maintaining his or her Christian belief. J. L. Schellenberg claims that you may hold your perspective to be true only when you can offer non-question-begging justification that competing claims are false. However, he says, the nature of religious diversity is such that no believers can offer such objective justification and therefore are in no position to claim their beliefs to be true.[7]

David Basinger, representative of most Plantinga critics, contends that the burden of proof, in such circumstances, shifts to the exclusivist; he writes: "Unless it can be demonstrated on epistemic grounds that are (or should be) accepted by all rational people that proponents of the competing perspectives are not actually on equal epistemic footing, the exclusivist must consider his challenger on equal epistemic footing and is thus obligated to engage in belief assessment."[8] Basinger maintains that religious exclusivism is a justified position to hold so long as the quest for truth is acknowledged as a basic epistemic duty. He formulates this duty as follows: "If a religious exclusivist wants to maximise truth and avoid error, she is under a *prima facie* obligation to attempt to resolve significant epistemic peer conflict."[9] Although Basinger does not contend that the exclusivist is required in such circumstances to resolve the epistemic conflict, she must at least *attempt* a resolution of the issues raised by awareness of diversity. And Robert McKim writes that "disagreement about an issue or area of inquiry provides reason to think that each side has an obligation to examine beliefs about the issue."[10] Recognized disagreement on matters religious shifts the burden of proof onto the believer. The shifting of the burden of proof is often based on the assumption that the Christian must concede that he or she holds beliefs on the same epistemic grounds as his or her interlocutor: The two interlocutors stand on equal epistemic grounds (religious experience). Even supposing that Christian belief may be prima facie warranted without the support of evidence, critics often claim that hearing the voice of disagreement creates an obligation for the Christian to examine and defend personal beliefs.

Plantinga, however, denies that the Christian theist must concede that she stands on equal epistemic grounds with her interlocutor. She will believe, graced by the Internal Witness of the Holy Spirit, that she "has been epistemically favored in some way," which blessing God has "not so far bestowed upon the dissenters." The Christian will believe, therefore, that in spite of the apparent epistemic parity, she is "in a better position, epistemically speaking,"[11] than those who reject her beliefs.

This chapter will proceed as follows. First, I will briefly consider Plantinga's conception of warrant; I shall assume, for the sake of argument, that his account of warrant is the correct account. Second, I shall consider Plantinga's defense of exclusive Christian belief in the face of the challenge of religious diversity. Third, I shall argue that there is no 'one-size-fits-all' approach to these matters. That is, I shall argue that the claim by Plantinga's critics that all Christians thusly apprised of religious diversity are either unwarranted or under an obligation to provide non-question-begging evidence for their Christian beliefs is wrong. There are a variety of proper epistemic responses that can be made in such circumstances (one size here does not fit all). And I shall argue that Plantinga's paradigmatic Christian, who need not surrender warranted Christian belief when made keenly aware of religious diversity, is one of but many proper epistemic responses that can be made in such circumstances (again, one size does not fit all here). Indeed, in the final section I shall show how, given our less than ideal believing conditions, many Christians who are keenly aware of religious diversity could lose warrant for their Christian beliefs.

Before turning to Plantinga's defense of Christian exclusivism, let us first briefly consider his account of warranted Christian belief.

WARRANT AND PROPER FUNCTION

Plantinga calls the special property that turns true belief into knowledge 'warrant.' Very roughly put, a belief B has *warrant* for one if and only if B is a) produced by one's properly functioning cognitive faculties b) in circumstances to which those faculties are designed to apply; in addition, c) those faculties must be designed for the purpose of producing true beliefs.[12] So, for instance, my belief that *there is a butterfly flitting around me* is warranted if a*) it is produced by my properly functioning perceptual faculties (not by, say, wish fulfillment or drugs) and if b*) no one is tricking me by dangling an exact painted replica of a butterfly in front of me[13] (that person has messed up my cognitive environment); and, finally, c*) our perceptual faculties have been designed for the purpose of producing true beliefs.

Belief in (1) may be warranted, according to Plantinga, if it is produced by a properly functioning cognitive faculty in the appropriate circumstances. He famously contends that belief in God may be properly basic – a noninferential (foundational) but justified belief. The properly functioning cognitive faculty relevant to producing (1) is, following Calvin, the *sensus divinitatis*. The *sensus divinitatis* produces belief in God in the appropriate circumstances, such as when one is on a mountain top and taken with the majestic glory of it all, or when one feels guilty and unclean for all that one has done or when one hears a beautiful piece of music. In those circumstances, the belief that God created all of this, or that God is good and beautiful, may rightly well up inside oneself without support or even consideration of an argument. Although Plantinga initially denigrated and even castigated theistic arguments,[14] he has since come to believe that such arguments are likewise adequate to warrant belief in 1.[15]

Plantinga contends that one's Christian beliefs may be warranted if the believer meets the relevant warranting conditions. He argues that, on the available historical evidence, the probability that the full panoply of Christian beliefs (including the incarnation and resurrection of Jesus) is true is quite low, too low to warrant Christian belief on the basis of that evidence.

However, historical evidence is not the only way of warranting Christian beliefs. Plantinga contends that it is possible that God has given us information about himself and his redemptive plans in the Bible and that God endorses that information through the internal testimony of the Holy Spirit. The Holy Spirit works in our hearts (passions and will) to help us come to accept and trust in the truths of the gospel. The Holy Spirit effects the proper cognitive (belief, knowledge) and affective (trust, commitment, gratitude) attitudes in the heart/minds of Christian believers. Plantinga does not contend that Christian beliefs are warranted but that they can be warranted if there is a God who is reconciling the world to himself in Christ Jesus and who has sent the Holy Spirit to open our hearts and minds to God. That is, Christian belief can be warranted if (1) and (2) are true.[16]

Plantinga, it should be noted, is an epistemological externalist. To understand externalism, let us first consider epistemological internalism.[17] The central contention of internalism is that the justifying conditions of a belief are somehow internal to the believing agent; whatever it is that justifies belief is something to which the believer has fairly direct cognitive access. Justification is a property of beliefs that can be 'seen' or 'grasped' simply by looking within, by carefully examining one's own beliefs. If any of one's beliefs fail to have the right sort of justificational luster or aura, they ought to be discarded. Plantinga rejects internalism because one's beliefs can have all of the internal luster necessary for maximally justified beliefs yet still lack knowledge. For beliefs to be warranted to the degree that constitutes knowledge, external conditions must obtain. But that places the relevant warranting conditions external to the mind. Note briefly the portions of Plantinga's definition that are not within one's immediate or direct cognitive purview – whether or not one's faculties are functioning properly, whether or not one's faculties are designed by God, whether or not one's faculties are designed for the production of true beliefs, whether or not one is using one's faculties in the environment intended for their use. We cannot determine if our beliefs are warranted simply by attending to our beliefs. Warranted belief depends crucially upon whether or not conditions obtain that are not under our direct rational purview. Indeed, with respect to Christian belief, he concedes that he has not demonstrated that it is warranted, only that it might possibly be warranted if Christian belief is true. But he has not, arguing that it can't be done, offered a demonstration or proof of Christian belief.[18] So, with respect to Christian belief, the relevant warranting conditions may be satisfied, but they exceed our cognitive access. We can know (1) and (2) without being able to show or tell that we know (1) and (2).

Let us assume that Plantinga's accounts of warrant and warranted Christian belief are true.[19] Let us now turn to his defense of exclusive Christian belief.

PLANTINGA'S DEFENSE OF EXCLUSIVISM

Let us canvass Plantinga's defense of Christian exclusivity from the various charges that (1) and (2) are unjustified or unwarranted when one is made aware of religious diversity.

Historical Conditionedness. The argument from historical conditionedness alleges that if we had been born at a different time or place, we wouldn't have been a Christian or perhaps even a theist. The underlying claim is that our doxastic lives are governed more by conditioned, historical accident than by special access to unconditioned, transcendent truth and so are unwarranted or irrational. Insofar as Christian belief is thusly historically conditioned, it is, therefore, unwarranted or irrational. This argument does not purport to refute Christian belief ((1) and (2)); rather it purports to undermine the rationality or warrant of Christian belief.

Plantinga simply concedes the obvious truth of historical conditionedness while denying its alleged epistemic import. He notes that it is in general true that had people been born in different times and places, they would have believed different things. But he goes on to point out that there are no devastating epistemic consequences from the admission of conditionedness. Consider the following examples:

> Had Einstein been born in the eighteenth century, he would not have believed special relativity; nothing follows about special relativity. Many now think it is wrong to treat someone with hatred or contempt or indifference on the mere grounds that they are of a different race: their views are not automatically unwarranted just because they might have believed otherwise if they had been brought up in Nazi Germany or ancient Sparta. Perhaps we should think, instead, that if they had been brought up in Nazi Germany or ancient Sparta, they wouldn't have known something they *do* know.[20]

Plantinga has long argued that warrant is relative to time, place, and circumstance. But the fact that one might have believed something in different circumstances does not undermine the warrant that one might have for believing it now. For example, although I now see that there's a book on my desk, it surely is not unwarranted by virtue of the fact that if I were in a different epistemic situation (say on the top of the Grand Teton), I would have believed something entirely different. Or suppose I believe now that it's wrong to discriminate on the basis of skin color; my warrant is not diminished by the fact that if I had been born in the U.S. South in 1852, I likely would have believed otherwise. The bottom line: if the relevant warranting conditions are met and my belief is true, my belief is warranted.

Moral Perniciousness. Some claim that maintaining exclusive religious beliefs in the face of sincere practitioners of other religions is morally pernicious. If, so the argument goes, one's beliefs cannot be supported by evidence (and so one lacks arguments to persuade dissenters), one holds one's beliefs arbitrarily. But if one's beliefs are held arbitrarily (and there are no arguments to persuade dissenters), then in denigrating the beliefs of those with whom one disagrees, one is thereby being egoistic, arrogant, or prideful. While conceding that believers must consider themselves privileged (they believe the truth and those who disagree with them believe what is false), Plantinga contends that this charge creates a moral dilemma: by demonstrating that continuing to believe what others disagree about is impossible to avoid; if such practices are morally pernicious, then everyone must be morally pernicious. It you reject, withhold, or accept (1) and (2), there are always people with whom you disagree. So, in affirming, denying, withholding belief in (1) and (2), the pluralist places one in a moral dilemma: No matter what one's propositional attitude is, one is thereby arrogant or egoistic. Plantinga's final argument faces the charges of moral perniciousness straight on. Plantinga contends that arrogance and egoism are more properly applied to persons, not to beliefs:

> I must concede that there are a variety of ways in which I can be and have been intellectually arrogant and egoistic; I have certainly fallen into this vice in the past, will no doubt fall into it in the future, and am not free of it now. Still, am I really arrogant and egoistic just by virtue of believing something I know others don't believe, where I can't show them that I am right? Suppose I think the matter over, consider the objections as carefully as I can, realize that I am finite and furthermore a sinner, certainly no better than those with whom I disagree, and indeed inferior both morally and intellectually to many who do not believe what I do. But suppose it *still* seems clear to me that the proposition in question is true: am I really immoral in continuing to believe it?[21]

The best one can do in such a situation, both epistemically and morally, is to continue to hold one's belief in all due epistemic and moral humility. That is all that can be asked or expected of finite, human believers. Plantinga holds no moral regard for those who, in such circumstances, use such beliefs as a source of moral or spiritual pride. But people are not morally or spiritually prideful simply by virtue of holding beliefs that others disagree with.

Diversity and Probability. This objection to exclusive Christian belief contends that it is unjustified to affirm (1) and (2) in opposition to one's religious competitors. The probability of Christian belief, even if initially judged to be more likely than its religious competitors, might be less than the combined probability of its competitors (it is more likely that the denial of one's religious beliefs – all of the competitor religious beliefs disjoined with the logical connective 'or' – is much greater than the probability of one's religious belief). The initial probability in favor of any particular religious belief would be outweighed by the likelihood that another religious belief might be right. This sort of consideration should lead one to believe that the probability of one's particular belief is too low to merit acceptance.[22]

Plantinga rejects this line of reasoning because it commits a category mistake: It assumes that Christian belief is a hypothesis that requires the evidential support of some body of data or some set of beliefs. But what is the relevant body of evidence with respect to which Christian belief must be judged more probable? Plantinga notes, quite correctly, that "if it is the set of beliefs *actually accepted* by the believer, then, of course, the probability of her beliefs will be 1."[23] Suppose someone contends that there is some other, privileged subset of one's beliefs with respect to which Christian belief must be probable; that is, Christian belief is rational only if it is supported by some more fundamental propositions. But that assumes what Plantinga has argued powerfully against for the past twenty-five years. Many, many beliefs, even belief in God, are properly basic if they are produced immediately in the appropriate circumstances by our (properly functioning) cognitive faculties. They should not be treated as hypothetical beliefs, held tentatively, if at all, until and if the evidence is shown to support them. Christian belief is perfectly rational, if Plantinga's argument is correct, if accepted in a basic, that is, noninferential, way.

Diversity and Warrant. We shall, following Plantinga, take Gutting as representative of those who hold that awareness of religious diversity undermines the rationality or justification of Christian belief. Recall Gutting's claim that Christian belief is unjustified and immoral because a) there is no evidence to support specifically Christian doctrines and b) there is widespread disagreement about Christian belief. Plantinga's initial critique of Gutting's view proceeds by way of counterexample. Suppose that you are accused of a crime for which you had ample motive, opportunity, and ability. However, when the crime occurred you were taking a solitary hike in the mountains (which you can't prove to anyone else). Your belief that you were hiking is a) not based on an argument, b) can't be proven to those who've charged you with the crime, and c) is disputed by others. By Gutting's criterion, your belief is unjustified and immoral. But are you really guilty of epistemological egoism? Surely not. Because you remember that you were hiking in the mountains, you have a source of knowledge not available to those with whom you disagree. You may be in the minority of one on this belief, but you are surely not an epistemological egoist for holding it: Indeed, your belief is morally permissible, even warranted, in such circumstances.

But, in the case of the diversity of religious beliefs, aren't we required to treat similar cases similarly? Plantinga's *alethic* response to this is that the Christian won't believe that those beliefs incompatible with hers are similar because she believes them to be false. But one might reply that the issue is not alethic parity; it is rather *epistemic* parity. Epistemic parity is

> parity with respect to what is internally available to the believer. What is internally available includes, for example, detectable relationships between the belief in question and other beliefs you hold; so internal parity would include parity of propositional evidence. What is internally available to the believer also includes the *phenomenology* that goes with the belief in question: the *sensuous* phenomenology, and also the nonsensuous phenomenology involved, in doxastic evidence, in the belief's just having the feel of being *right*.[24]

But the Christian, on this account, will not believe that her beliefs are on an epistemic par with those beliefs incompatible with hers, for her internal markers with respect to her Christian beliefs provide doxastic evidence for her: Christian beliefs seem to her to be true; they have the right phenomenology of seeming. And the beliefs she rejects will have the internal markers of false beliefs.

But perhaps the critic means to suggest that the relevant epistemic parity is that the phenomenology that accompanies Christian belief (for the Christian) is the same as the phenomenology for those who hold non-Christian religious beliefs (for the non-Christian). For the sake of argument, Plantinga concedes that "those of a different religious tradition have the same sort of internally available markers – evidence, phenomenology, and the like – for their beliefs as the Christian has for [Christian beliefs]".[25] His concession here is tempered: He does not concede that the beliefs of the interlocutors are on an epistemic par, all things considered. Rather, they are on an epistemic par only in the sense that the beliefs have the same 'internally available markers'.

Consider the following example. Suppose I think racism is wrong and you think it is right. I might agree that our beliefs share the same internally available markers, but does it follow from that that I must believe that our beliefs are on an epistemic par, all things considered, and that I must give up or withhold my nonracist belief until I learn of a good argument to support it (one that should, if you were functioning properly, convince you)? Surely not, because I don't really think that our beliefs are on an epistemic par, all things considered.[26] I will likely think that you've made a mistake (culpably or nonculpably). And the same will go for the Christian believer. Plantinga writes:

> [The believer] may agree that she and those who dissent are equally con-vinced of the truth of their belief, and even that they are internally on a par, that the internally available markers are similar, or relevantly similar. Still, she must think that there is an important epistemic difference: she thinks that somehow the other person has made a mistake, or has a blind spot, or hasn't been wholly attentive, or hasn't received some grace she has, or is blinded by ambition or pride or mother love or something else; she must think that she has access to a source of warranted belief the other lacks. If the believer concedes that she *doesn't* have any special source of knowledge or true belief with respect to Christian belief – no *sensus divini-tatis*, no internal instigation of the Holy Spirit, no teaching by a church inspired and protected from error by the Holy Spirit, nothing not available to those who disagree with her – *then*, perhaps, she can properly be charged with an arbitrary egoism, and *then*, perhaps, she will have a defeater for her Christian belief. But why should she concede these things? She will ordi-narily think (or at least *should* ordinarily think) that there are indeed sources of warranted belief that issue in these beliefs.[27]

Although her Christian beliefs may be mistaken, if she nonculpably believes them, she thereby is relieved of the charge of epistemological egoism. Her belief in the internal instigation of the Holy Spirit entails that she will nonarbitrarily and nonegoistically believe that she is in a better epistemic position than her interlocutors.[28] She may be *mistaken* in these beliefs, Plantinga contends, but she is not *culpable* for holding them. So she can be rational and even justified in holding her Christian beliefs.[29] And, if Plantinga's account of warranted Christian belief is true, then those who accept Christian belief, under the specified warranting conditions, are in an epistemically advantaged position (not of their own doing and so no source of pride, arrogance, or egoism); hence, their belief is neither on an epistemic par with their interlocutors' nor is it arbitrary. If Christian belief is true, it is probably warranted. The critic's claim that all Christians thusly apprised of belief competitors but lacking evidence in support of (1) and (2) are unwarranted, unjustified, or irrational is untenable. Plantinga has offered a model of warranted Christian belief in which Christian belief can be warranted in the face of belief competitors, even if the Christian should lack a compelling argument in favor of (1) and (2).

DECREASING WARRANT

Suppose we concede Plantinga's point, that if Christian belief is true, then it may be warranted in spite of widespread disagreement about (1) and (2) by sincere truth seekers. If Christians' cognitive faculties are working appropriately in the environment for which they were created (and are appropriately truth-aimed), then their Christian beliefs can be warranted. And if Christians' faculties are sufficiently enlivened by the instigation of the Holy Spirit (and Christianity is true), then their Christian beliefs can be warranted even in the face of widespread disagreement. The circumstances under which this will work include but are not restricted to the following: All of the relevant warranting conditions must be satisfied and the Christian's epistemic situation must be favorable; that is, she must nonculpably be in a situation that is such that the internal markers for her Christian belief are on an epistemic par or stronger than what she adjudges of the beliefs of religious competitors, and she (believes she) has access to a source of knowledge (warrant?) that her interlocutor does not. In such circumstances, warranted Christian belief is possible in the face of religious diversity. It's possible, but is it necessary or even likely?

Plantinga routinely speaks of '*the* (Christian) believer' throughout his defense of Christian belief in the face of religious diversity. The Christian believes this and asserts that; the believer will deny this and reject that. For example, in response to Gutting, he writes: "In each of these cases, the believer in question doesn't really think the beliefs in question are on a relevant epistemic par." He goes on to say that "she [the Christian believer] must think that there is an epistemic difference".[30] One gets the impression from the body of his argument that no Christian, faced with belief competitors, will find her Christian beliefs difficult to maintain; nor will her rationality, justification, or warrant decrease. *The* Christian will triumph over the challenge of religious diversity because of what she must think.

But, once again, Plantinga's response, like his critic's contentions, is not a one-size-fits-all response (we might think that Plantinga's shoe fits only the ideal Christian believer). There is a variety of Christian believers affected in a variety of ways by awareness of religious diversity, eliciting a variety of equally valid responses. Plantinga has set up one situation that provides a model of what a Christian could or even must think if her belief is to be warranted in the face of religious diversity. But how many Christians are in that epistemic situation?

Plantinga himself concedes that few of us may be in the ideal believing situation described in his lengthy defense of warranted Christian belief. While noting that Christian belief can, if true, have warrant sufficient for knowledge, he concedes: "Of course this hardly settles the issue as to whether Christian belief (even if true) has or can have warrant in the circumstances in which most of us actually find ourselves."[31] The focus of his book then shifts to a consideration of many of the difficulties for Christian belief that the Christian believer typically faces. Plantinga further concedes, at the end of his dismissal of the challenge of religious diversity, that religious diversity need not but could create epistemic problems for the Christian. He writes:

> But don't the realities of religious pluralism count for *anything*? Is there nothing at all to the claims of the pluralists? Could that really be right? Of course not. For at least some Christian believers, an awareness of the enormous variety of human religious responses does seem to reduce the level of confidence in their own Christian belief. It doesn't or needn't do so by way of an *argument*. Indeed, there aren't any respectable arguments from the proposition that many apparently devout people around the world dissent from (1) and (2) to the conclusion that (1) and (2) are false or can be accepted only at the cost of moral or epistemic deficiency. Nevertheless, knowledge of others who think differently can reduce one's degree of belief in Christian teaching. From a Christian perspective, this situation of religious pluralism is itself a manifestation of our miserable human condition; and it may indeed deprive Christians of some of the comfort and peace the Lord has promised his followers.[32]

In addition, Plantinga concedes that awareness of religious diversity can (but need not) reduce one's warrant and, hence, can reduce one's claim to know Christian belief. In what follows I shall describe at least one way in which religious diversity can reduce one's warrant.

As noted, Plantinga concedes that in some cases awareness of religious diversity can reduce one's degree of belief in (1) and (2). In this section,

I explore the phenomenology of belief for a Christian who, in the face of religious diversity, is faced with decreasing warrant and even unbelief. I draw clues from Plantinga's text itself that support this phenomenology. In the preceding quotation, Plantinga spoke of our miserable human condition, which "may . . . deprive Christians of some of the comfort and peace the Lord has promised his followers." This passage is ambiguous. It may be that we are nonculpably in a miserable epistemic condition: The world is religiously ambiguous without sufficient clues to settle the various religious options. Another way of putting this is that the available evidence (and here I construe evidence quite broadly to include the grounds of basic beliefs) underdetermines religious options. If the world is religiously ambiguous, underdetermining one's religious beliefs, then we are indeed in a miserable human condition. Or Plantinga, following Calvin, might attribute our misery to our own culpability: We are in an epistemic darkness of our own choosing; one of the noetic effects of sin is morally culpable religious doubt and despair. From the inside and from the available evidence, it may be difficult or even impossible to tell if religious difference is due to a fundamentally ambiguous world or to the noetic effects of sin. Let us consider the belief journey of, say, Jennifer, as she becomes increasingly aware of 'our miserable human condition'.

How might Jennifer's exclusive Christian beliefs be negatively affected by her increasing awareness of religious diversity? The first thing to note is that there is no such thing as *the* epistemic situation with respect to the Christian believer. Each believer is different, and so each believer's epistemic situation will be different. In each case, one's epistemic situation will depend, in part, on one's degree of belief in (1) and (2), as well as one's degree of belief in the counterclaims.[33] What precisely are the counterclaims? They are beliefs that explicitly or implicitly deny the truth of (1) and (2), including, for example, the central claims of Islam, Judaism, Buddhism, or Hinduism.[34] How are these beliefs presented to Jennifer, and what claim do they have to her serious epistemic consideration? Since they are not Jennifer's first-person beliefs, they are presented to her through the testimony of others, her Buddhist and Muslim friends.[35] Claims thusly presented must be weighed against a host of background beliefs or assumptions (including one's general beliefs about the ways of the world and the sincerity of the speaker). In Jennifer's case, it is precisely the moral character of the (surprisingly upright) speaker that is so troubling to her; she believes, as do many Christians, that we are dead in our trespasses and sins and can only be morally and spiritually enlivened by the work of the Holy Spirit. Jennifer has befriended both a Muslim and a Buddhist and has become a sympathetic listener to their stories. Here she finds herself face-to-face with her non-Christian friends who, near as she can tell, are at least as, if not more, morally upright than she is.

Let us suppose, with Plantinga, that Christian belief is true, that Jennifer's belief in God is initially warranted by her properly functioning *sensus divinitatis*, and that her Christian belief is initially warranted by the internal instigation of the Holy Spirit.[36] Does it follow from this that Jennifer will hold (1) and (2) to a sufficient degree to outweigh the testimonial evidence against her beliefs? That is, since warrant is defeasible, can Jennifer's warrant be decreased by the testimony of those who reject (1) and (2)? Again, we cannot speak here, as Plantinga typically does, of *the* Christian believer. We are, after all, considering *Jennifer* who is trying to do her best in *her* miserable human condition. The best that can be expected of Jennifer is for her to examine her internal markers and determine if the markers for (1) and (2) are strong enough to resist the incursion of beliefs contrary to (1) and (2) offered in the testimony of others. In Jennifer's case, these circumstances serve to reduce her warranted Christian beliefs. How might this happen in Jennifer's case?

Consider Jennifer's generic belief in God (that the world was created by an almighty, all-knowing, perfectly good, personal being). Let us suppose, as Plantinga contends, that Jennifer's belief in God can be warranted in two ways: by one's properly functioning *sensus divinitatis* and/or by theistic arguments. As she comes in contact with sincere practitioners of other religions, she begins to think that there might be empirical evidence against the *sensus divinitatis*. As she studies her belief competitors, she becomes aware that while some religions do maintain belief in God as described here, others, such as Hinduism, countenance a panoply of gods, while still others, including various forms of Buddhism, deny the existence of gods; belief in a pantheon of gods seems endemic in primitive cultures,[37] and some worldviews, such as various forms of Daoism, believe that there is no ultimate spiritual or personal Reality but that Reality nonetheless exerts a moral force.[38] Jennifer entertains but is increasingly suspicious of Plantinga's contention that everyone has a sense of God that it is quite often suppressed or distorted by sin. She finds it increasingly difficult to maintain that people culpably reject (1) the more she personally comes in contact with sincere practitioners of other religions who, from all appearances, are more spiritually and morally advanced than she is. Thus aware, appeals to the noetic effects of sin seem to Jennifer to be self-deceptive, hopelessly ad hoc or somehow circular. In addition, theistic arguments begin to seem question-begging, quaint, and parochial.

In order to shore up her flagging belief in (1), she turns to Plantinga, who himself gives her reason to distrust beliefs that are not widely shared; he writes: "Philosophy itself is a good candidate for a certain degree of measured skepticism: in view of the enormous diversity of competing philosophical views, one can hardly claim with a straight face that what we have in philosophy is *knowledge*; the diversity of views makes it unlikely that the relevant segments of the design plan are sufficiently reliable."[39] Jennifer thinks, 'Why not say the same of religious beliefs? At any rate, why not say the same of religious belief if one were to judge as sincere the moral and spiritual attainments of practitioners of other religions?' All of these considerations work on Jennifer, reducing the vivacity of her internal markers concerning belief in God.

With respect to distinctly Christian belief, Jennifer finds herself in a similarly unsettling situation.[40] She looks for independent, fairly compelling evidence of the existence of God and the truth of Christian belief to increase her confidence in theistic and Christian belief. She asks not 'Is belief in God warranted?' but 'Is there any reason to think that God exists and that Jesus was his Son?' She carefully reads Warranted Christian Belief where Plantinga argues that on the available historical evidence, Christian belief is unlikely.[41] So she finds little relief from her growing doubts about (1) and (2). And when presented with a historical case for Christianity, appeals to the evidence ring hollow; they seem to her more like special pleading than compelling argument.[42] Jennifer prays nightly for the Holy Spirit to enliven her flagging convictions, to give her a sign, or to direct her to some convincing evidence. But her prayers are in vain. And as she continues to speak with practitioners of other religions, she is increasingly convinced of their sincerity. She finds she can no longer believe that her Christian convictions have anything special to recommend them over the convictions of her non-Christian friends; her internal markers are on an epistemic par with those of her friends. And she thinks it self-interest or self-deception to believe that she has a special source or divine knowledge that her friends lack.

Jennifer's journey toward decreased conviction began with Plantinga's assumption that her Christian beliefs were warranted, at least initially, by the *sensus divinitatis* and the instigation of the Holy Spirit. But her experience was different from 'the Christian' of which Plantinga speaks, the paradigmatic believer in ideal conditions. Jennifer's journey was through less than ideal conditions, which, for many, constitute the real conditions within which they find themselves. What began as prima facie warranted became prima facie unwarranted. Her current lack of warrant is prima facie as well. Should the veracity of her internal markers increase through, say, the work of the Holy Spirit or consideration of evidence for (1) and (2), to the point where it exceeds her judgments of the internal markers of her non-Christian friends, then her belief may again be warranted.[43] But lacking sufficient convictions, her exclusive Christian beliefs may be rational and even justified, but they are scarcely warranted.

CONCLUSION

There are a variety of responses to the problems that religious diversity raises for exclusive Christian belief, ranging from atheism to radical denial of any truth in other religions. And many of these responses can involve a legitimate increase or decrease of warrant. It is simply not the case, as Plantinga's critics contend, that warrant for Christian belief must decrease in the face of religious diversity. And it's not the case that warrant can or will remain the same for all Christian believers in similar situations. I do not offer Jennifer as the paradigmatic case or model of genuine Christian belief in the face of religious diversity. Jennifer's case may not be typical of many Western Christians because most Western Christians have little sustained personal contact with, say, Muslims or Buddhists. It's difficult to make judgments about sincerity and moral and spiritual progress on the basis of sensational news stories, reading texts of other religions, or in chance encounters at the airport. Only when one meets and gets to know well a Muslim or a Buddhist is one in a position to make judgments of sincere moral and spiritual progress. I have shown how the facts of religious diversity may work in the life of a religious believer in such a way that they reduce warrant. Again, I have not argued anything that Plantinga hasn't already conceded; he would agree that things could work this way but need not. But, given his talk about the 'the Christian' throughout his essay, one might get the impression that his few final paragraphs, which concede that religious diversity could have serious effects on the Christian believer, are simply throw-offs or rare exceptions. I have developed epistemic circumstances in which such doxastic troubles seem more likely.

Notes

1. I use the term 'religious diversity' rather than 'religious pluralism' throughout the chapter. I reserve 'religious pluralism' for John Hick's Kantian explanation of religious diversity.

2. Hick's quasi-Kantian explanation of religious diversity affirms a plurality of transformational responses to the ultimate divine reality. Believing that the divine Reality "cannot be encompassed in human terms," he distinguishes "the Real *an sich* (in him/her/itself) and the Real as humanly experienced and thought" (John Hick, *Problems of Religious Pluralism*, New York: St. Martin's Press, 1985, p. 39). This divine Reality is capable of being experienced in a multitude of ways. The Kantian distinction between phenomena and noumena is apparent. We can have access to the phenomenal world of religious experience, of appearances as categorized by human cognitive powers, but not to the divine noumenal world. What we do not, indeed cannot, encounter in these experiences is Reality in itself. Religious assertions are relegated to the realm of appearance.

3. Plantinga has written two primary essays on the challenges that religious diversity poses to exclusive Christian belief. The first essay, "Pluralism: A Defense of Religious Exclusivism" (in Thomas D. Senor, ed., *The Rationality of Belief and the Plurality of Faith*, Ithaca and London: Cornell University Press, 1995) was expanded and developed with the main ideas intact. We will focus on the expanded essay, "Postmodernism and Pluralism" (in Alvin Plantinga, *Warranted Christian Belief*, New York and Oxford: Oxford University Press, 2000, pp. 422–457).

4. Plantinga adds provisos that one is an exclusivist only if one is keenly aware of religious diversity such that it has given one pause to question one's Christian belief and also if one believes that there are no demonstrative arguments to settle the truth of religion (Plantinga, "Postmodernism and Pluralism," p. 440).

5. This may be purely pedantic. To believe *p* is to believe that *p* is true. And if one believes that *p* is true, then one will believe that the denial or contrary of *p* is false. Hence, if one believes (1) and (2), one will also reject propositions that are incompatible with (1) and (2). However, disbelief in propositions that are incompatible with (1) and (2) may not be explicit. One may affirm (1) and (2) yet merely dispositionally reject propositions incompatible with (1) and (2). Our term of art, exclusive Christian belief, is reserved for the belief of those who believe (1) and (2) and have explicitly entertained the proposition *beliefs incompatible with (1) and (2) are false*. So exclusive Christian belief is the explicit, not merely dispositional, belief in (1) and (2) and in the rejection of beliefs incompatible with (1) and (2).

6. Gutting as quoted in Plantinga, "Postmodernism and Pluralism," p. 449.

7. John Schellenberg, "Religious Experience and Religious Diversity: A Reply to Alston," in K. Meeker and P. Quinn, eds., *The Philosophical Challenge of Religious Diversity*, New York: Oxford University Press, 2000, p. 213.

8. David Basinger, *Religious Diversity: A Philosophical Assessment*, Aldershot: Ashgate, 2002, pp. 26–27.

9. Ibid., p. 11.

10. Robert McKim, *Religious Ambiguity and Religious Diversity*, Oxford: Oxford University Press, 2001, p. 140.

11. Alvin Plantinga, "Ad Hick," *Faith and Philosophy* 14.3, 1997, p. 296.

12. I have stated this succinctly, roughly, partially, and without nuance. For a full discussion, see Plantinga, *Warranted Christian Belief*, pp. 153–161.

13. Artist Conrad Q. Bakker, one of my former colleagues, held a 'garage sale' that consisted entirely of his artistic renditions of garage sale stuff, including, for example, typewriters, exercise bicycle, and tools. Many visitors were fooled, some (looking for a bargain on real hammers) unhappily.

14. See Alvin Plantinga and Nicholas Wolstertorff, eds., *Faith and Rationality: Reason and Belief in God*, Notre Dame, IN, and London: University of Notre Dame Press, 1983, pp. 63 ff.

15. For Plantinga's most recent discussion of theistic arguments, see Kelly James Clark, *Readings in the Philosophy of Religion*, Peterborough, Ontario: Broadview Press, 2000, pp. 126–137.

16. And so the only way to argue that they can't be thusly warranted is to demonstrate that Christian belief is false.

17. Plantinga discusses internalism and externalism in Alvin Plantinga, *Warrant: The Current Debate*, New York and Oxford: Oxford University Press, 1993, chap. 1.

18. Plantinga, *Warranted Christian Belief*, pp. 271–280.

19. Plantinga's account of warrant has been criticized and defended in Jonathan Kvanvig, ed., *Warrant in Contemporary Epistemology*, Lanham, MD: Rowman & Littlefield, 1996.

20. Plantinga, *Warranted Christian Belief*, p. 428.

21. Ibid., p. 447.

22. Ibid., pp. 441–442; see also Schellenberg, "Religious Experience and Religious Diversity," p. 147.

23. Plantinga, *Warranted Christian Belief*, p. 442.

24. Ibid., p. 451.

25. Ibid., p. 452.

26. This example is a lot more persuasive from the perspective of nonracist beliefs. It should be noted that it would work in a similar fashion if told from the perspective of this racist. This sort of example, from, say, the perspective of the racist, is often offered as a counterexample to Plantingian epistemology. It is precisely at this point that some would demand a compelling argument for racist beliefs. David Silver, in his critique of Plantinga, contends that Plantinga's justification here is circular and that warranting conditions require independent evidence. He argues: "[Exclusivists] should provide independent evidence for the claim that they have a special source of religious knowledge . . . or they should relinquish their exclusivist religious beliefs" (David Silver, "Religious Experience and the Facts of Religious Pluralism," *International Journal for Philosophy of Religion* 49.1, 2001, p. 11). He rejects Plantinga's example here because the racist is required, on his view, to support his belief with independent evidence (presumably the same would hold for the antiracist). The justified antiracist, he optimistically opines, will believe that he or she possesses a moral proof that would persuade a properly functioning racist. I seriously doubt that racists simply (and

culpably?) ignore the empirical evidence (say, that members of another race are dumber than they are) and so doubt that the issue of racism can be compelled by independent moral arguments. I suspect that people are racists because that is what they've been taught and, in the face of empirical evidence contrary to some racist beliefs, will simply believe that members of another race are not, perhaps for nonempirical reasons, fully human and therefore fully deserving of human rights. I take it that moral disagreement is interminable precisely because we have no independent moral grounds to settle many moral matters (including, for example, abortion, euthanasia, and racism). I do believe that racists are more likely to change if they should meet and get to know a member of another race than if presented with empirical arguments. But my belief that they are more likely to change in such circumstances is more a psychological than epistemological claim. However, in the next section I will argue that such psychological factors can produce epistemically relevant results.

27. Plantinga, *Warranted Christian Belief*, p. 453.

28. Silver contends that in such a situation, on Plantinga's own epistemological assumptions, one thereby acquires via testimony an undefeated defeater of Christian belief. One might think, as Silver has charged, that the Christian in this position should withhold belief when a belief produced by testimony from a person one believes to be sincere contradicts a basic belief (assuming there's no independent evidence to settle the matter). However, Plantinga's moral examples suggest that Plantinga is more properly attuned to how one adjudicates conflicting beliefs. He seems to suggest that in such cases, one must compare the strength of inclination to one's basic belief to the strength of inclination to accept the testimony of the person one disagrees with; the strongest inclination wins.

29. It does so because warrant comes in degrees, which degrees are measured by one's degree of belief. Plantinga writes: "In general (for a person S with properly functioning faculties in an appropriate environment...) the more firmly S believes p, the more likely it is that p is true" (Alvin Plantinga, *Warrant and Proper Function*, New York and Oxford: Oxford University Press, 1993, p. 18). In some cases, the degree to which one's Christian belief is warranted will be equal to or less than the degree of belief one has in the sincerity and veracity of those with whom one disagrees. Let us proceed here by way of example. Recall the person accused of a crime in one location but who remembers hiking alone in the mountains many miles away at the same time; this person had the motive and ability to commit the crime and is widely believed to have committed it by those who've examined the evidence. Is the accused warranted in her belief that she did not commit the crime in the face of a) widespread disagreement and b) evidence against her belief? Plantinga contends, quite rightly, that the accused is warranted because the internal markers of her memory belief vastly exceed the internal markers of her belief that other, sincere truth seekers disagree with her on an important matter and in the evidence against her:

> No doubt there are subsets S of her total set of beliefs with respect to which Christian belief is indeed improbable; perhaps, in fact, it is improbable with respect to the rest of what she believes (supposing, for the moment, that there is some neat way to segregate

her Christian belief from her other beliefs). But how is that relevant? The same will be true, no doubt, with respect to many other beliefs she holds in perfect rationality. She is playing bridge and is dealt all the sevens and eights. The odds against this are pretty formidable; there are many alternatives that are at least equally probable; does that mean that her belief that she was dealt all the sevens and eights is irrational? Of course not. The reason, clearly, is that this belief has a source of warrant independent of any it gets by way of its probabilistic relations to her other beliefs. The same goes for Christian belief. If there is a source of warrant for Christian belief that is independent of any it acquires by way of probabilistic relations to other beliefs, then the fact (if it is a fact) that Christian belief isn't particularly likely with respect to those others doesn't show anything of much interest. It certainly doesn't provide a defeater for Christian belief. (Plantinga, *Warranted Christian Belief*, p. 442).

Her accusers, on the other hand, may be rational and justified in holding their beliefs; what makes their beliefs rational or justified is that the internal markers of the evidence and its believed bearing on the conclusion are quite strong (stronger than the counterevidence). The accused can be warranted in maintaining her belief while the accusers can be rational and justified in rejecting that very same belief. The best one can do in such situations is accede to the strongest internal markers of one's beliefs (even in cases of being nonculpably mistaken about the truth of one's beliefs).

30. Plantinga, *Warranted Christian Belief*, p. 453.

31. Ibid., p. 357.

32. Ibid., p. 456.

33. Jerome Gellman concurs; reevaluation of foundational religious beliefs is not required. When faced with the apparent defeater of religious diversity, the exclusivist can employ the G. E. Moore shift and, holding firm to his or her foundational religious belief, rationally reject the competing claim (Jerome Gellman, "Religious Diversity and the Epistemic Justification of Religious Belief," *Faith and Philosophy* 10.3, 1993, pp. 345–364, and "Epistemic Peer Conflict and Religious Belief: A Reply to Basinger," *Faith and Philosophy* 15.2, 1998, pp. 229–235). More recently, Gellman has come to hold that foundational beliefs may, but need not, be reconsidered when one becomes aware of religious diversity. Sympathetic awareness of religious diversity may make the Christian lose some confidence in his or her foundational beliefs (in Plantinga's terms, her internal markers may decrease in vivacity or luminosity). Gellman holds that such a decrease in confidence is possible but not necessary ("In Defense of Contented Religious Exclusivism," *Religious Studies* 36.4, 2000, p. 403).

34. There may be, for example, Buddhist beliefs that are consonant with (1) and (2) or that are compatible with other Christian teachings. We are only concerned with those claims that are explicitly or implicitly contrary to (1) and (2).

35. We often simply accept what other tells us. Indeed, a vast portion of human knowledge is thusly acquired. Reid calls the disposition to accept what others tell us the 'credulity disposition'. The credulity disposition is unlimited in children but, through experience, we learn to critically assess what others tell us. In cases of beliefs produced by the credulity disposition that are contrary to deeply held prior beliefs (perhaps also acquired by the credulity disposition), reason must help us determine which of the competing beliefs to accept. Plantinga discusses

the operation of the credulity disposition in *Warrant and Proper Function*, pp. 77 ff.

36. If Christian belief is false, then the internal markers of Christian belief are not produced by the instigation of the Holy Spirit and, hence, may prove likely to falter in the face of counterevidence. There is much more to be said about this, perhaps something about self-deception or wish fulfillment, but we shall pass over it for the sake of length.

37. I have argued that this is even so in the ancient Hebrew scriptures. See Kelly James Clark, "The Gods of Abraham, Isaiah and Confucius," *Dao: A Journal of Comparative Philosophy* 5.1, 2005, 109–136.

38. In China, I once defended the notion that belief in God is warranted by one's properly functioning *sensus divinitatis*. My commentator said that I only believed that because I was an American Christian and that if I were more aware of China's religious history, I wouldn't so blithely accept it. I take it that his argument was not simply that my belief was conditioned and thereby unmerited but that there is empirical evidence to assert that it is simply false that all peoples everywhere have an innate sense of divinity.

39. Plantinga, *Warrant and Proper Function*, p. 19.

40. I doubt that Plantinga would disagree with the basic thrust of this argument (although he may disagree with some details). As noted at the beginning of this section, Plantinga is keenly aware that the facts of diversity can undermine Christian belief.

41. Many people contend that Plantinga owes us an account of the historical truth of Christianity. However, Plantinga can only owe us this a) if he promised such an account and b) he is able to pay. Similar claims have been made about the free will defense in which Plantinga successfully demonstrates that God and evil are logically compossible through an admittedly implausible and probably false defense (see Alvin Plantinga, *God, Freedom, and Evil*. Grand Rapids, MI: Eerdmans, 1974, pp. 7–57). Some of his critics contend that, at that point, Plantinga owes a theodicy (as though Plantinga knows what God's reason is for allowing evil but is maliciously keeping it to himself; if Plantinga knew what God's reasons were for allowing evil, he would tell us). If Plantinga could make the historical case for Christian belief, he would offer it to the world.

42. Of course, this is not always the case. Some people are moved from unbelief back to belief by consideration of the historical evidence. My point is that epistemic situations differ, and the internal markers for the alleged evidence and its force on Christian belief differ for different people. At this point, evidence that would compel luminous and vivacious Christian belief would be most welcome.

43. Although evidentially inclined philosophers would object, Pascalian considerations might also be relevant here. If the will and passions are involved in attaining and maintaining belief (and unbelief) in God, noncognitive factors may prove salutary. Pascal's famous wager concludes that one ought to wager that God exists. But placing a wager and actually believing in God's existence are very different matters. Since our beliefs are not always within our conscious

or direct control, Pascal suggests that if you want to become a believer, you should do the things that believers do:

You want to find faith and you do not know the road. You want to be cured of unbelief and you ask for the remedy: learn from those who were once bound like you and who now wager all they have. These are people who know the road you wish to follow, who have been cured of the affliction of which you wish to be cured: follow the way by which they began. They behaved just as if they did believe, taking holy water, having masses said, and so on. That will make you believe quite naturally." (Blaise Pascal, *Pensées*, A. J. Krailsheimer, trans, New York: Penguin Books, 1995, p. 418.)

Pascal suggests this approach because he believes the primary obstacle to religious faith is the passions, not the intellect. Unbelievers, he contends, don't need an increase of proofs to salve the intellect; they require, rather, the decrease of the influences of the passions on the will. By following the religious practices of those who are availing themselves of the means of grace, one might diminish the effect of the passions on one's will. This may open the way for one to receive the gift of faith. This is Pascal's advice for moving from unbelief to belief. He suggests that the doubter may need to learn his belief by doing what believers do and, by getting the body into the right positions, the soul may soon follow. Again, these may seem odd reflections for a philosopher, but they are in line with the account of warranted Christian belief offered by Plantinga; Plantinga's account involves both belief and affections, intellect and will (indeed, the will is primary with respect to Christian belief).

8 Plantinga's Replacement Argument

PETER VAN INWAGEN

INTRODUCTION

Alvin Plantinga has recently turned his attention to materialism. More precisely, he has turned his attention to the thesis that philosophers of mind call materialism.[1] This thesis can be variously formulated. In this essay, I will take "materialism" to be the conjunction of the following two theses:

(1) Human persons – what human beings refer to when they use the first-person-singular pronoun – are *substances*. They are substances in the strict and philosophical sense: They persist through time, retaining their identities while changing various of their accidental properties;[2] they are not grammatical fictions; they are not "modes of substance"; they are not logical constructs on shorter-lived things (they are not *entia successiva*); they are not abstract objects (they are not, for example, things analogous to computer programs); they are not events or processes.[3]

(2) These substances, these human persons, are wholly material. They are (if current physics is to be believed) composed entirely of up-quarks, down-quarks, and electrons, so related by the electromagnetic and color forces as to compose matter in its solid, liquid, and gaseous phases. They are, in two words, living organisms – or, if not *whole* living organisms, then parts of living organisms (human brains, brains-plus-central-nervous-systems, brain stems, cerebral hemispheres, cerebral cortices – or perhaps even *luz* bones or tiny, almost indestructible material things unknown to physiology . . .). They have no immaterial part.[4]

Plantinga's position as regards materialism can be summed up in the words of President Calvin Coolidge's well-known summary of the preacher's position on sin: He's against it. That is to say, he not only rejects materialism, not only thinks it false, but thinks it of great – as one might say – *human importance* to convince his philosophical audience that it is false. In that respect, Plantinga's position vis-à-vis materialism is unlike *my* position vis-à-vis dualism (that is, the conjunction of thesis 1 and the denial of thesis 2).[5] I think that dualism is false, but I don't think it's particularly important – in the matter of how human beings live their lives – whether others share this belief.[6] If this were another paper about Plantinga on materialism, I might try to convince my readers that he was wrong to think that the question whether we are material things was of great "human importance" – a question whose importance was comparable to, say, the importance of the question whether materialism in the strong sense mentioned in note 1 is true, or the question whether human persons are substances in the strict and philosophical sense, or the question whether any moral judgments are objectively true, or the question whether human persons survive death. In my view, the question whether human persons are material is indeed "an important philosophical question" in the sense in which, say, the question whether there are Platonic universals, or the question whether causation can be analyzed in terms of constant conjunction, are important philosophical questions. But we philosophers can perhaps forgive nonphilosophers if they are not much interested in either of these two "important" questions; it is much harder to forgive them – it is much harder to *understand* them – if they are not interested in the question whether "the cosmos is all that there is or was or ever will be," or the question whether they will have a post mortem existence.

This is not that paper. My business here is with a much more narrowly defined and technical issue. I propose to examine a certain argument of Plantinga's, an argument for the falsity of materialism, an argument he calls "the replacement argument."[7]

THE REPLACEMENT ARGUMENT

1

I begin with a statement of the conclusion of the replacement argument:

> I am not identical with any material substance; that is to say (since we are presupposing that I am a substance), I am an immaterial substance.

The replacement argument, like the central argument of *Meditations on First Philosophy*, is conducted in the first person. Plantinga's text is both a record of Alvin Plantinga's going through the argument "for his own case" and an invitation to each of his readers to go through the same argument (mutatis mutandis) for his or her own case. In my presentation of the argument, I will go through the argument for my own case: The pronoun 'I' in the statement of the conclusion of the argument and in the presentation of the argument in the sequel refers to *me*. When one has gone through the argument and discovered that one is not identical with any material substance (Plantinga contends), one will see that anyone else could go through the same chain of reasoning for his or her own case and discover thereby that he or she is not identical with any material substance. Having seen that this is so, one will, of course, conclude that no human person is identical with any material substance – that every human person is an immaterial substance. I am willing to grant that if Plantinga's reasoning (adapted to my own case) convinces me that I am not identical with any material substance, it should convince me that every human person is an immaterial substance. I will, therefore, consider only the first-person chain of reasoning that is supposed to convince me that I am not identical with any material substance.

The first step in this chain of reasoning is intended to lead me to the conclusion that I am not identical with a *certain* material substance, my body. Once I have reached this conclusion (Plantinga contends), it will be evident to me that, for any material substance, a parallel chain of reasoning would establish the conclusion that I was not identical with *that* material substance: that I was not identical with my brain, my brain-plus-my-central-nervous-system, my brain stem, one of my cerebral hemispheres, my cerebral cortex, and so on.[8] I will grant that if one application of the replacement argument proves that I am not identical with my body, other, exactly parallel, applications would prove that I was not identical with any other material substance. I will therefore consider only the argument for the conclusion that I am not identical with my body. (And, anyway, I am one of those materialists who believes that one is identical with one's body – in a sense of 'one's body' that I shall spell out in a moment. I, in fact, believe that none of the other items in the foregoing list of "material person-candidates" exists.)[10]

Here is the general strategy of the argument. I am to consider (guided by Plantinga's statement of the argument for his case) a certain imaginary episode or adventure – imaginary but *possible* – that I survive and during which my body ceases to exist. And I am to conclude from the possibility of that imaginary adventure that I am not identical with my body. I certainly have no logical objection to this dialectical strategy. If it is indeed possible for me to survive my body's ceasing to exist, then to assert (in the face of this possibility) that I am identical with my body would be to deny a very attractive modal principle: that $x = y \rightarrow \sim \Diamond x \neq y$, or, in plain English, that a thing and itself cannot part company.[11] (Similarly, if someone wanted to convince me that the Morning Star was not identical with the planet Venus, and if that person proposed to prove this to me by asking me to consider an imaginary – but possible – astronomical catastrophe that destroyed the planet Venus and left the Morning Star unscathed, I should have no logical objection to this strategy.) Of course, I believe that any application of this strategy will yield an argument with a false premise – almost certainly the premise that the imagined adventure is a possible adventure – for, as I have said, I believe that I *am* identical with my body, and that conclusion follows jointly from this belief of mine and the obvious logical validity of the proposed argument. But that is no reason to refuse to consider the argument: For all I know, considering the imaginary adventure on which the argument turns will convince me that it is more plausible to believe that that adventure is possible than it is to believe that I am (as I have always supposed) identical with my body.

The question on which the cogency of the replacement argument turns, therefore, is the following: Is the adventure Plantinga describes possible? – or, more cautiously, is it more plausible to suppose that it is possible than it is to suppose that I am identical with my body?

2

I proceed to a statement of the replacement argument for the conclusion that I am not identical with my body. I begin with a description of the imaginary-but-possible adventure that (if Plantinga is right) I should survive and my body would not.

Following Plantinga's procedure in laying out the description of *his* adventure, I first give my body a proper name: I say, "Let 'B' be a proper name of my body." But this thing I am supposed to do raises a question: What do I mean by 'my body'? Well, *a* (human) body is, I suppose, a living human organism – a thing that a biologist would classify as a member of the species *Homo sapiens*. But what do I mean when I say of a certain body, a certain living organism, that it is *my* body? This is not a trivial question, since a definition of 'my body' that one philosopher favored might well be rejected as tendentious by other philosophers. For example: 'the body with which I interact causally' (given that a thing can interact causally only with things other than itself). In "Philosophers and the Words 'Human Body',"[12] I contended that it was not possible to define '*x*'s body' in a way that was neutral with respect to all historically important theories of the person-body relation – I contended, that is, that any possible definition of '*x*'s body' would presuppose the truth or the falsity of at least one of the historically important theories of the person-body relation. For present purposes, however, it will suffice to have a definition of 'my body' that is neutral with respect to dualism and materialism (with respect to the affirmation of 1 and 2, on the one hand, and the affirmation of 1 and the denial of 2 on the other). And such a definition is possible:

> My body $=_{df}$ the living human organism such that it is possible for me to bring about changes in that organism without bringing about changes in any other organism (other than such organisms as it may have as proper parts) – and which is such that causing changes in it can cause changes in me and in no other person.[13]

This definition is not "neutral with respect to all historically important theories of the person-body relation," for it presupposes the falsity of epiphenomenalism and occasionalism (that is, the thesis that I *have* a body in this sense presupposes the falsity of both these historically important theories). But it is, I believe, neutral as between dualism and materialism. B, therefore, is to be understood as a proper name for a certain living human organism, that living human organism in which I can bring about changes "directly."

The adventure that is central to the replacement argument is, as one might have expected, an adventure that involves the rapid replacement of various parts of my body. The argument comes in two versions, a "macroscopic" version and a "microscopic" version. In the former, the parts of my body that are rapidly replaced are largish, visible parts like my hands and feet and my left cerebral hemisphere. In the latter, the parts are smallish, invisible parts – atoms, perhaps, or cells. I will consider only the macroscopic version of the argument. (I will later briefly explain why it will not be necessary for my purposes to consider the microscopic version.)

Here, then, is the macroscopic version of the replacement argument. We suppose first that, for some time now, my brain has had a certain odd property: At any given moment, one of my two cerebral hemispheres is "dormant" and the other "active"; at any given moment, the hemisphere that is active at that moment is then "doing all that a brain ordinarily does"; at midnight of each day, all the "relevant" "data" or "information" (I reproduce Plantinga's scare-quotes) that was then stored or tokened (or whatever the word should be) in the active hemisphere is copied to[14] the dormant hemisphere; the dormant hemisphere then becomes active and the active hemisphere dormant. If I am awake when this rather complex event happens, I shall not notice it. Any train of thought that I may be engaged in at the time will proceed without interruption. The first part of that train of thought will be tokened in one cerebral hemisphere and the remainder in the other, and the "hemisphere switching" will have no phenomenological consequences whatever.

I do not know whether the recurring sequences of events that are entailed by my brain's having this "odd property" are physically possible.

And I do not know whether, if they are possible and if they were actually to occur, they would have the phenomenological consequences (or lack thereof) that are claimed for them. But I am inclined to think that Plantinga is right to suppose that they are at least metaphysically possible and that he is right to suppose that I should notice nothing if one of them occurred when I was awake (that the sequence of events would be the physical correlate of a single, unified episode of consciousness). At any rate, I will not dispute either of these things.

We now consider some partition (*in intellectu*) of B into largish, visible parts (nonoverlapping); the following partition, let us say: My left and right legs (LL and RL), my left and right arms (LA and RA), my lower torso (LT), my upper torso (UT), my neck (N), my head, exclusive of my neck and my cerebrum (H), and my left and right cerebral hemispheres (LB and RB). (The reader is advised at this point to make a visual aid: a "gingerbread man" outline of a human figure with the labels 'LL' etc. attached to the appropriate sections of the figure.) Our imaginary adventure consists in the sequential replacement (in the order mentioned) of each of these parts of B by perfect duplicates (which had been grown in a vat or something like that). Plantinga (speaking of his own case), imagines that this sequential replacement occurs while he is reading the *South Bend Tribune*. (As a staunch Kathleen Wilkes–style advocate of realism in philosophical examples, I am compelled, in adapting Plantinga's argument to my own case, to substitute the *Chicago Tribune* for the *South Bend Tribune* – for only in very distant possible worlds do I ever open the *South Bend Tribune*.) The sequence of replacements is integrated with the dormant/active cycle of my cerebral hemispheres in this manner: The sequence of replacements begins just before midnight; whichever of my cerebral hemispheres was dormant before midnight is replaced with a duplicate and is then annihilated; midnight comes, and the "relevant information" tokened in the active hemisphere is copied to the (newly installed) dormant hemisphere, which is then activated; simultaneously with its activation, the hemisphere that had been active is rendered dormant; it is then replaced with a (dormant) duplicate and annihilated.

Now, following Plantinga's example, I am to consider this imaginary episode and I am asked to reason as follows:

If this process occurs rapidly – during a period of one microsecond, say – B will no longer exist. I, however, will continue to exist, having been reading the comic page during the entire process.

The story is rather complicated. Let us set it out in the form of a time line. I shall suppose, as Plantinga has invited me to suppose, that the sequence of replacements takes exactly one microsecond. Let it begin just before midnight, at the instant t. At t, RB is dormant and LB is active. The numbers represent nanoseconds (thousandths of a microsecond).

t	LL is replaced and annihilated
$t + 100$	RL is replaced and annihilated
$t + 200$	LT is replaced and annihilated
$t + 300$	RA is replaced and annihilated
$t + 400$	LA is replaced and annihilated
$t + 500$	UT is replaced and annihilated
$t + 600$	N is replaced and annihilated
$t + 700$	H is replaced and annihilated
$t + 800$	RB (dormant) is replaced with a duplicate (RB*), also dormant, and annihilated
$t + 800 - t + 900$	The information in LB (active) is copied to RB* (dormant)
$t + 900$	RB* is activated and LB rendered dormant
$t + 1000$	LB is replaced with a (dormant) duplicate and annihilated.

The one-microsecond interval $t - t + 1000$ is (we suppose) a subinterval of a twelve-second interval during which I read (and, in the words of *The Book of Common Prayer*, inwardly digest) that day's "Doonesbury" strip: At the start of the longer interval, I glance at the first panel; at the end of it, having reached the fourth and final panel, got the point, and chuckled, I have formed the intention to go on to "The Boondocks." This whole twelve-second mental episode proceeds without interruption. When the one-microsecond sequence of replacements occurs, I don't notice a thing: It has "no phenomenological consequences whatever." It is evident that I exist throughout the twelve-second interval ("I, however, will continue to exist, having been reading the comic page during the entire process") and that B does not – for the one-microsecond sequence of replacements has destroyed B.

This story is evidently metaphysically possible, and its metaphysical possibility establishes that it is metaphysically possible for both the following two propositions to be true.

I exist throughout a certain interval.

B ceases to exist at some point in that interval.

And, as we have seen, this metaphysical possibility logically implies that I am not identical with B. (Here endeth the statement of the argument.)

3

But why, one might ask, am I to suppose that the sequence of replacements destroys B? Well, I am willing to grant that it does. B is a living human organism, and a certain "minimum assimilation time" is required for an object to become a part of an organism – and this minimum assimilation time is certainly greater than one microsecond (and, a fortiori, greater than 100 nanoseconds, the interval between the successive replacements in the story). Consider, for example, an eye transplant. Suppose that x is a detached but viable human eye.[15] Suppose that x is not a part of Alice and then becomes a part of Alice. How long does it take for x to become a part of Alice? How quickly can this happen? Well, it certainly can't happen instantaneously. There cannot be two "adjacent" intervals (two intervals such that a certain mathematical instant t is the least upper bound of one them and the greatest lower bound of the other) such that x is not a part of Alice at any instant that belongs to the earlier interval and is a part of Alice at every instant that belongs to the later one. Assimilation, whatever else it may be, is a causal process, and causal processes take time.[16] This much can be said a priori. And we know enough a posteriori to say more. If t is the first instant at which x is "spatially in place," is at that place in Alice's eye socket at which the surgeon wants it to be (supposing, unrealistically, that being in place is a condition that can be achieved instantaneously), there will be an interval following t during which x is not a part of Alice, and we know enough about rate at which chemical reactions occur to know that this interval will be greater than one microsecond (much less, so to speak, 100 nanoseconds). But we need not appeal to any empirical facts (which do have a way of turning into empirical nonfacts). The a priori point is sufficient for our purposes: If the intervals one microsecond and 100 nanoseconds should turn out to be "too long," we can simply adjust the intervals between replacements in the example.

Now consider any partition (again, *in intellectu*) of an organism into n nonoverlapping parts $P_1, P_2, \ldots, P_n$. If the Ps are replaced sequentially by duplicates, and if the interval between successive replacements is less than the minimum assimilation time (or, even better, if the whole sequence of replacements takes place in an interval less than the minimum assimilation time), the organism will thereby be destroyed.[17] No doubt the "replacement Ps" will pretty quickly come to compose an organism – a duplicate of the original organism – but it will not be the original organism.

I have conceded that the sequence of replacements, if it is sufficiently rapid, will destroy B because that thesis is a consequence of the metaphysic of living organisms that I endorse. (Neglecting the point that, according to that metaphysic, neither the "objects replaced" nor the "replacement objects" exist.) Plantinga devotes considerable space and philosophical ingenuity to an attempt to refute that metaphysic. It will perhaps not astonish the reader to learn that I believe that this attempt is a failure, but this is not the place to discuss that attempt. All that is relevant for our purposes is that he and I agree that a sufficiently rapid replacement of the parts of a living organism will destroy that organism – and, in particular, that the episode of rapid replacement that he imagines would destroy B.

This, then, is a macroscopic version of the replacement argument. There is no need for us to consider the microscopic version, for I am willing to concede that a sufficiently rapid replacement of the cells or the elementary particles of which B is composed would destroy B. My reasons for thinking this – they are, of course, based on a theory of material composition that Plantinga rejects – are essentially the same as the reasons I have given for thinking that a sufficiently rapid replacement of its macroscopic parts (given some partition of B into macroscopic parts) would destroy B.

ANALYSIS

The question comes down to this. Why should I accept – why should anyone accept – the following premise of the replacement argument: that I should continue to exist throughout the twelve-second interval that contained the one-microsecond replacement episode? After all, if I am identical with B, this premise is false. It therefore requires some sort of defense.

Plantinga does not offer an explicit argument for this premise. But examination of his text suggests an argument, an argument I will call the argument from continuous consciousness. (I am thinking particularly of the sentence "I, however, will continue to exist, having been reading the comic page during the entire process.") One might plausibly contend that Plantinga *presupposes* this argument, or that he regards the argument as so obvious that he believes that it is unnecessary to state it, that contemplating the replacement story – contemplating the version of the story adapted to the reader's own case – will cause the argument to be present in the reader's mind. I formulate the unstated argument in these words:

During the twelve-second interval, a single episode of conscious awareness occurs. If a single episode of conscious awareness occurs during a certain interval, a single person must be the subject of that episode. I am the subject of the earlier parts of this episode. Since a single person is the subject of the whole episode, I am therefore the subject of the final parts this episode – and I therefore exist at the end of the twelve-second interval.

This argument is, in my judgment, valid. But are its premises true? In particular, is its first premise true: 'During the twelve-second interval, a single episode of conscious awareness occurs'? Not in my view. Plantinga's *modus ponens* (if indeed the *modus ponens* is Plantinga's) is my *modus tollens*:[18]

> I do not exist at the end of the twelve-second interval. But if any person is present throughout the twelve-second interval, it is I. No person, therefore, is present throughout that interval. If, therefore, a single episode of conscious awareness occurs during the twelve-second interval, no one person is its subject. And if a single episode of conscious awareness occurs during a certain interval, a single person must be the subject of that episode. It is, therefore, false that during the twelve-second interval a single episode of conscious awareness occurs.

If you asked me what I should expect, phenomenologically speaking, if I were about to be subjected to a replacement procedure like the one Plantinga has imagined, I would reply that (considerations pertaining to an afterlife aside) I should expect my consciousness to come to an abrupt end at the moment the replacements were made. My phenomenological expectations would be identical with those I should have if I were told that I was about to be vaporized by the explosion of a hydrogen bomb. And this is no mere bloodless conviction of the intellect. I value my own continued existence and continued consciousness as much as most people do, but I would sacrifice no present pleasure or other good (e.g., a sum of money that I might leave to my loved ones) to bribe the powers-that-be to substitute my undergoing the replacement procedure at *t* for my being vaporized at *t*.

I will concede that if, as I began to read "Doonesbury," I had been ignorant of the fact that the series of replacements was about to commence, then, at the end of the twelve-second interval there would exist *someone* who believed that he had just had the experience of reading the four panels of a comic strip.[19] But, in my view, this person would be wrong. He would not have existed when the twelve-second interval began. He would have been *brought into existence* by the series of replacements and by the subsequent "coalescing" – Plantinga's nice word – of the "replacement parts" into the whole that is himself. At the moment the replacement parts began to form a whole, his consciousness would have been "switched on" all in an instant;

he would be created remembering, as Russell said in another connection, "a wholly unreal past" (or perhaps it would be more accurate to say, having wholly unreal memories of a real past).

I have discussed what is essentially the argument from continuous consciousness in §16 of *Material Beings* (pp. 205–207). I said there (the 'you' is an interlocutor who had presented a case different from Plantinga's replacement story, but not entirely unlike it):

> You say that a "continuous consciousness" is present in a certain situation over a certain interval. [But you *also* hold that the presence of a continuous consciousness implies the continuous presence of a conscious thinker. If *that* is so, then to] find out whether a certain situation contains a "continuous consciousness" . . . we have first to find out whether that situation contains a continuously conscious thinker. We can't do things the other way round. We can't find out whether a situation contains a continuously existent thinker by first finding out whether it contains a "continuous consciousness." (pp. 205–206)

The reader who desires a fuller discussion of this point is directed to this section of *Material Beings*.

To sum up: The argument from continuous consciousness has a premise that I (I who am attempting to go through the replacement argument "for my own case") see no reason to accept, namely, that a single, continuous conscious episode would occur during the replacement episode; therefore, I have no reason to accept the premise of the replacement argument that the argument from continuous consciousness was supposed to establish: that I should exist throughout the replacement episode (I know of no reason to accept that premise of the replacement argument other than the reason that was supposed to be provided by the argument from continuous consciousness). I have not, I concede, said anything that should convince Plantinga that either of these premises is false. I have not said anything that should convince *anyone* that either of these premises is false. But it is not my business to convince Plantinga (or anyone) of anything. It is, rather, Plantinga's business to convince *me* of something: that I am not identical with B. And this he has not done. Perhaps the replacement argument will convince others that they are not identical with their bodies – perhaps, indeed, it will convince some or even all of those who have read the present essay of this. I do not claim for this essay the power to turn its readers into people who will be unmoved by the replacement argument. But its readers will understand why *I* am unmoved by it.[20]

Notes

1. As opposed to the following stronger thesis, which is also called materialism: Everything – or every concrete thing or everything that has causal powers – is material. One might well accept materialism in the sense of the present essay but reject this stronger thesis; that, in fact, is my own position.

2. In this essay, I presuppose an "endurantist," as opposed to a "perdurantist," account of persistence. I think that most of, if not all, my arguments could be translated into perdurantist terms, but they would have to be presented in forms that were very different from the forms in which I shall present them. Since both Plantinga and I are endurantists, I see no point in trying to present my arguments in forms acceptable to perdurantists.

3. Many philosophers of mind reject thesis 1 and would call themselves materialists (if, for no other reason, because they are materialists in the strong sense of note 1). Plantinga and I, however, agree that thesis 1 is true. It will therefore be convenient for me to treat the "materialism-dualism" dispute as a dispute about whether "human substances" (on whose existence Plantinga and I agree) are material or immaterial substances.

4. Or at any rate, they have no nonphysical part. Perhaps electrons (for example) are too small (or "too weird") to be classified as material objects. But electrons are certainly physical things, since they have properties like mass that are uncontroversially physical properties.

5. Strictly speaking, dualism is the conjunction of these two theses with the thesis that matter exists (or that material things exist). The conjunction of thesis 1 and the denial of thesis 2 and the thesis that matter exists is what some philosophers call *substance* dualism – a species of dualism that is opposed to *property* dualism. In my view, however, substance dualism is the only dualism – property dualism being (depending on the words that are used to formulate it) either an unintelligible thesis or a thesis that is not really a species of dualism. For more on my difficulties with the idea of property dualism, see my essay "A Materialist Ontology of the Human Person," in Dean Zimmerman and Peter van Inwagen (eds.), *Persons: Human and Divine*, forthcoming from Oxford University Press.

6. I do think it's important for *Christian* dualists to take special care not to allow their dualism to weaken or to undermine the importance of the doctrine of the Resurrection of the Dead. And I do think that there's some danger of dualism's having such consequences.

7. The argument is presented in Plantinga's essay "Against Materialism." The section of the paper devoted to the argument (Section 1) is entitled, appropriately enough, "The Replacement Argument: An Argument from Possibility."

8. It is a nice question whether some version of the replacement argument can be used to show that I am not identical with my *luz* bone or with some tiny, almost indestructible material thing unknown to physiology. Since I am willing to stipulate that I am neither of these things, I will not consider this nice question.

9. What I am granting here is not entirely trivial. Consider this argument of Moore's: I am closer to my head than I am to my feet; therefore, I am not my

body. Whether or not this argument does show that I am not my body, it is evident that no parallel argument shows that I am not, e.g., my brain.

10. For reasons that I have spelled out in *Material Beings*, Ithaca, NY: Cornell University Press, 1990.

11. And it is also to deny Leibniz's Law, which is perhaps even more attractive than this modal principle, for if I shall exist on Thursday, and if my body will not exist on Thursday, then, if I and my body are identical (Leibniz's Law assures us), I both have and lack the property "being a thing that will exist on Thursday." The Law of Noncontradiction (which is, if possible, even more attractive than Leibniz's Law) therefore implies that if I and my body are identical and if I shall exist on Thursday and my body will not exist on Thursday, then Leibniz's Law is false.

12. In Peter van Inwagen (ed.), *Time and Cause: Essays Presented to Richard Taylor*, Dordrecht: D. Reidel, 1980, pp. 283–299.

13. This is the definition of 'my body' that I used in *Metaphysics* (2nd ed., Boulder, CO, and London: Westview Press and Oxford University Press, 2002) pp. 169–170. It was first suggested to me by Frances Howard-Snyder in conversation.

14. Plantinga says "transferred." I prefer to say "copied," and that is the word I shall use. Information is not, after all, a liquid that can be pumped from one place to another – however useful the metaphor of a "flow of information" may be in some contexts. To speak of transferring something from place A to place B strongly suggests that, after the transfer, the "something" is no longer in place A. My paradigm of a "transfer of information" (if one must use the phrase) is this: Imagine two boards, on each of which there are *n* on-off switches arranged spatially in the same way; someone takes note of the on-off positions of the switches on one of the boards and turns the counterpart of each of the switches on the other board to the same position. After that has been done, the information that had been (and still is) "tokened in" the pattern of "ons" and "offs" on the one board will be tokened in the (now identical) pattern on the other board. This paradigm should make it clear why I prefer to speak of "copying" than of "transferring" information.

15. According to my metaphysic of material things, there are no such things as human eyes, detached or undetached, but I will concede their existence for present purposes. That is, since we are considering an abstract point in the metaphysics of assimilation, I will not insist that the example I am about to offer be consistent with my beliefs about the ontology of the material world – with the answer to the "Special Composition Question" that I accept. A similar point applies to LL and RB and all the other "parts" that figure in my version of Plantinga's imaginary episode: I don't, in fact, think that they exist, but I am willing to concede their existence "for the sake of argument."

16. As Plantinga points out, if this principle can be established on no other grounds, it follows from the fact that causal influence can propagate no faster than the speed of light.

17. In the language used to discuss assimilation in *Material Beings*, the organism will be destroyed because its life will have been "disrupted" (p. 147).

18. John Pollock once said to me, "Al and I accept all the same arguments. It's just that the ones he thinks are proofs, I think are reductios, and the ones he thinks are reductios, I think are proofs."

19. Actually, I'm wary of conceding even that much. I am inclined to think that – for "Kripke-Putnam" reasons – the newly created "someone" would not speak or understand English or any other language. And I doubt whether it would be possible to believe that one had just had the experience of reading the four panels of a comic strip without having a language. But I'll let that worry go, since it's not relevant to our present concerns.

20. As will the readers of §16 of *Material Beings*. The argument of the final section of this essay is little more than a recapitulation of an argument presented in that section of the book.

Appendix: Two Dozen (or so) Theistic Arguments

ALVIN PLANTINGA

PREFACE TO THE APPENDIX (JULY 2006)

What follows are notes for a lecture on theistic arguments given in a summer seminar in philosophy of religion in Bellingham, Washington, in 1986. Although the last twenty years have seen a good bit of interesting work on theistic arguments (for example, on the fine-tuning arguments),[1] the notes, while shortened a bit, are unrevised. My intention had always been to write a small book based on these arguments, with perhaps a chapter on each of the main kinds. Time has never permitted, however, and now the chances of my writing such a book are small and dwindling. Nevertheless, each, I think, deserves loving attention and development. I'm not sure they warrant publication in this undeveloped, nascent, merely germinal form, but Deane-Peter Baker thought some people might find them interesting; I hope others will be moved to work them out and develop them in detail.

I've argued in *Warranted Christian Belief* and elsewhere that neither theistic nor full-blown Christian belief requires argument for justification or rationality or (if true) warrant. One can be justified and rational in accepting theistic belief, even if one doesn't accept theism on the basis of arguments and even if in fact there aren't any good theistic arguments. The same holds for Christian belief, which of course goes far beyond theism: One doesn't need arguments for justified and rational Christian belief. If theistic belief is true, furthermore, then, so I say, it can have warrant sufficient for knowledge for someone, even if he or she doesn't believe on the basis of theistic arguments, and even if in fact no good theistic arguments exist. That said, of course, it doesn't follow that there *aren't* any good theistic arguments, and as a matter of fact, so the title of this section intimates, there *are* good theistic arguments – at least two dozen or so. I hasten to add that the arguments as stated in the notes aren't really good arguments; they are merely argument sketches, or maybe only pointers to good arguments. They await that loving development to become genuinely good.

But what makes a theistic argument (or, for that matter, any other philosophical argument) a *good* one? Forty years ago, when I first wrote about theistic arguments in *God and Other Minds*, this question was much easier to answer. Then I was implicitly accepting some variety of classical foundationalism; the answer to this question is reasonably clear from that perspective. Of course, there is more than one variety of classical foundationalism; for the moment let's go with John Locke's version. As usual with these matters, there are problems connected with saying just what Locke had in mind. Perhaps the following will serve as a rough and ready account:

> (L) A belief is properly basic for S just if it is incorrigible (like such beliefs as *I'm being appeared to redly*) or self-evident for S or "evident to the senses" for S; and a belief that isn't properly basic for S is rationally acceptable for S if and only if it deductively follows from or is sufficiently probable with respect to S's properly basic beliefs.

It is then reasonably clear what it is for an argument to be good. It must take as premises propositions that are properly basic for all or most people, and proceed via self-evidently valid deductive steps to the conclusion, or else it must make it evident that the conclusion is sufficiently probable with respect to all or most people's foundations.

Of course even here there are problems. An argument of the form *p*, therefore *p*

won't be a good argument even if *p* is properly basic for everyone. Such an argument, of course, is question-begging or circular, and a good argument will be neither; but under just what conditions is (or isn't) an argument question-begging or circular? That's not easy to say. Is circularity an epistemic property? Is it person-relative? Can it be characterized formally? These are hard questions. Furthermore, what is incorrigible will of course vary from person to person, as will what is evident to the senses. (It's evident to the senses for me that I am sitting before a computer; since I am alone in the room that is not evident to the senses for anyone else.) Less obviously, what is self-evident also varies from person to person; as Thomas Aquinas said, some propositions are self-evident only to the learned.

Another source of difficulty is the fact that self-evidence, or *intuitive support*, as perhaps we can better call it, comes in degrees. Simple logical and arithmetical propositions such as $2 + 1 = 3$ and the corresponding conditional of modus ponens (better, some instance of it) have maximal intuitive support (are maximally self-evident); propositions like *Nothing has properties in possible worlds in which it doesn't exist* and *There aren't any things that don't exist* have some but much less than maximal intuitive support. This leads to trouble with the previous explanation of goodness for an argument: On that account as it stands, a good argument could take as premises propositions that have some but less than maximal intuitive support, and take as conclusion the denial of a proposition that has maximal intuitive support. Indeed, this isn't merely possible; consider the self-exemplification paradox. Some properties exemplify themselves and hence also exemplify the property *self-exemplification*; others do not. But then what about the property of non-self-exemplification? Sadly enough, it exemplifies itself if and only if it does not, which entails a contradiction. Here the premises (*There is such a property as self-exemplification, All properties have complements, . . .*) all have at least some intuitive support; the argument is such that each step follows self-evidently from previous steps; but the *denial* of the conclusion has near maximal intuitive warrant. So there are complications; still, the basic structure of the right answer is fairly clear, and a little Chisholming will presumably suffice to deal appropriately with the complications.

Classical foundationalism, however, is mistaken, as is now widely recognized. Given that it *is* mistaken, how shall we say what makes for goodness in an argument? That's a wholly nontrivial question. To make a beginning, we might say that an argument is maximally good if it meets the conditions for goodness appropriate to classical foundationalism. There are arguments that meet that condition, particularly in mathematics and logic; think, for example, of the argument for the conclusion that there is no greatest prime.[2] The theistic arguments that follow, however, do not meet that exalted standard; few if any philosophical arguments do. Perhaps a few do. Descartes's *cogito* meets that condition: that I think is incorrigible for me, and it is self-evident that if I think (or am appeared to redly, or for that matter go for a walk), then I exist. A *reductio* that by self-evident steps displays a contradiction in a philosophical position is a philosophical argument, and there are arguments of that type. But the vast majority of philosophical arguments don't meet that standard; some of those, presumably, are nevertheless good; so what constitutes goodness for a philosophical argument, given the demise of classical foundationalism?

We can effect one small but comforting simplification: Adding additional premises can turn any argument into one that is deductively valid, one where the premises entail the conclusion by steps each of which has near maximal intuitive support. (If worst comes to worst, we can always add as a premise a conditional whose antecedent is the conjunction of the premises and whose consequent is the conclusion.) So we need worry only about the premises. What conditions will the premises of a good argument have to meet? Must they be justified, rational, warranted? Here, the first problem is that all three of these virtues are had by different propositions for different people. So perhaps we'll have to say that goodness, for an argument, is person relative; an argument isn't in the first instance, good simpliciter, but for a given person S. Then we can go on to say that an argument is good überhaupt (in a derived sense) just if it is good for a sufficiently large class of people, or perhaps of people meeting certain conditions of rationality.

Well, then, shall we say that an argument is good for S if each of the premises is justified (in the deontological sense, so that p is justified for me just if I am within my intellectual rights in accepting it) for S? But what about the self-exemplification paradox? For some reason or other, I might be such that I simply can't help believing each of the premises; in that case, I am within my rights in accepting them all; if so, the argument, by the current consideration, is good for me. But surely it isn't. There are various expedients one might try to amend this account; but there is probably no hope along these lines. Given the fact that beliefs (for the most part, anyway) are not under our voluntary control, and given that one is within one's rights in accepting a belief when one can't help accepting it, a standard in terms of justification is going to be much too permissive.

Shall we say that an argument is a good one for S just if each of the premises of the argument *has warrant* for S? Say that a belief is warranted for a person S, give or take a few bells and whistles, if it is produced in S by cognitive faculties that are functioning properly in an appropriate cognitive environment according to a design plan that is successfully aimed at the truth (Plantinga, *Warrant and Proper Function*, 1993). Unfortunately, that environmental condition produces a problem: Whether an argument is good, for S, should not depend, in this way, upon S's cognitive environment. Even if I'm a brain in a vat, so that my cognitive environment is defective and my beliefs lack warrant, some arguments ought to be good, for me – including ones that involve as premises beliefs that, due to my envatted condition, do not have warrant for me.

Shall we say that an argument is good for S just if each of the premises of p is *rational*, where a belief is rational if a rational human being – one whose rational faculties are functioning properly – could believe or accept p? First, we'd have to add that a rational person could accept *all* the premises of the argument. (It's not enough that each be such that it can be accepted by a rational person; it must also be that a rational person could accept them all.) Even so, this criterion will be extremely permissive; an extremely wide variety of premises can, at least in principle, meet this condition. Each of the premises of the self-exemplification paradox can be rationally accepted, and a person can be rational even if he or she accepts them all – at least until that person sees the connection between premises and conclusion. Perhaps this problem can be skirted as follows. Note that one can hold a belief with varying degrees of firmness, and that rationality in this sense attaches to the firmness with which a belief is held as well as to the content of the belief itself. So perhaps we could say, with respect to the self-exemplification paradox, that a rational person will accept the denial of the conclusion more firmly than he or she accepts the premises – more exactly, there is at least one of the premises such that rationality dictates accepting the denial of the conclusion more firmly than that premise; we could then amend the criterion for goodness appropriately.

Still, this criterion is too liberal. Consider a person who has been brought up to believe some wild and implausible proposition – for example, the earth is on the back of a turtle, which is on the back of another turtle, so that it's turtles all the way down. A person brought up to believe this could believe it rationally. But now consider an argument whose conclusion is that there are infinitely many turtles and whose premises were the foregoing story about turtles. Is such an argument a good argument? I should think not.

As good a suggestion as any moves in quite a different direction. Peter van Inwagen suggests that an argument is a good one if it meets the following condition: It would convince an audience of ideal agnostics when the argument is presented in an ideal fashion, and when there is an ideal critic present who is permitted to criticize the argument:

> An argument for p is a success just in the case that it can be used, under ideal circumstances, to convert an audience of ideal agnostics (agnostics with respect to p) – to belief in p – in the presence of an ideal opponent of belief in p.[3]

'Ideal', here, means pretty much what you think it does; we might add that the ideal agnostics in the audience take the conclusion to be about as probable as its denial with respect to the opponent's beliefs. But here too there are questions. Presumably, we are to suppose that ideal agnostics are rational in the proper function sense; but perhaps it isn't possible to be both rational and agnostic with respect to the conclusion. Could one be rational and also agnostic with respect to the question whether there is or has been a past? Whether there are people? An external world? If not, any argument for any of these conclusions – even if patently ridiculous – will be a good argument on the present suggestion; since there aren't any neutral observers, it will be vacuously true that every neutral observer would accept the conclusion of the argument.

This problem is particularly poignant in the present connection; for according to one of the live options in the epistemology of religious belief, a rational person will have a powerful inclination to believe that there is such a person as God. Of course, we are thinking, here, of the *human* cognitive design plan. Might there not be other design plans that didn't dictate this inclination to believe these propositions? No doubt there could be. Could we say, then, that an argument with the conclusion that *p* is a good one if it would convince an audience of ideal agnostics who had a design plan like the human, except that the design plan specifies no inclination to believe *p* or its denial? Perhaps.

A problem still remains, however: Whether the argument will convince someone depends in part on what else that person believes. Suppose I am neutral with respect to the question whether there are infinitely many unicorns, but, having read my David Lewis, believe that if it is possible that there be unicorns, there are infinitely many. (I'm also neutral with respect to the question whether unicorns are possible.) You argue that there are infinitely many unicorns by arguing that it's possible that there be unicorns (and your argument for that premise is such that it would convince an ideal agnostic). Then your argument for there being infinitely many unicorns would convince *me* – but not, perhaps, someone who doesn't share my belief that if it is possible that there be unicorns, then there are infinitely many of them. In the same way, one ideal agnostic might believe a conditional whose antecedent is one or more of the premises and whose consequent is the conclusion of the argument; but another might believe a conditional whose antecedent is one or more of the premises and whose consequent is the *denial* of the conclusion of the argument. There is no reason to believe that all ideal agnostics would react in the same way to the argument.

We could go further with attempts to patch up this sort of account of goodness for an argument; and we could go further with the question whether there *are* any plausible accounts of goodness for an argument. Let us instead simply note that it is difficult indeed to give a good criterion for argumentative goodness; and then let me instead briefly go on to say what the following arguments can be thought to be good *for* – that is, what they can plausibly be expected to accomplish.

Well, from the point of view of atheism, I suppose they aren't good for much of anything. So suppose we think about the matter from the point of view of theism, or, better, Christian belief: What are theistic arguments good for, from that perspective? One suggestion, perhaps endorsed by Aquinas, is as follows: The function of arguments for the existence of God is to transform faith into knowledge, *scientia. Fides quarens intellectum.* But can they actually accomplish this function? *Scientia* is a pretty exalted epistemic condition: According to Aquinas, one has *scientia* of a proposition *p* just if one sees *p* to follow from propositions one sees to be true – where the seeing is a matter of self-evidence. I don't believe that any of the theistic arguments or all of them taken together can fulfill this function.

Furthermore, as I've argued here, theistic arguments are not needed for justification, or rationality, or, if true, warrant. But then what *are* these arguments good for? At least four things. First, they can move someone closer to theism – by showing, for example, that theism is a legitimate intellectual option. Second, they reveal interesting and important connections between various elements of a theist's set of beliefs. For example, a good theistic argument reveals connections between premises and conclusions, connections that in some cases can also contribute to the broader project of Christian philosophy by showing good ways to think about a certain topic or area from a theistic perspective. Examples would be the arguments from counterfactuals, numbers, propositions, sets, and properties. Third, the arguments can strengthen and confirm theistic belief. Not nearly all believers hold theistic belief in serene and uninterrupted certainty; most are at least occasionally subject to doubts. Here these arguments can be useful. I wake up in the middle of the night: I am assailed by doubts about the truth of theism itself. But then I remember that (as I think) there wouldn't even be such a thing as objective right and wrong, good and evil, if there weren't such a person as God; the doubt recedes. (Other arguments – for example, the arguments from proper function and contingent counterfactuals, and perhaps also the arguments from propositions, properties, and sets – can work the same way.) Finally, and connected with the last, these arguments can increase the warrant of theistic belief. For me as for most, belief in God, while accepted in the basic way, isn't maximally firm and unwavering; perhaps it isn't nearly as firm as my belief in other minds. Then perhaps good theistic arguments could play the role of confirming and strengthening belief in God; in that way they might increase the degree of warrant belief in God has for me. Indeed, such arguments might increase the degree of warrant of that belief in such a way as to nudge it over the boundary separating knowledge from mere true belief; they might in some cases therefore serve something like that Thomistic function of transforming belief into knowledge.

These are some of the roles theistic arguments can play, even if they are not needed for justification, rationality, or warrant.

TWO DOZEN (OR SO) THEISTIC ARGUMENTS (1986)

I've been arguing that theistic belief does not (in general) *need* argument either for deontological justification or for positive epistemic status (or for Foley rationality or Alstonian justification); belief in God is properly basic. But it doesn't follow, of course, that there aren't any good arguments. Are there some? At least a couple of dozen or so.

Swinburne: Good argument is one that has premises that everyone knows. Maybe there aren't any such arguments, and if there are some, maybe none of them would be good arguments *for* anyone. (Note again the possibility that a person might, when confronted with an arguent he sees to be valid for a conclusion he deeply disbelieves from premises he know to be true, give up (some of) those premises; in this way you can reduce someone from knowledge to ignorance by giving that person an argument seen to be valid from premises he or she knows to be true.)

These arguments are not coercive in the sense that every person is obliged to accept their premises on pain of irrationality. Maybe just that some or many sensible people do accept their premises (oneself).

What are these arguments like, and what role do they play? They are probabilistic, either with respect to the premises or with respect to the connection between the premises and conclusion, or both. They can serve to bolster and confirm ('helps' à la John Calvin), perhaps to convince.

Distinguish two considerations here: 1) You or someone else might just *find yourself* with these beliefs; so using them as premises gets an effective theistic arg for the person in question. (2) The other question has to do with warrant, with conditional probability in an epistemic sense: Perhaps in at least some of these cases, if our faculties are functioning properly and we consider the premises, we are inclined to accept them; and (under those conditions) the conclusion has considerable epistemic probability (in the explained sense) on the premises.

Add Aquinas's fifth way: this is really an argument from proper function, I think.

I. Half a Dozen (or so) Ontological (or Metaphysical) Arguments

(A) The Argument from Intentionality (or Aboutness). Consider propositions: the things that are true or false, that are capable of being believed, and that stand in logical relations to one another. They also have another property: aboutness or intentionality (not intensionality, and not thinking of contexts in which coreferential terms are not substitutable *salva veritate*).

Represent reality or some part of it *as being thus and so*. This crucially connected with their being true or false. Diff from, e.g., sets (which is the real reason a proposition would not be a set of possible worlds, or of any other objects).

Many have thought it incredible that propositions should exist apart from the activity of minds. How could they just *be* there, if never thought of? (Sellars, Rescher, Husserl, many others; probably no real Platonists besides Plato before Frege, if indeed Plato and Frege were Platonists.) (And Frege, that alleged arch-Platonist, referred to propositions as *gedanken*.) Connected with intentionality. *Representing things as being thus and so*, being about something or other – this seems to be a property or activity of *minds* or perhaps *thoughts*. So extremely tempting to think of propositions as ontologically dependent upon mental or intellectual activity in such a way that either they just are thoughts, or else at any rate couldn't exist if not thought of. (According to the idealistic tradition beginning with Kant, propositions are essentially *judgments*.) But if we are thinking of human thinkers, then there are far too many propositions: at least, for example, one for every real number that is distinct from the Taj Mahal. On the other hand, if they were divine thoughts, no problem here. So perhaps we should think of propositions as divine thoughts. Then in our thinking we would literally be thinking God's thoughts after him.

(Aquinas, *De Veritate*: "Even if there were no human intellects, there could be truths because of their relation to the divine intellect. But if, *per impossibile*, there were no intellects at all, but things continued to exist, then there would be no such reality as truth.")

This argument will appeal to those who think that intentionality is a characteristic of propositions, that there are a lot of propositions, and that intentionality or aboutness is dependent upon mind in such a way that there couldn't be something *p* about something where *p* had never been thought of.

(B) The Argument from Collections. Many think of sets as displaying the following characteristics (among others) (1) No set is a member of itself (2) sets (unlike properties) have their extensions essentially; hence sets are contingent beings and no set could have existed if one of its members had not; (3) sets form an iterated structure: at the first level, sets whose members are nonsets, at the second, sets whose members are nonsets or first-level sets, etc. Many (Cantor) also inclined to think of sets as *collections* – i.e., things whose existence depends upon a certain sort of intellectual activity – a collecting or "thinking together" (Cantor). If sets *were* collections, that

would explain their having the first three features. But of course there are far too many sets for them to be a product of human thinking together; there are many sets such that no human being has ever thought their members together, many that are such that their members have not been thought together by any human being. That requires an infinite mind – one like God's.

A variant: perhaps a way to think together all the members of a set is to attend to a certain property and then consider all the things that have that property: e.g., all the natural numbers. Then many infinite sets are sets that could have been collected by human beings; but not nearly all – not, e.g., arbitrary collections of real numbers. (axiom of choice)

This argument will appeal to those who think there are lots of sets and either that sets have the above three properties or that sets are collections.

Charles Parsons, "What Is the Iterative Conception of Set?" in *Mathematics in Philosophy*, pp. 268 ff.

Hao Wang, *From Mathematics to Philosophy*, chap. 6: iterative and constructivist (i.e., the basic idea is that sets are somehow constructed and are constructs) conception of set.

Note that on the iterative conception, the elements of a set are in an important sense prior to the set; that is why on this conception no set is a member of itself, and this disarms the Russell paradoxes in the set theoretical form, although of course it does nothing with respect to the property formulation of the paradoxes. (Does Chris Menzel's way of thinking about propositions as somehow *constructed* by God bear here?)

Cantor's definition of set (1895): "By a "set" we understand any collection M into a whole of definite well-distinguished objects of our intuition or our thought (which will be called the "elements" of M)." *Gesammelte Abhandlungen mathematischen und philosophischen*, ed. Ernst Zermelo, Berlin: Springer, 1932, p. 282.

Shoenfield (*Mathematical Logic*) 1967 writes: "A closer examination of the (Russell) paradox shows that it does not really contradict the intuitive notion of a set. According to this notion, a set A is formed by gathering together certain objects to form a single object, which is the set A. Thus before the set A is formed, we must have available all of the objects which are to be members of A" (238).

Wang: "The set is a single object formed by collecting the members together" (238).

Wang (182): "It is a basic feature of reality that there are many things. When a multitude of given objects can be collected together, we arrive at a set. For example, there are two tables in this room. We are ready to view them as given both separately and as a unity, and justify this by pointing to them or looking at them or thinking about them either one after the other or simultaneously. Somehow the viewing of certain objects together suggests a loose link which ties the objects together in our intuition."

(C) The Argument from (Natural) Numbers. (I once heard Tony Kenny attribute a particularly elegant version of this argument to Bob Adams.) It also seems plausible to think of *numbers* as dependent upon or even constituted by intellectual activity; indeed, students always seem to think of them as "ideas" or "concepts," as dependent, somehow, upon our intellectual activity. So if there were no minds, there would be no numbers. (According to Kronecker, God made the natural numbers and man made the rest – not quite right if the argument from sets is correct.) But again, there are too many of them for them to arise as a result of human intellectual activity. We should therefore think of them as among God's ideas. Perhaps, as Christopher Menzel suggests (special issue of *Faith and Philosophy*), they are properties of equinumerous sets, where properties are God's concepts.

There is also a similar argument re *properties*. Properties seem very similar to *concepts*. (Is there really a difference between thinking of the things that fall under the concept *horse* and considering the things that have the property of being a horse?) In fact many have found it natural to think of properties as reified concepts. But again, there are properties, one wants to say, that have never been entertained by any human being; and it also seems wrong to think that properties do not exist before human beings conceive them. But then (with respect to these considerations) it seems likely that properties are the concepts of an unlimited mind: a divine mind.

(D) The Argument from Counterfactuals. Consider such a counterfactual as

(1) If Neal had gone into law he would have been in jail by now.

It is plausible to suppose that such a counterfactual is true if and only if its consequent is true in the nearby (i.e., sufficiently similar) possible worlds in which its antecedent is true (Stalnaker, Lewis, Pollock, Nute). But of course for any pair of distinct possible worlds W and W*, there will be infinitely many respects in which they resemble each other, and infinitely many in which they differ. Given agreement on these respects and on the degree of difference within the respects, there can still be disagreement about the resultant total similarity of the two situations. What you think here – which possible worlds you take to be similar to which others *überhaupt* will depend upon how you *weight* the various respects.

Illustrative interlude: *Chicago Tribune*, June 15, 1986:
"When it comes to the relationship between man, gorilla and chimpanzee, Morris Goodman doesn't monkey around.

"No matter where you look on the genetic chain the three of us are 98.3% identical," said Goodman, a Wayne State University professor in anatomy and cell biology.

"Other than walking on two feet and not being so hairy, the main different between us and a chimp is our big brain," said the professor.... the genetic difference between humans and chimps is about 1.7%.

"How can we be so close genetically if we look so different? There's only a .2% difference between a dachshund and a Great Dane, yet both look quite different [sic]," Goodman said.

"He explained that if you look at the anatomies of humans and chimps, chimps get along better in trees than people, but humans get along better on the ground. (Or in subways, libraries and submarines.)"

How similar *überhaupt* you think chimps and humans are will depend upon how you rate the various respects in which they differ: composition of genetic material, hairiness, brain size, walking on two legs, appreciation of Mozart, grasp of moral distinctions, ability to play chess, ability to do philosophy, awareness of God, etc. End of Illustrative interlude.

Some philosophers as a result argue that counterfactuals contain an irreducibly *subjective* element. E.g., consider this from van Fraassen:

"Consider again statement (3) about the plant sprayed with defoliant. It is true in a given situation exactly if the 'all else' that is kept 'fixed' is such as to rule out the death of the plant for other reasons. But who keeps what fixed? The speaker, in his mind.... Is there an objective right or wrong about keeping one thing rather than another firmly in mind when uttering the antecedent?" (*The Scientific Image*, p. 116)

This weighting of similarities therefore doesn't belong in serious, sober, objective science. The basic idea is that considerations as to which respects (of difference) are more important than which is not something that is given in *rerum natura*, but depends upon our interests and aims and plans. In nature apart from mind, there are no such differences in importance among respects of difference.

Now suppose you agree that such differences among respects of difference do in fact depend upon mind, but also think (as in fact most of us certainly do) that counterfactuals are objectively true or false: you can hold both of these if you think there is an unlimited mind such that the weightings it makes are then the objectively correct ones (its assignments of weights determine the correct weights). No human mind, clearly, could occupy this station. God's mind, however, could; what God sees as similar is similar.

Joseph Mendola, "The Indeterminacy of Options," *APQ*, April 1987, argues for the indeterminacy of many counterfactuals on the grounds that I cite here, substantially.

(E) The Argument from Physical Constants. (Look at Barrow and Tipler, *The Anthropic Cosmological Principle)*

Carr and Rees ("The Anthropic Principle and the Structure of the Physical World" (*Nature*, 1979): "The basic features of galaxies, stars, planets and the everyday world are essentially determined by a few microphysical constants and by the effects of gravitation.... several aspects of our Universe – some which seem to be prerequisites for the evolution of any form of life – depend rather delicately on apparent 'coincidences' among the physical constants" (p. 605).

If the force of gravity were even slightly stronger, all stars would be blue giants; if even slightly weaker, all would be red dwarfs. (Brandon Carter, "Large Number Coincidences and the Anthropic Principle in Cosmology," in M. S. Longair, ed, *Confrontation of Cosmological Theories with Observational Data*, 1979, p. 72.) According to Carter, under these conditions there would probably be no life. So probably if the strength of gravity were even slightly different, habitable planets would not exist.

The existence of life also depends delicately upon the rate at which the universe is expanding. S. W. Hawking, "The Anisotropy of the Universe at Large Times," in Longair, p. 285: "...reduction of the rate of expansion by one part in 1012 at the time when the temperature of the Universe was 1010 K would have resulted in the Universe's starting to recollapse when its radius was only 1/3000 of the present value and the temperature was still 10,000 K" – much too warm for comfort. He concludes that life is only possible because the Universe is expanding at just the rate required to avoid recollapse.

Davies, P. C. W., *The Accidental Universe*, 1982: "All this prompts the question of why, from the infinite range of possible values that nature could have selected for the fundamental constants, and from the infinite variety of initial conditions that could have characterized the primeval universe, the actual values and conditions conspire to produce the particular range of very special features that we observe. For clearly the universe is a very special place: exceedingly uniform on a large scale, yet not so precisely uniform that galaxies could not form; ... an expansion rate tuned to the energy content to unbelievable accuracy; values for the strengths of its forces that permit nuclei to exist, yet do not burn up all the cosmic hydrogen, and many more apparent accidents of fortune." (p. 111).

And what is impressive about all these coincidences is that they are apparently required for the existence of life as we know it (as they say).

Some thinkers claim that none of this ought to be thought surprising or as requiring explanation: no matter how things had been, it would have been exceedingly improbable. (No matter what distribution of cards is dealt, the distribution dealt will be improbable.) This is perhaps right, but how does it work? And how is it relevant? We are playing poker; each time I deal I get all the aces; you get suspicious: I try to allay your suspicions by pointing out that my getting all the aces each time I deal is no more improbable than any other equally specific distribution over the relevant number of deals. Would that explanation play in Dodge City (or Tombstone)?

Others invoke the *Anthropic Principle*, which is exceedingly hard to understand but seems to point out that a necessary condition of these values of the physical constants being observed at all (by us or other living beings) is that they have very nearly the values they do have; we are here to observe these constants only because they have the values they do have. Again, this seems right, but how is it relevant? What does it explain? It still seems puzzling that these constants should have just the values they do. Why weren't they something quite different? This is not explained by pointing out that we are here (a counterexample to Hempelian claims about explanation). Like "explaining" the fact that God has decided to create me (instead of passing me over in favor of someone else) by pointing out that I am in fact here, and that if God had not thus decided, I wouldn't have been here to raise the question.

From a theistic point of view, however, no mystery at all and an easy explanation.

(F) The Naive Teleological Argument. Swinburne: "The world is a complicated thing. There are lots and lots of different bits of matter, existing over endless time (or possibly beginning to exist at some finite time). The bits of it have finite and not particularly natural sizes, shapes, masses, etc; and they come together in finite, diverse and very far from natural conglomerations (viz. lumps of matter on planets and stars, and distributed throughout interstellar space). . . . Matter is inert and has no powers which it can choose to exercise; it does what it has to do. Yet each bit of matter behaves in exactly the same way as similar bits of matter throughout time and space, the way codified in natural laws. . . . all electrons throughout endless time and space have exactly the same powers and properties as all other electrons (properties of

attracting, repelling, interacting, emitting radiation, etc.), all photons have the same powers and properties as all other photons etc., etc. Matter is complex, diverse, but regular in its behaviour. Its existence and behaviour need explaining in just the kind of way that regular chemical combinations needed explaining; or it needs explaining when we find all the cards of a pack arranged in order." (*The Existence of God*, 288)

Newton: "Whence arises all this order and beauty and structure?"

Hume *Dialogues*: "Cleanthes: Consider, anatomize the eye. Survey its structure and contrivance, and tell me, from your own feeling, if the idea of a contriver does not immediately flow in upon you with a force like that of sensation. The most obvious conclusion, surely, is in favour of design, and it requires time, reflection and study to summon up those frivolous, though abstruse objections which can support infidelity."

The idea: the beauty, order and structure of the universe and the structure of its parts strongly suggest that it was designed; it seems absurd to think that such a universe should have just been there, that it wasn't designed and created but just happened. Contemplating these things can result in a strong impulse to believe that the universe was indeed designed – by God.

(Hume's version may be very close to a wholly different style of "argument": one where the arguer tries to help the arguee achieve the sort of situation in which the *Sensus Divinitatis* operates.)

(G) Tony Kenny's Style of Teleological Argument

(H) The Ontological Argument

(I) Another Argument Thrown in for Good Measure. Why is there anything at all? That is, why are there any *contingent* beings at all? (Isn't that passing strange, as S says?) An answer or an explanation that appealed to any contingent being would of course raise the same question again. A good explanation would have to appeal to a being that could not fail to exist, and (unlike numbers, propositions, sets, properties and other abstract necessary beings) is capable of explaining the existence of contingent beings (by, for example, being able to create them). The only viable candidate for this post seems to be God, thought of as the bulk of the theistic tradition has thought of him: that is, as a necessary being, but also as a concrete being, a being capable of causal activity. (Difference from S's Cosmo Arg: on his view God a contingent being, so no answer to the question "Why is there anything (contingent) at all?"

II. Half a Dozen Epistemological Arguments

(J) The Argument from Positive Epistemic Status. Clearly many of our beliefs do have positive epistemic status for us (at any rate most of us think so, most of us accept this premise). As we have seen, positive epistemic status is best thought of as a matter of a belief's being produced by cognitive faculties that are functioning properly in the sort of environment that is appropriate for them. The easiest and most natural way to think of proper functioning, however, is in terms of design: a machine or an organism is working properly when it is working in the way it was designed to work by the being that designed it. But clearly the best candidate for being the being who has designed our cognitive faculties would be God.

This premise of this argument is only a special case of a much broader premise: there are many natural (nonartifactual) things in the world besides our cognitive faculties such that they function properly or improperly: organs of our bodies and of other organisms, for example. (Tony Kenny's design argument)

Objection: perhaps there is indeed this initial tendency to see these things as the product of intelligent design; but there is a powerful defeater in evolutionary theory, which shows us a perfectly natural way in which all of these things might have come about without design.

Reply: (1) Is it in fact plausible to think that human beings, for example, have arisen through the sorts of mechanisms (unguided random genetic mutation and natural selection) in the time that according to contemporary science has been available? The conference of biologists and mathematicians ("Mathematical Challenges to the NeoDarwinian Interpretation of Evolution," ed. Paul Morehead and Martin Kaplan, Philadelphia, Wistar Institute Press; the piece by Houston Smith.) The chief problem: most of the paths one might think of from the condition of not having eyes, for example, to the condition of having them will not work; each mutation along the way has to be adaptive, or appropriately connected with something adaptive. (2) There does not appear to be any decent naturalistic account of the origin of life, or of language.

(K) The Argument from the Confluence of Proper Function and Reliability. We ordinarily think that when our faculties are functioning properly in the right sort of environment, they are reliable. Theism, with the idea that God has created us in his image and in such a way that we can acquire truth over a wide range of topics and subjects, provides an easy, natural explanation of that fact. The only real competitor here is nontheistic evolutionism; but

nontheistic evolution would at best explain our faculties' being reliable with respect to propositions which are such that having a true belief with respect to them has survival value. That does not obviously include moral beliefs, beliefs of the kind involved in completeness proofs for axiomatizations of various first order systems, and the like. (More poignantly, beliefs of the sort involved in science, or in thinking evolution is a plausible explanation of the flora and fauna we see.) Still further, true beliefs *as such* don't have much by way of survival value; they have to be linked with the right kind of dispositions to behavior. What evolution requires is that our *behavior* have survival value, not necessarily that our beliefs be true. (Sufficient that we be programmed to act in adaptive ways.) But there are many ways in which our behavior could be adaptive, even if our beliefs were for the most part false. Our whole belief structure might (a) be a sort of by-product or epiphenomenon, having no real connection with truth, and no real connection with our action. Or (b) our beliefs might be connected in a regular way with our actions, and with our environment, but not in such as way that the beliefs would be for the most part true.

Patricia Churchland (*JP* 84, Oct. 87) argues that the most important thing about the human brain is that it has evolved; hence (548) its principle function is to enable the organism to move appropriately. "Boiled down to essentials, a nervous system enables the organism to succeed in the four F's: feeding, fleeing, fighting and reproducing. The principle chore of nervous systems is to get the body parts where they should be in order that the organism may survive.... Truth, whatever that is, definitely takes the hindmost." (Self-referential problems loom here.) She also makes the point that we can't expect perfect engineering from evolution; it can't go back to redesign the basics.

(L) The Argument from Simplicity. According to Swinburne, simplicity is a prime determinant of *intrinsic probability*. That seems to me doubtful, mainly because there is probably no such thing in general as intrinsic (logical) probability. Still we certainly do favor simplicity; and we are inclined to think that simple explanations and hypotheses are more likely to be true than complicated epicyclic ones. So suppose you think that simplicity is a mark of truth (for hypotheses). If theism is true, then some reason to think the more simple has a better chance of being true than the less simple; for God has created both us and our theoretical preferences and the world; and it is reasonable to think that he would adapt the one to the other. (If he himself favored antisimplicity, then no doubt he would have created us in such a way that we would, too.) If theism is not true, however, there would

seem to be no reason to think that the simple is more likely to be true than the complex.

(M) The Argument from Induction. Hume pointed out that human beings are inclined to accept inductive forms of reasoning and thus to take it for granted, in a way, that the future will relevantly resemble the past. (This may have been known even before Hume.) As Hume also pointed out, however, it is hard to think of a good (noncircular) reason for believing that, indeed the future will be relevantly like the past. Theism, however, provides a reason: God has created us and our noetic capacities and has created the world; he has also created the former in such a way as to be adapted to the latter. It is likely, then, that he has created the world in such a way that in fact the future will indeed resemble the past in the relevant way. (And thus perhaps we do indeed have a priori knowledge of contingent truth: perhaps we know a priori that the future will resemble the past.) (Note here the piece by Aron Edidin: "Language Learning and a Priori Knowledge," *APQ*, October 1986 (Vol. 23/4); Aron argues that in any case of language learning a priori knowledge is involved.)

This argument and the last argument could be thought of as exploiting the fact that according to theism God has created us in such a way as to be at home in the world (Wolterstorff).

(N) The Putnamian Argument (the Argument from the Rejection of Global Skepticism). Hilary Putnam (*Reason, Truth, and History*) and others argue that if metaphysical realism is true (if "the world consists of a fixed totality of mind independent objects," or if "there is one true and complete description of the 'the way the world is'"), then various intractable skeptical problems arise. For example, on that account we do not know that we are not brains in a vat. But clearly we do know that we are not brains in a vat; hence metaphysical realism is not true. But of course the argument overlooks the theistic claim that we could perfectly well know that we are not brains in a vat even if metaphysical realism is true: we can know that God would not deceive us in such a disgustingly wholesale manner. So you might be inclined to accept (1) the Putnamian proposition that we do know that we are not brains in a vat, (2) the anti-Putnamian claim that metaphysical realism is true and antirealism a mere Kantian galimatias, and (3) the quasi-Putnamian proposition that if metaphysical realism is true and there is no such person God who has created us and our world, adapting the former to the latter, then we would not know that we are not brains in a vat; if so, then you have a theistic argument.

Variant: Putnam and others argue that if we think that there is no conceptual link between justification (conceived internalistically) and truth, then we should have to take global skepticism really seriously. If there is no connection between these two, then we have no reason to think that even our best theories are any more likely to be true than the worst theories we can think of. We do, however, know that our best theories are more likely to be true than our worst ones; hence . . . you may be inclined to accept (1) the Putnamian thesis that it is false that we should take global skepticism with real seriousness, (2) the anti-Putnamian thesis that there is no *conceptual* link between justification and truth (at any rate if theism is false), and (3) the quasi-Putnamian thesis that if we think there is no link between the two, then we should take global skepticism really seriously. Then you may conclude that there must be a link between the two, and you may see the link in the theistic idea that God has created us and the world in such a way that we can reflect something of his epistemic powers by virtue of being able to achieve knowledge, which we typically achieve when we hold justified beliefs.

Here in this neighborhood and in connection with antirealist considerations of the Putnamian type, there is a splendid piece by Shelley Stillwell in the '89 *Synthese* entitled something like "Plantinga's Anti-realism," which nicely analyzes the situation and seems to contain the materials for a theistic argument.

(0) The Argument from Reference. Return to Putnam's brain in a vat. P argues that our thought has a certain *external* character: what we can think depends partly on what the world is like. Thus if there were no trees, we could not think the thought *there are no trees*; the word 'tree' would not mean what it does mean if in fact there were no trees (and the same for other natural kind terms – water, air, horse, bug, fire, lemon, human being, and the like, and perhaps also artifactual kind terms – house, chair, airplane, computer, barometer, vat, and the like). But then, he says, we can discount brain in vat skepticism: it can't be right, because if we were brains in a vat, we would not have the sort of epistemic contact with vats that would permit our term 'vat' to mean what in fact it does. But then we could not so much as think the thought: we are brains in a vat. So if we were, we could not so much as think the thought that we were. But clearly we can think that thought (and if we couldn't we couldn't formulate brain in vat scepticism); so such skepticism must be mistaken.

But a different and more profound skepticism lurks in the neighborhood: We *think* we can think certain thoughts, where we can give general descriptions of the thoughts in question. Consider, for example, our thought that there are trees. We think there is a certain kind of large green living object that grows and is related in a certain way to its environment; and we name this kind of thing 'tree'. But maybe as a matter of fact we are not in the sort of environment we think we are in. Maybe we are in a sort of environment of a totally different sort, of such a sort that in fact we can't form the sort of thoughts we think we can form. We think we can form thoughts of certain kind, but in fact we cannot. That could be the case. Then it isn't so much (or only) that our thoughts might be systematically and massively mistaken; instead it might be that we can't think the thoughts we think we can think. Now as a matter of fact we can't take this skepticism seriously; and, indeed, if we are created by God we need not take it seriously, for God would not permit us to be deceived in this massive way.

(P) The Kripke-Wittgenstein Argument from Plus and Quus (See Supplementary Handout)

(Q) The General Argument from Intuition. We have many kinds of intuitions: (1) logical (narrow sense and broad sense): the intuitions codified in propositional modal logic – if it could be the case that the moon is made of green cheese, then it is necessary that that could be so; (2) arithmetical, set theoretical and mathematical generally; (3) moral; (4) philosophical (Leib's Law; there aren't any things that do not exist; sets don't have the property of representing things as being a certain way; neither trees nor numbers are either true nor false; there are a great number of things that are either true or false; there is such a thing as positive epistemic status; there is such a property as being unpunctual; and so on). You may be inclined to think that all or some of these ought to be taken with real seriousness, and give us real and important truth. It is much easier to see how this could be so on a theistic than on a nontheistic account of the nature of human beings.

A couple of more arguments: first, the argument from the causal theory of knowledge: many philosophers think there is a problem with our alleged knowledge of abstract objects in that they think we can't know truths about an object with which we are not in the appropriate causal relation. They then point out that we are not in much of any causal relation with abstract objects, and conclude, some of them, that there is a real problem with our knowing anything about abstract objects (e.g., Paul Benacerraf). But if we think of abstract objects as God's thoughts, then he is in causal relation with them, and also with us, so that there should be no problem as to how it is that we could know something about them. (On the causal theory of knowledge, if you think of abstract objects as just *there*, and as not standing in causal relations, then the problem should really be that it is hard to see how even God could have any knowledge of them.)

There is another realism/antirealism argument lurking here somewhere, indicated or suggested by Wolterstorff's piece in the Tomberlin metaphysics volume. It has to do with whether there are really any joints in reality, or whether it might not be instead that reality doesn't have any joints, and there are no essential properties of objects. Instead, there is only de dicto reality (this could be the argument from de re modality) with all classifications somehow being done by us. Interesting. Also another topic for Christian philosophy.

Another argument.... Thomas Nagel, *The View from Nowhere*, 78ff. Thinks it amazing that there should be any such thing as the sort of objective thinking or objective point of view that we do in fact have. Perhaps it is really amazing only from a naturalist point of view. He says he has no explanation. Maybe you find it amazing, maybe you don't. (I'm not sure I see why it is amazing yet.) He argues cogently that there is no good evolutionary explanation of this: first, what needs to be explained is the very possibility of this, and second, suppose that is explained, he goes on to argue that evolution gives us no good explanation of our higher mental abilities. The question is whether the mental powers necessary for the making of stone axes, and hunter-gatherer success, are sufficient for the construction of theories about subatomic particles, proofs of Gödel's theorem, the invention of the compact disc, and so on. He thinks not. So he is really on to something else: not so much 'objective thinking' as higher mental powers involved in these striking intellectual accomplishments.

The evolutionary explanation would be that intellectual powers got started by going along for the ride, so to speak, and then turned out to be useful, and were such that improvements in them got selected when we came down from the trees. (At that point a bigger brain became useful. Don't whales have an even bigger one?) A sort of two-part affair, the first part being accidental. So then the second part would be selected for survival value or advantage. But of course the question is whether this gives the slightest reason to think these theories have any truth to them at all. And he fails to mention the fact that all that really gets selected is behavior; there are various combinations of desire and belief that can lead to adaptive actions even if the belief is completely mistaken.

III. Moral Arguments

(R) Moral Arguments (actually R1 to Rn). There are many different versions of moral arguments, among the best being Bob Adams's favored version

("Moral Arguments for Theistic Belief," in C. Delaney, *Rationality and Religious Belief*, Notre Dame): (1) One might find oneself utterly convinced (as I do) that morality is objective, not dependent upon what human beings know or think, and that it cannot be explained in terms of any "natural" facts about human beings or other things; that it can't ultimately be explained in terms of physical, chemical or biological facts. (2) One may also be convinced that there could not be such objective moral facts unless there were such a person as God who, in one way or another, legislates them.

Here consider George Mavrodes' argument that morality would be 'queer' in a Russellian or nontheistic universe (in "Religion and the Queerness of Morality," in *Rationality, Religious Belief and Moral Commitment*, ed. Audi and Wainwright).

Other important arguments here: A. E Taylor's (*The Faith of a Moralist*) version, and Clem Dore's (and Sidgwick's) Kantian argument from the confluence of morality with true self-interest, some of the other arguments considered by Bob Adams in the above-mentioned paper, and arguments by Hastings Rashdall in *The Theory of Good and Evil*, and by W. R. Sorley, *Moral Values and the Idea of God* which we used to read in college.

(R*) The Argument from Evil. Many philosophers offer an antitheistic argument from evil, and perhaps they have some force. But there is also a theistic argument from evil. There is real and genuine evil in the world: evil such that it isn't just a matter of personal opinion that the thing in question is abhorrent, and furthermore it doesn't matter if those who perpetrate it think it is good, and could not be convinced by anything we said. And it is plausible to think that in a nontheistic or at any rate a naturalistic universe, there could be no such thing. So perhaps you think there is such a thing as genuine and horrifying evil, and that in a nontheistic universe, there could not be; then you have another theistic argument.

How to make this argument more specific?: "what Pascal later called the 'triple abyss' into which mankind has fallen: the libidinal enslavement to the egotistical self: the *libido dominandi*, or lust for power over others and over nature; the *libido sentiendi*, or lust for intense sensation; and the *libido sciendi*, or lust for manipulative knowledge, knowledge that is primarily used to increase our own power, profit and pleasure" (Michael D. Aeschliman, "Discovering the Fall," *This World*, Fall 1988, p. 93).

How think about utterly appalling and horrifying evil? The Christian understanding: it is indeed utterly appalling and horrifying; it is defying

God, the source of all that is good and just. It has a sort of cosmic significance: in this way it is the other side of the coin from the argument from love. There we see that the deep significance of love can't be explained in terms of naturalistic categories; the same goes here. From a naturalistic perspective, there is nothing much more to evil – say the sheer horror of the Holocaust, of Pol Pot, or a thousand other villains – than there is to the way in which animals savage each other. A natural outgrowth of natural processes.

Hostility, hatred, hostility towards outsiders or even towards one's family is to be understood in terms simply of the genes' efforts (Dawkins) to ensure its survival. Nothing perverted or unnatural about it. (Maybe can't even have these categories.) But from a theistic pint of view, deeply perverted, and deeply horrifying. And maybe this is the way we naturally see it. The point here is that it is objectively horrifying. We find it horrifying: and that is part of its very nature, as opposed to the naturalistic way of thinking about it where there really can't be much of anything like objective horrifyingness.

On a naturalistic way of looking at the matter, it is hard to see how there can really be such a thing as evil (though of course there could be things we don't like, prefer not to happen): how could there be something that was bad, worthy of disapproval, even if we and all other human beings were wildly enthusiastic about it? On naturalistic view, how make sense of (a) our intuition that what is right or wrong, good or evil, does not depend upon what we like or think, and (b) our revulsion at evil – the story the prophet Nathan told David, at the sort of thing that went on in Argentina, Stalin's Russia, Hitler's Germany (*Sophie's Choice*); the case mentioned in Surin's book about the young child who was hanged and remained living for half an hour after he was hanged; the fact that the Nazis were purposely trying to be cruel, to induce despair, taunting their victims with the claim that no one would ever know of their fate and how they were treated; the thing from Dostoevsky, who says that beasts wouldn't do this, they wouldn't be so artistic about it. Compare dying from cancer with the sort of horror the Germans did: the second is much worse than the first, somehow, but not because it causes more pain. It is because of the wickedness involved, a wickedness we don't see in the cancer. An appalling wickedness.

There seems to be a lot more to it than there could be on a naturalistic account of the matter. So the naturalist says: evil is a problem for you: why would a good God permit evil, or all that evil? But evil also a problem for him: There really isn't any evil (or isn't any of a certain sort, a sort such that in fact we think there is some of that sort) on a naturalistic perspective. (This needs working out, but I think there is something to it.)

IV. Other Arguments

(S) The Argument from Colors and Flavors (Adams and Swinburne). What is the explanation of the correlation between physical and psychical properties? Presumably there *is* an explanation of it; but also it will have to be, as Adams and Swinburne say, a personal, nonscientific explanation. The most plausible suggestion would involve our being created that way by God.

(T) The Argument from Love. Man-woman, parent-child, family, friendship, love of college, church, country – many different manifestations. Evolutionary explanation: these adaptive and have survival value. Evolutionarily useful for male and female human beings, like male and female hippopotami, to get together to have children (colts) and stay together to raise them; and the same for the other manifestations of love. The theistic account: vastly more to it than that: reflects the basic structure and nature of reality; God himself is love.

(U) The Mozart Argument. On a naturalistic anthropology, our alleged grasp and appreciation of (alleged) beauty is to be explained in terms of evolution: somehow arose in the course of evolution, and something about its early manifestations had survival value. But miserable and disgusting cacophony (heavy metal rock?) could as well have been what we took to be beautiful. On the theistic view, God recognizes beauty; indeed, it is deeply involved in his very nature. To grasp the beauty of Mozart's D Minor piano concerto is to grasp something that is objectively there; it is to appreciate what is objectively worthy of appreciation.

(V) The Argument from Play and Enjoyment. Fun, pleasure, humor, play, enjoyment. (Maybe not all to be thought of in the same way.) Playing: evolution: an adaptive means of preparing for adult life (so that engaging in this sort of thing as an adult suggests a case of arrested development). But surely there is more to it than that. The joy one can take in humor, art, poetry, mountaineering, exploring, adventuring (the problem is not to explain how it would come about that human beings enjoyed mountaineering: no doubt evolution can do so. The problem is with its significance. Is it really true that all there is to this is enjoyment? Or is there a deeper significance? The

Westminster Shorter Catechism: the chief end of man is to glorify God and enjoy him (and his creation and gifts) forever).

(W) Arguments from Providence and from Miracles

(X) C. S. Lewis's Argument from Nostalgia. Lewis speaks of the *nostalgia* that often engulfs us upon beholding a splendid land or seascape; these somehow speak to us of their maker. Not sure just what the argument is; but suspect there is one there.

(Y) The Argument from the Meaning of Life. How does thought about the meaningfulness or meaninglessness of life fit in? Sartre, Camus, Nagel.

(Z) The Argument from (A) to (Y). These arguments import a great deal of unity into the philosophic endeavor, and the idea of God helps with an astonishingly wide variety of cases: epistemological, ontological, ethical, having to do with meaning, and the like of that.

Notes

1. See, e.g., Neil A. Manson, *God and Design* (London and New York: Routledge, 2003).
2. Suppose p is the greatest prime. Consider the product P of p with all the primes q1, q2, . . . smaller than p, and add 1. P + 1 won't be divisible by any of p or q1, q2, . . . qn; it is therefore prime, but greater than p. *Reductio*; hence there is no greatest prime.
3. *The Problem of Evil* (Oxford: Clarendon Press, 2006), p. 47.

Select Bibliography

Books by Plantinga

(ed.) *The Ontological Argument*. Garden City, NY: Doubleday, 1965.

God and Other Minds: A Study of the Rational Justification of the Belief in God. Ithaca, NY: Cornell University Press, 1967; rev. ed. 1990.

The Nature of Necessity. Oxford: Clarendon Press, 1974.

God, Freedom, and Evil, Grand Rapids, MI: Eerdmans, 1974.

Does God Have a Nature? Milwaukee, WI: Marquette University Press, 1980.

(ed.), with Nicholas Wolterstorff. *Faith and Rationality: Reason and Belief in God*. Notre Dame, IN, and London: University of Notre Dame Press, 1983.

Warrant: The Current Debate. New York and Oxford: Oxford University Press, 1993.

Warrant and Proper Function. New York and Oxford: Oxford University Press, 1993.

The Analytic Theist: An Alvin Plantinga Reader, ed. James F. Sennett, Grand Rapids, MI: Eerdmans, 1998.

Warranted Christian Belief. New York and Oxford: Oxford University Press, 2000.

Essays in the Metaphysics of Modality, ed. Matthew Davidson. New York and Oxford: Oxford University Press, 2003.

Books about Plantinga

James Beilby, *Epistemology as Theology: An Evaluation of Alvin Plantinga's Religious Epistemology*. Aldershot: Ashgate, 2006.

James Beilby (ed.), *Naturalism Defeated? Essays on Plantinga's Evolutionary Argument Against Naturalism*. Ithaca, NY, and London: Cornell University Press, 2002.

Jonathan Kvanvig (ed.), *Warrant in Contemporary Epistemology: Essays in Honor of Plantinga's Theory of Knowledge*. Lanham, MD: Rowman & Littlefield, 1996.

James E. Tomberlin and Peter van Inwagen (eds.), *Alvin Plantinga*. Dordrecht: Reidel, 1985.

Index